Taking Back the River

A true story

Sheila A. O'Quirke

Copyright © 2012 by Sheila A. O'Quirke
ISBN 978-0-615-65882-7

All rights reserved
Printed in the United States of America

Cover design by Amy Parish
Photo shot by Amy Parish
Front cover charcoal drawing by Everton Tsosie

CONTENTS

Acknowledgements 3

Author's Note 5

Preface 6

Part One

The Fragmenting of a Child's Soul 8

Part Two

Naïve Wife and Child Mother 56

Part Three

Temporary Band-Aids and Mind-Altering Men 86

Part Four

Recovering My Spirit: A Fierce and Sudden Hunger 155

Part Five

Losing My Grip: Post Traumatic Stress Disorder 197

Part Six

A Warrior Gains Strength from every Death 221

Part Seven

Taking Back the River 263

List of Characters 348

Epilogue 350

I Want to Live Before I Die 351

Acknowledgements

Linda Valdez, my friend and "sister"
For standing by me for over 30 years

Maria Brock, my little "sister"
For her selflessness and for appreciating my need to keep it *real*

Melinda Garcia, PhD
For "seeing" me and for challenging me

Tatanka Nazi Chante Wasake, my Wicasa (Teacher)
For his legacy, humility, and unconditional love

Pete Spotted Horse
For his unfailing friendship and sense of humor

Molly, my canine sister
For blessing me in innumerable ways

My dog park buddies at Triangle Park, Albuquerque
For their support, friendship, and our shared love for our canine friends

To my friends at the Villa Nueva Senior Apartments
For their friendship, support, and validation

To the *sandpaper* people, those who rubbed me the wrong way
For gifting me with hard lessons

To those who deliberately hurt me emotionally, physically, and sexually
For gifting me with the opportunity to realize the strength of my spirit

Author's Note

Due to the nature of this book, I suggest that you seek counseling or a support group, should you be triggered by any of the material.

A large portion of my story includes treatment modalities that enabled *me* to heal. I am not promoting any specific type of therapy or spiritual belief. The book is about *my* process—*my* journey to wholeness. If you read something that resonates with your spirit—pay attention to that.

Most of the names in this book have been changed in order to maintain dignity and privacy.

For information regarding lectures or to schedule one, you can reach me at my email address: strongheartiam@yahoo.com

Preface

I was 35 years old when I began to ponder questions like: "Who am I and what's my purpose on this planet?" Up until then, my identity was dependent on who I was in relation to everyone else. I was a chameleon: adapting myself to situations and to other's expectations of how I should act, think, and feel. For years I struggled with demons. I attempted suicide several times; I saw death as the only way out of a miserable existance. I was often asked, "Don't you ever smile?" For the majority of my life, there wasn't a lot to smile about.

But at the age of 35, I recognized in me a thirst I'd never known; the need for a spiritual connection—for knowledge—for truth. The answers didn't come over night, in fact, I found that for me, the long road was the shortest way home. I'd invested so much time and energy into hating myself that it was hard to give that up. It kept me on the merry-go-round of addiction and recovery, spaning many years. But as I began the difficult work of healing and facing myself, I was able to see the value—the gift—in having a rough life. I knew there was a reason for all the horror I'd experienced.

My purpose for writing this book is two-fold. I needed to revisit and put to rest, some of those dark places that still haunted me. The other reason is that I have a responsibility to others, to tell my story as candidly as I lived it; to share what I have been taught; to let you know that you are not alone.

For me, *Taking Back the River* is symbolic of many things. The river is within me. It is the life force that sustains my spirit. It has been a lifelong process of clearing away debris: old tapes in my head that told me I'm no good; energy blocks in my throat that cut off my voice from speaking my truth; the fire in my gut from years of abuse; a culture that says I'm a bitch if I dare to stand up for myself; a society that prefers that I'm *nice* instead of real; a core belief that tells me that the needs of others are more important than my own. All those feelings and beliefs became the stagnation of my internal river, leaving me feeling stuck, exhausted, and deadened.

In my decision to take back the river, I have also committed to returning to my *wild woman* soul: the *me* that refuses to be defined by any person, institution, or religion. It's about me reclaiming my intuitive and wise self. It means connecting with my childlike innocense, allowing for spontoneity and experiencing more of life through the senses; getting in touch with my instinctual nature—like a dog. Maybe that's why the Creator has seen fit to put canines into my life to care for.

So now, I invite you to take this journey with me on my earthwalk through pain, struggle, and finally, to the empowered essence of who I truly am.

Part One
The Fragmenting of a Child's Soul

I stood up in my crib, holding on to the wooden railing and looking out the bedroom window. The room was dark, except for the bright glow of the moon as it shone through the sheer, white, lacy curtains. I felt so alone in my crib. My mother was gone. I had a sense of my loss, but didn't fully understand why she was no longer there. I could make out the still form of my father as he lay in his bed, just a few feet away. I wanted to be in bed next to him. I needed him to hold me. I had to wake him up, but didn't have the language to call out to him and tell him how afraid I was. So I started crying. It worked. He woke up, lifted me from my crib, and put me in bed next to him. I felt safer in his arms. That was my first childhood memory in our little house in San Diego, California.

I was born to Joyce Wanda Argo and Robert James O'Quirke on June 10, 1951, in Chicago, Illinois. My birth mother was Cherokee, and her people were from northern Kentucky. My great-uncle, Joe, said that at some point, the family decided to move to Indiana, "because they were still huntin' down the Cherokee," herding them off to Oklahoma like cattle. My mother's grandparents found a way to assimilate into the white community they lived in. They became ashamed of being Indian. To be Indian back then was a disgrace; it was worse than being black, I was told. Now, everybody wants to claim Indian blood. But my grandparents bought into seeing themselves the way whites did and passed their shame down to their offspring. And *that* was the *real* shame. It was around 1940 when my mother's people moved to Chicago, probably to look for work.

My father's paternal grandparents were a long line of Burkes and Sheehans from County Cork, Ireland. His maternal grandparents were from Bohemia and their surname was Lahvic. Unfortunately, I never knew my dad's side of the family, but even so, that gypsy blood runs through me. Just how my parents met, was never mentioned. I only know that it must have been about five years after my dad returned to his home in Chicago, after serving in WWII as a Lieutenant Navy pilot, in the South Pacific.

My mother was sickly as a child with rheumatic fever. After I was born, her doctor cautioned her about attempting another pregnancy because of her illness. She had wanted to give my father a son and so, ignoring her doctor's advice, became pregnant for the second time.

I was a year old when we left Chicago. My dad was tired of the bitterly cold winters and thought that the further west we went, the more suitable the weather would be for all of us.

We set out for California on old route 66 in a *woody* station wagon. My father decided on San Diego, because there was a Naval Base there and he liked the area. He soon found a job working in a plant called, Conair, while my mother stayed home taking care of me. About a month after we arrived in San Diego, my mother developed pneumonia. This compounded her already poor health problems, especially since she was also in her eight month of pregnancy. My dad took her to the hospital where her condition rapidly worsened. A priest was summoned and she received the Last Rites. She held on long enough to bring my brother, Matthew, into the world.

We had a housekeeper after my mother's death. I didn't like her at all and did my best to drive her away. Once, I flooded the bathroom sink. Another time, I crapped in the bathtub. I couldn't have been more than three years old. I'm guessing that I thought if I could get rid of the housekeeper, I'd have a full-time dad.

I sensed my father's guilt about my mother's death, and about me not having a mother anymore. I took advantage of his guilty feelings. He bought me whatever I asked for, but what I really wanted was to feel safe with him; to know that he would never leave me. The fear of abandonment followed me throughout most of my adulthood. It was the most terrifying feeling. I would subconsciously choose men who were unable to be there for me emotionally, just like my dad, because he was stuck in his grief over losing his wife. Or I'd unknowingly choose men who would end up leaving me suddenly, and not return, as my mother had.

My dad would pick me up and carry me, or hold me on his lap whenever I asked him to, but it wasn't enough.

It was worse for my baby brother, Matthew. My father hardly paid any attention to him at all. My brother slept in the second bedroom with the housekeeper, who provided him with his care. In his grief, I think my father subconsciously resented Matthew for being the cause of my mother dying. And my mother's sisters blamed my dad for "killing their sister."

I was about three years old, and I dreaded the times when we *visited* my mother, as my dad called our trips to her grave. My mother was buried at the Naval Base in San Diego, next to the ocean. We would arrive at the cemetery and as soon as we got to her gravesite, my dad would begin to sob. I needed him to be strong and in control for me, and I felt helpless when he cried. Once, as he was driving us to the cemetery I said, "Daddy, if you cry, I'm gonna run away."

When we were in front of her grave, he cried and I ran. I ran and ran, through tombstones I ran, my dress flying in the breeze coming off of the ocean. I could hear him calling, "Sheila, come back." I don't remember going there after that day.

Around that time I was obsessed with horses. When I was about three and a half, my dad bought me a cowgirl outfit with leather fringes on the skirt bottom and a cowboy hat. I was so proud of that outfit. "Daddy, will you buy me a pony?" I pleaded. I must have thought, *now that I have my cowgirl outfit, having a pony should surely follow.* Instead, he'd take me to the carnivals and let me go on the pony rides, but that didn't quite cut it. I wanted my own pony. Other times, he'd take me to the supermarket and leave me bouncing up and down on the coin operated horses, feeling very silly, while he went in to shop.

My love of trees began early. Since we didn't have any trees in our yard, I'd go to the house across the street, and climb their tree. Well, one day, I fell from the tree and landed on my head. My dad rushed me to the hospital, where I was examined by a doctor. I remember my dad being worried. As for me, it did nothing in the way of preventing me from wanting to get right back up there and balance my little fanny on a branch.

Here's a little incident I was told about when I was already an adult. Apparently, I'd made friends with another three or four-year-old girl from the neighborhood. One day, I came in the house and asked my dad if my friend could come in and play. When he said she could, I brought my little black girlfriend inside. It's wonderful the way children don't distinguish one race from another. I was told that the little black girl was my first friend. I'm glad I wasn't brought up to be prejudice against blacks.

It was between the ages of three and four that I began to feel secure in knowing that my dad wasn't going to leave me, as my mother had. I remember being a happy and untroubled little girl, who loved her dad. And then, one night, when I was four years old and Matthew was three, my father told us to come to the living room; he said he wanted to talk to us. By the tone of his voice, I could tell that it was serious. My brother and I sat on the couch. I was holding my little black patent-leather purse full of M & M's. He told us that our mother was dead. I, of course, knew that. Then he said that my brother and I would have to live with someone else, because he had to go to school to learn how to be a policeman. He lost me at, "live with someone else," as my awareness became focused solely on my purse full of candy. I disappeared inside of it. Candy would later become a means of escape as well as comfort for me.

Years later, I found out that my dad had asked his sister, Marion, in Chicago, if she would keep Matthew and me for a while. She declined; she already had three kids of her own. He then asked my mother's sister, Juanita, who had recently moved to L.A. She also refused. Juanita's excuse was that her husband was an alcoholic. So my dad located a couple who did foster care.

"Now tell me if you don't like them, and we can find another family," my dad said, as we stood on the front porch, facing the huge front door for the first time. I heard my father's words and felt his love. I heard-*choice*: that we could make our own decision as to where we wanted to live, and that as the older sister, it was up to me to make that decision for Matthew and me. It was too big a decision for someone so young. After that day, I failed in my responsibility to my little brother.

My dad rang the doorbell. As we waited for the door to open, a door I can't remember walking through, I knew it didn't matter where we lived, because my father wouldn't be there with us. We sat in the Howleys' living room as the grownups talked. They were nice enough. My father seemed to favor them, so when we left their house and he asked me if I liked them, I told him, "Yes."

Living with the Howleys was akin to a prison sentence. "I'll come visit you every two weeks," my father said. Two weeks is a long time for a child, but in that house, it became an eternity. I was to discover that the Howleys had two faces: one for my father and one for my brother and me.

Our new home was in Bostonia, a suburb of San Diego. The living room faced the street. I'd spend hours gazing out that window, waiting for my father to come. Beyond the living room was the kitchen, which faced the back of the house. To the left of the kitchen was a dining room that was never used because we all ate our meals in the big kitchen. Beyond that, there were two bedrooms separated by a bathroom. The bedroom to the left belonged to the Howleys. The one to the right was mine. It was a nice room with a bed, a dresser, and a closet. Atop the dresser was my parents' wedding picture, which did little in the way of making me feel more secure. There were two windows; one of which faced the backyard, where there were fruit trees, chickens, and a vegetable garden. To the right of the big kitchen, were more bedrooms, for my brother as well as the other foster kids that came and went.

The feeling in that house was one of oppression. The foster parents hardly spoke to each other. I don't remember

ever hearing them laugh, and there was certainly no laughter or spontaneity among us kids. We knew our place and we knew the rules:
Rule #1 You will call us Ma'am and Sir. Rule #2 Children are to be seen and not heard.
Rule #3 No talking at the table.

Rule #4 You don't leave the table until you've eaten everything on your plate (Once I had to leave the table to vomit from something I had to eat)
Rule #5 Keep your mouth shut about what goes on in the house. This was an unspoken rule, but understood, nonetheless.

  I was born with black hair. It fell out and was replaced with blond—that turned light brown—then went to reddish brown. By the age of five, I had beautiful multicolored long hair. I don't think that my father had ever cut it. One day, Mrs. Howley made one long braid and then whacked it off, and cut me some thick bangs. I looked like the boy on the Dutch Cleanser container. I was mortified. I felt naked and vulnerable.

  There was a hutch cabinet in the dining room with pretty little teacups and saucers. They were only there for decoration. I used to wish that I could play with them. Beyond the dining room was the parlor. It was there in that room, in the eerie half-light of the lamp, accentuating the darkness, that Mr. Howley would make me stand before him and take my clothes off. He'd look for any infraction committed by me, just for an excuse to see me naked and strap my bottom with the belt. For example, once we were at Mass and I made the sign of the cross with the wrong hand. Hell, I was left handed. I knew, by the look he gave me, what would be awaiting me when we got home. But before he would put my naked body over his knee, I would feel his eyes moving up and down my little girl body. It gave me such an ugly feeling and I knew it was wrong. I don't know where his wife was at those times, except that she wasn't there.

Sometimes in the morning, after his wife had left, Mr. Howley would summon me to his bedroom. He'd be lying in bed on his stomach and would make me massage his back. He progressed to having me sit on his lap in that dreaded parlor. He'd tell me what a pretty girl I was. I came to hate that I was pretty. He would unzip his pants, take my hand, and pull it toward his genitals, wrapping my little fingers around his penis. I remember trying to pull my hand away. I was forced to masturbate this man, my foster father. Those are the only conscious memories I have of a sexual nature, but I believe that he also fondled me. I hated him, but feared him more. I don't remember him telling me not to tell my father, but it must have been implied, because I never did. It was my secret, and it filled me with shame. I did wonder why my dad never suspected anything. Didn't he know his own daughter? Couldn't he tell that I was becoming withdrawn and unhappy? Did he even care?

When children don't get their needs met, it's not uncommon for them to compensate, by wanting to take care of others. That's where codependency has its roots. So it's not surprising, that when I was about five years old, I told my dad I wanted to be a nurse when I grew up. One day, when he came for his regular visit, he handed me a children's book called, *Nurse Nancy*. At another visit, he brought me a toy medical kit with the stethoscope, thermometer, and fake pills. Then, one Christmas, my father gave me a toy pickup truck. I must have told him that's what I wanted because at some point, I stopped wanting to be a girl. It wasn't safe.

My foster father wasn't the only sicko in the family. On several occasions, Mrs. Howley took me to the bathroom and had me lie naked on my stomach, on the cold bathroom floor, while she gave me enemas. We weren't alone, either. A neighbor lady would be standing there too. So there I was, at my most vulnerable, with two adults towering over me. I wanted to disappear into the tile floor, straight down into the earth.

My foster mother was cold and mean to me and I feared her just as much, if not more than, Mr. Howley. Thinking back now, it seemed that she wore the pants in the family. Mr. Howley must have felt that the only way for him to feel in control, or to feel like a man, was to molest little girls.

I finally resigned myself to my unfortunate existence in that house. It wasn't easy being in an environment where the adults who were supposed to care for you, didn't even like you. It was downright terrifying at times.

My father was going to the Highway Patrol Academy in Sacramento, and for two years, he told Matthew and me that he would come for us when he finished the school. Well, he finished and then moved to the town of Compton, in L.A. County, because that's where his "beat" was. Once, he picked us up and took us to his apartment. I didn't understand why we couldn't be together and live with our dad, but I didn't ask him; I was afraid he'd get mad and leave us in the home forever. My dad was good to Matthew and me, and he was never angry with us, but at that point in my life, I didn't trust him. I just remember thinking that I shouldn't expect anything good to happen in my life. I felt I was just plain bad, and that I deserved all that was happening to me. I was so confused. I knew my dad loved me. He called me "princess" and always made me feel special, and then he was gone.

On one of my dad's visits, he brought me a little wooden rocking chair. I loved to sit in it and rock. It was one of the ways I would soothe myself. Another way was to take a portion of my dress, twist it around and then suck on the cloth.

One night, after all of us kids were in bed asleep, my foster mother woke me up and told me to come to the living room. When I got there, she and her cohort, Mr. Howley, were sitting on the couch. She spoke to me in her stern way, and said that I had scratched up the headboard on my bed. I didn't know what she was talking about. I never would have done such a thing. I hadn't even noticed if it was scratched. I did nothing in that house to bring attention to myself, good or bad. I feared them too much. If anything, I tried to be invisible. So for my punishment, I was forced to get on my knees in front of my rocking chair, and start scratching it. When my little paws got tired and I had to stop, she yelled, "Scratch, scratch, scratch!" Mr. Howley didn't say a word the whole time. I felt helpless and trapped. When my fingers became tired and numb, and when I'd successfully managed to scratch the entire chair, she was finally satisfied with my work, and I was ordered back to bed. My beautiful rocking chair was as marred and ugly as I felt inside.

I was sitting at the dinner table when my dad came for his visit, soon after that incident. I watched as he followed the two of them to my bedroom. I was afraid he'd believe that I really *did* scratch that headboard. When they came back out, I studied my dad's face, which showed concern, but that was all, and I knew that he wouldn't mention it to me. So, a crazy thing happened that wasn't acknowledged by my dad. Since I was a precocious child, I figured it out. My foster parents were setting me up to look like a liar, just in case I spilled the beans about how they were treating me. They probably told my dad, "See, she even scratched her rocking chair."

Kindergarten was a nice respite from the house of horrors. I liked the play kitchens and doll houses, the naps, and the graham crackers and milk. It was a world unto itself with its magic, adventure, and discovery. The teacher was young and seemed warm and kind. I really liked kindergarten. What I liked most was that it was a safe place.

But when I was in the first grade, I began behaving oddly. I would find things; such as, paper clips, bobby pins, and safety pins, and take them to the main office, telling whoever was behind the counter, that I was turning them in to the lost and found. It was I who was lost, and wanted desperately to be found, by a caring adult who would acknowledge my existence. I wanted someone to see that I was hurting and needed to be saved.

It was in the first grade that I began to feel different from the other kids. They talked about their mothers and fathers, whereas, I lived in the "home." They played and were happy. I was miserable and had secrets. At recess, I played alone and sang songs to myself that were popular in the early 50's.

There was a boy that I liked in my first grade class. Once, I picked some wildflowers in the school yard and put them in my hair, hoping he'd notice. I was starved for attention. When he told me I was pretty, I continued to put flowers in my hair.

During lunch, if it was a nice day, we'd all sit at a picnic table to eat. When we finished, we had to line our lunch boxes up outside the classroom door, and return to the playground.

Well, one such very nice day, turned very bad for me. I'd finished my lunch of a bland type of sandwich and carrot and celery sticks, and was still hungry. Breakfast that morning had probably been a piece of toast, floating in a bowl of milk. I never had cookies or other sweets. When I put my lunch box up that day, I decided to open up one of the others, and found some graham crackers. I was eating them like a little mouse, when the bell rang.

All the children came running up to the classroom, I was caught red-handed. My special admirer began yelling at me for stealing his graham crackers. Of all the kids' lunch boxes I could have stolen from, it had to be his! If I'd known that was going to happen, I could've kept searching the lunch boxes and stolen something really good…like a Twinkie or a pink snow ball cake. It was a shameful experience, with all the kids staring at me, as if I were the scum of the earth.

When we went inside, I took my seat, lay my head down on my desk, and started crying. The teacher came over to me and led me to the front of the classroom. All eyes were upon me. She sat me on her lap and held me as I continued to cry. I must have felt safe enough to cry with that caring woman, because I never cried at home. After that, the boy stopped talking to me altogether. I hated first grade.

Daydreaming became one of my survival mechanisms. If I hadn't found times to space out, I might have gone crazy. I daydreamed whenever I could, usually at school, because I dared not let my guard down at home. I daydreamed by day, and at night, I'd have awful dreams, like one that I had about witches wearing pointed hats. They were stirring a huge black pot, and inside the pot was my father. He was being cooked! I must have been terrified that something would happen to my father; that I would have to live in that house forever.

When he'd come for his visits, my dad would often take me to get an ice cream cone, or he'd buy me a new dress. There was one I remember in particular. It had different colored polka dots on it, and it became my favorite. One day, one of the other little foster girls was wearing that dress. I was upset that Mrs. Howley put it on her. Nothing was sacred in the "home."

I'd take Matthew outside to play every chance I got. We'd go across the street and play with the kids who lived there, or I'd take him down the street to visit an older couple who seemed to really like us. The man would do things to make us laugh, like wiggling his ears. I felt safe at their house. But inside the house where we lived, I don't remember us playing at all, not with each other, or with the other foster kids.

When I was about six years old, my dad told Matthew and me that he'd be coming for us as soon as he could find us a new mother. He started bringing different women with him when he came to visit us. We'd all go to the drive-in movies or out to eat. As far as I was concerned, any woman would do.

Finally, when I was seven years old, he brought Paula to the house and told Matthew and me that they were getting married. I thought she was very pretty. She was petite and had black hair. My dad said they would be back in a couple of weeks to take us home. It was the news I'd been waiting to hear for so long. After they left, I heard Mrs.

Howley say to her husband, "Did you see that woman? She's an Indian!" (Native American). I was confused by her reaction and was glad that my new mother was Indian.

Psychologically speaking, whatever trauma a child experiences, can have damaging effects for life. But if the child receives treatment for the trauma, as well as love and validation from parental figures, the chances for the child's self-esteem and healthy development can be increased. Well, that was not to be my fate.

It was a beautiful summer day when my dad and Paula came to take us to our new home. I remember sitting in the back seat of my dad's car. As we drove away, the Howleys were in the front yard waving, appearing to be a loving couple, sad to see us leaving. I had no tears to shed. I was anything but saddened to see the last of those people. I didn't even wave goodbye, but looked at them instead, with a smirk of victory on my freckled face. I was finally leaving that hell-hole, with renewed trust in my father, and dirty little secrets forgotten, in the wake of that glorious day of freedom.

I liked our two-bedroom apartment in Lynwood, a suburb of L.A. County. Matthew and I finally had our own bedroom together. I liked my new mother, Paula. She was only 23 years old, 14 years younger than my dad, and was lots of fun. While my dad was at work, she'd take Matthew and me on picnics and to the movies. We had snacks and toys and the freedom to play outside and run wild. I was in charge of the running wild part.

Sometimes my new mother would get out the reel-to-reel tape recorder, and make up stories for us to act out. I remember a cowboy story where Matthew was in charge of the sound affects for trotting horses. I started to feel like a kid again.

I let my guard down. I knew my dad wasn't going anywhere so I must have felt safe enough to let my anger seep out. I became a brat toward my dad and would make fun of his thinning hair; I let it out with my little brother by bossing him around. He was a very sweet boy, but I would make fun of him too. Once I made a mud pie and made Matthew take a bite. The poor little guy did whatever I told him. I regret not being a good big sister to him when we were kids. But I was only seven years old, and didn't know how to get those feelings out, so I took them out on the ones closest to me.

We had a fun summer and I entered second grade, but before long, I felt the tension between my parents and realized that the cause of that tension was Matthew and me. My mom was pregnant, which may have been part of it. She was upset that my brother and I weren't helping out with chores. So I decided that I'd start washing dishes. I had to stand on a stool to reach the sink, but I felt like I better help out, because I didn't want my new mother to be upset anymore.

My mom would let me play dress up in her clothes. Boy, I was like a kid let loose in a candy store. I wanted to experience all the things I wasn't able to before, and all at once. I had pop-beads for necklaces and plastic Cinderella shoes with glitter in them. For Halloween we went trick-or-treating for the first time, and got to eat our candy whenever we wanted. Sugar! My first addiction.

My new mom had a mother and four sisters. Paula's mom was Quechan and Yaqui Indian, from Fort Yuma,

California. Her dad was Mexican, but she never knew him. I loved going to their house on 11th Street, in downtown L.A. My brother and I were part of a bigger family now, and I loved it. My own Cherokee grandmother, I later learned, was an alcoholic and living in L.A. at the time. Not once did she try to see my brother and me. My new grandmother, Lela, would be the only grandparent I'd ever know, and I loved her dearly. I really enjoyed lying on my aunt's beds, watching as they dressed up for their dates. There was laughter in that house. There was teasing and scolding, just like in a real family.

We went to Mass every Sunday, and although my brother had been baptized Catholic at birth, I had not. So I became a full-fledged Catholic at the age of seven. There was solace for me in attending the Mass, even though I still didn't have much of an understanding of who God was.

At some point, I began to notice a subtle change in the way my father interacted with me. He wasn't as attentive as he'd been after we first left the foster home. I felt that my mother was jealous of our relationship. So I stopped acting like a brat toward my dad and backed off from seeking his attention, because I thought I should.

I was eight years old when I had a new baby brother. Donald had light brown hair and green eyes. Not long after he was born, we moved to Paramount, another suburb of L.A. County. It was a nice two-bedroom house, with a front and backyard, with an enclosed patio. In the backyard, there was the perfect tree for climbing.

The next door neighbors were the O'Neils. They were an Irish Catholic family with six kids, and they came over to introduce themselves right away. One of the girls,

Anne, was my age, and one of the boys, Patrick, was Matthew's age. The O'Neils had a huge yard with apricot, plum, and peach trees. Anne had a dollhouse that we often played in.

When I was in the second grade, I discovered I had writing abilities. I wrote a story about a duck, with pictures to go with it, and put it in booklet form. I punched holes in the side of it and strung it with yarn. I was very proud of my first book.

I joined the Brownies and wore pennies in my brown loafers, as was the custom in the late 50's. I liked wearing the uniform, but mostly I liked going to the meetings and eating cookies.

When I was about nine years old, my mother began losing patience with me because, as I understood it, I had become withdrawn. Looking back, it was probably because of all the feelings I had stuffed about what had happened to me in the foster home, as well as my dad having pulled away from me. She'd slap me, or hit me with the belt for being too quiet and for not smiling and talking.

This drastic change in her behavior toward me was a shock, and I withdrew even further. I was under a lot of pressure, trying to figure out how I was supposed to act. She thought she could whip me into this happy, talkative child. She only hit me though, when my dad wasn't around. Now I had even more secrets to keep from him. But I kept my mouth shut, and kept her secret, because I didn't want to get beat.

She would often wake me up in the middle of the night to wash walls with her. This only happened when my dad was working graveyard. My mom told me several years later that *her* mother would get her out of bed to wash walls too. I wasn't a stranger to adults and their "crazy making" ways, so I just did what I was told.

One night, as my mom and I were washing the living room wall, I felt the need to tell her about what had happened in the foster home. I'd already shared a little about the Howleys with her, and was building up to the big one. So that night, as I began to talk about them she said, "I'm sick of hearing about those people. Don't talk about them again!" Wham! A steel door shut on the subject of my abuse, not to be brought up again until several years later.

When I was in the third grade, I had a teacher who was very kind to me. I had written some poems and she praised me, telling me to never stop writing them. Once, at the end of the school day, after all the other kids had left, she walked me to the bus. I told her that I wished she was my mother. Once again, I wanted to be saved, and I knew it wasn't going to be my father.

Recess in the third grade meant playing marbles, usually by myself. I had my own little cloth bag of big and small cat eyes and "steelies," as they were called. If I wasn't playing marbles, I was sitting in the grass making chain necklaces out of dandelion flowers. Sometimes I'd play jacks with the other girls.

When I was in the fourth grade, Matthew and I started going to Catholic school. I liked wearing the blue plaid jumper and white blouse. Wearing a uniform made me feel as if I were a part of something, like I belonged. So began my years with the Sister Mary's and the corporal punishment, which was pretty much a given, if you attended parochial school back then.

I continued to play alone during recess. I'd spin on the monkey bars or participate in other forms of solitary play. My social skills were stunted and I didn't know how to initiate play; besides, I felt so awful about myself that I didn't think anyone would want to play with me. But once in a while, if invited, I'd join in on hopscotch and jumping rope with the other girls.

Sometimes I would go inside the church, because it was right there on school grounds, and make a "visit." I would pray to Our Blessed Mother to help me at home and to make my mother stop hurting me. I begged her to appear to me like she did to Bernadette. I felt desperate and afraid and didn't want to be alive if I had to be hit and slugged all the time, for reasons I didn't understand. I just wanted relief, but the relief never came.

I was a good kid; I did my chores and my homework. My crime was that I was just too quiet. My mother gave me nicknames like "Deadbeat," "Mousy," and "Dead Head."

I started wetting the bed when I was about ten. When that stopped I developed a couple of nervous conditions that were compulsive in nature. When I walked through the hallway I had to tap my hands twice on each wall, or I felt anxious. I also began blinking my eyes a lot. When I stopped the compulsive blinking, I went to habitual nose sniffing and clearing my throat. My mother's response to those nervous conditions of mine was to slap me, or yell at me to stop, which of course, only made me that much more anxious. The pressure and stress I experienced as a child would end up turning into depression in my teens.

It was 1960. Kennedy was president and rock and roll was really hot. I memorized every song I heard: *A Thousand*

Stars in the Sky, Johnny Angel, and *The Lion Sleeps Tonight,* to name a few. I only sang rock and roll songs when I was alone. Music became my refuge, my escape, my passion. I'd make up songs in my head. I had the words and melodies memorized so that my mom wouldn't find anything written down and get mad because I was hiding things from her. It's funny, I had to keep quiet about her abuse of me, but God forbid if she found out I was keeping secrets from *her.*

My whole existence was becoming one big lie. I became very good at keeping my true feelings to myself. I trusted no one. My candy addiction really took hold around that time. Sometimes on Sundays, when Matthew and I walked to Mass by ourselves, my mother would give me the little envelope with the offering of fifty cents to put in the basket. On the way to Mass, we would stop at the little grocery store and I'd buy us candy with that change. We had to eat it all before we got home. Once, when Matthew and I returned from Mass, he tattled on me. My mom searched my pockets and found a toy I bought from the nickel slot machine. It was a little, clear, plastic ball with a rubber ring inside. I believe I covered at least two mortal sins in that little caper. Needless to say, there were no more envelopes for *me* to take to Mass. Matthew was always telling on me for something. As I got older, it was, "Mother, Rita said a bad word." Hell, I learned how to swear from her, which is probably why she never got mad at me for it.

Life with my new mother wasn't all bad, though. In fact, most of the time it was good, but because she was so unpredictable, I was always on guard for the next assault. Sometimes, after my dad had just left to work the graveyard shift, she'd wake me up to watch the Carol Burnett Show with her, or the Late Show with Jack Parr, before Johnny Carson became the host.

I'll never forget the day I learned how to ride a bike. My dad bought me a used bike at the swap meet and repainted it. After he pushed me off a few times, it took, and I was off. I rode that bike every chance I got. Cruising the neighborhood became my new passion, my little slice of freedom. One time I was out riding and I saw a dollar bill in the street. To market, to market, to buy candy bars I went. I can't remember how many I bought, but at five cents apiece, I hit the jackpot.

I had the kind of roller skates that you tightened with a key over your shoes. I loved skating and have the scars on my knees to prove it. After I became good at skating, my dad started taking me to the ice rink. Those were some special times. Having been born and raised in Chicago, my dad was an avid ice skater. I loved the smell of the rink, and the way the skates sounded as they cut through the ice. I took to ice skating like I'd been born to it, and was soon skating backwards and in circles.

My 10th or 11th birthday landed on a Saturday, and my dad was going to take me to the ice rink. But before we left, my parents handed me a large box. Inside was a beautiful pair of white leather skates. I could've died and gone to heaven. I know now that the gift was my mom's idea, as well as having my dad take me ice skating. She realized that I had the need to spend more time with my dad and was always aware of what would make me happy in the way of gifts. She bought me a couple of Shirley Temple dolls because she knew how much I enjoyed watching her movies. She even rolled my hair up in socks so I'd have long, curly locks, like the young Shirley Temple did.

Right around 1960, a huge fad hit the nation with teenage girls—ratting hair. When I walked home from school, I'd pass the public high school and I knew who the *bad girls* were. They wore tight black skirts and had these big hairdos. I was fascinated with those girls. Those were the days when I'd come home from school and watch American Bandstand. I'd practice all the dances as they came out: the Mashed Potato, the Peppermint Twist, and the Pony.

Because I was so shy and was somewhat of a tomboy, my mom signed me up for different classes. First it was ballet lessons, then piano lessons, then charm school, where we had to perform skits and walk around with books on our heads. Finally, it was baton lessons. None of it worked. I preferred playing with my brothers Matthew and Donald; making roads in the dirt with Tonka trucks in the backyard, playing baseball in the street, or kick the can with the neighborhood kids, and climbing trees. I was glad my mom didn't force me to continue any of those lessons. But in her own way, she was trying to do something to help me come out of my shell, as she called it, and to be less of a tomboy. It's just that it was too late for me to want to be girly.

There was one thing that really captured my attention and enthusiasm—the Girl Scouts. I liked the idea of the merit badges, and with my mom's help, I earned them all. It gave me a feeling of accomplishment. I liked wearing the green dress with the green sash, full of all the patches that I'd earned. It made me feel important.

By the time I was 11years old, I had four brothers. After Donald, came Frankie, and then Kevin. I'd hoped for at least one sister, but after a while it didn't matter. My mother needed my help a lot more with each arrival. I loved holding them and playing with them when they were little.

Donald was becoming quite a little character. Unlike Matthew and me, he was a happy and spontaneous little boy. At a year old, Frankie was the cutest thing, with his big brown eyes, long eyelashes, and wavy dark hair. Kevin, the baby, had straight dark hair and brown eyes. Matthew had blond hair and blue eyes. Then there was me with reddish hair and green eyes. My dad had one blue eye and one green eye. We all looked so different from each other. As I got older, people often remarked on how my brothers and I didn't look like we were even related. Of course, that was never a problem for us. And we never referred to each other as step-brothers and step-sister.

I was becoming less and less sure of what pleased my mother, but hid my pain under superficial smiles and conversation. I went deeper and deeper into myself and hadn't a clue as to who I was. I began stealing candy from the grocery store on a regular basis, until I got caught by the manager. I'd buy candy with my milk money. We rarely had cookies or other sweets in the house, and when we did, I would sneak whatever I could as soon as my mom went outside. Sometimes my timing was terrible and she'd come walking in and ask me what I was eating. "Nothing," I'd say with cookie crumbs all over my mouth. I became quite the liar. The evidence would be glaring, but it was my story and I was sticking to it.

One Saturday afternoon, I was playing in the backyard by myself. I had climbed the tree and was perched on one of its branches, daydreaming. My mother came outside and I immediately climbed down as I was afraid I'd done something to displease her. After gauging her mood, I realized that she wasn't upset with me. Instead, she asked, "Do you want to go with me to the store?" When I hesitated, she said, "If you don't want to just say so." As soon as I told her that I wanted to stay home, I knew by the tightness in her face and the sharpness of her eyes, that I'd given the wrong answer. "Fine," she said, and left in the family station wagon.

I sat outside, thinking about how miserable I was. I'd heard about kids running away from home and felt that it was my only option. I went in the house and saw that my dad was in the living room watching TV. I don't remember where my brothers were, probably napping. I went to the kitchen and turned on the water faucet, acting like I was getting a drink of water. I needed to drown out my opening of the junk drawer to search for a sheet of paper and a pencil, without making my dad suspicious. Upon finding what I needed, I went back outside and sat in the patio in the backyard, to write my goodbye note. I wrote that I was running away because I didn't think my parents loved me. I signed it, "Love Sheila," and surrounded the words with a big heart.

I took off with no direction in mind. I quickly walked down a couple of side streets until I came upon the railroad tracks. I decided to walk on the tracks because I didn't want to be seen from the streets. As I was crossing a major intersection, I saw our blue Pontiac station wagon a few blocks away, and knew that it was probably my dad looking for me. I'd been gone for a couple hours by then. I ran down an alley and sat down to think about what I was going to do. It was starting to get dark, and only then, did I think about how I was going to eat and where I would sleep. In my impulsivity, I realized that I hadn't thought out my plan very well. I was a very naïve twelve year old.

Eventually, I knew I'd have to return home and I couldn't imagine what awaited me there. I was scared as I rounded the corner to our house. As I got closer, I saw several cars parked outside our house. I gingerly walked in the back door and then into the living room. I don't remember any of the visitors or what they said. I had eyes only for my parents, and what I could read from their expressions. My father looked relieved and my mother's eyes were bloodshot from crying. My parents didn't hug me and hold me close, saying how glad they were that I was back and that I was okay. Instead, my father, belt in hand, promptly escorted me to the bedroom I shared with my four brothers. Everyone, including my brothers, was still in the living room. As I lay on my bed, my dad spanked my bottom lightly, about five times, over my dress. My futile attempt at trying to communicate my desperation, had failed. I felt doomed to endure my mother's wrath.

My father had never spanked or hit me before. He didn't ask me about the letter I'd left. It was never talked about. My mother told everyone that I just wanted to go see some horses.

Because nothing of major importance was ever acknowledged by the adults in my life, I began to feel as if I were going crazy. When that sort of thing happens with children, it can cause them to disconnect from their *wild*, or, intuitive natures, and not trust what they see and feel. That's what happened with me. This lack of acknowledgement and validation created problems for me for the majority of my life. It made me question my own perceptions. I had a hard time deciphering between what was real and what I thought I imagined. I'd often have to ask others for a "reality check," because I didn't trust my own judgment. I was continually seeking validation from sources outside of myself.

After a couple of days of my mother ignoring me, she let me know how angry she was with me for running away. She said I was a troublemaker. Had my dad talked to her about the note I left, after all? Or was my running away an inconvenience to her because of how it may have made her look to the relatives and neighbors? When she was no longer upset with me, she handed me a new Girl Scout camera. She told me that was the reason she wanted me to go to the store with her that day. I then realized that she must've been hurt when I told her I didn't want to go.

One day, in 1962, we had to leave our home and my grandmother, aunts, uncles, and cousins. My dad had gotten a transfer from his beat in Compton, as a highway patrolman, to a town called Red Bluff, in the northern part of California. On the drive up, my mother was crying, and so was I. It was pretty traumatic, especially when we entered the town's city limits. I read the sign, "Red Bluff, population 6,000." I had been a city girl and wasn't looking forward to a new life in a small town where we didn't know anyone. It was quite an adjustment.

Our house had three bedrooms. My parents had one, three of my brothers were in another, and my baby brother Kevin and I, shared the third. Matthew and I began school at Our Lady of Mercy. I was in the middle of the sixth grade. I was getting used to changing schools, but it didn't make it any easier.

Red Bluff seemed like a town right out of the old west, real redneck-ville. Every year there was a western parade and we would all be dressed in Levis and cowboy shirts. I liked that part, it was the only time I was allowed to wear Levis. But my mom wore her regular clothes. I think she was the only Native woman in the whole town. My dad was totally into it. He even bought a pair of black cowboy boots and started wearing them with his highway patrol uniform.

One Sunday evening, my mom called me away from my homework to watch the Ed Sullivan Show. There was this new rock group, the Beatles, and she wanted me to see them. I sat in front of the black and white television set and fell instantly in love with the four boys with their amazing new sound in music and long hair as they sang, *I want to Hold Your Hand.* The next morning when I went to school, I found out that most of the girls had watched the Ed Sullivan Show. We couldn't stop talking about the rock group from England. We eventually learned all of their songs and even began speaking with an English accent.

In the seventh grade I won the spelling bee. It was the first time I'd won anything. I was proud of myself. I knew then that I loved words. I also loved art class and was a pretty decent artist, but somehow lost that ability along the way.

All of the girls in my seventh grade class were wearing bras, except me. I had no reason to. I was tall and lanky, with no figure whatsoever. I started with a training bra. I wondered what I was supposed to be training. I'd put tissue paper in mine so that it would appear that I had something to put in that training bra. I wanted so much to be like the other girls, because I'd been teased about my flat chest. Once, I put blue tissue in my bra, not realizing that it would show through my white blouse. I was the joke of the class for a week.

I didn't have many friends at school. I'd hang out by myself or with another girl who was shyer than I was. One of my friends was Jan Gorcey. Her dad was Leo Gorcey, a child star from the 1930's, who'd played in several movies as one of the *Dead End Kids*. I eventually tired of her. All she did was brag about what her life had been like while growing up in L.A., with maids and fancy clothes. I thought, *and look at you now. You're no better than any of us; you're wearing the same plain uniform we all have to wear and you're not rich anymore.*

Sister Mary Dominica was my eight grade teacher. She was hell on wheels. She enjoyed walking up and down the rows of students, swinging her ruler around or hitting you in the back with her big hands. I was getting it at school *and* at home.

My mother's abuse of me got worse. She started punching me in the face, and kicking me in the stomach after I'd fallen down from her blows. It was brutal. I'd get hit with whatever was handy. I had lots of black eyes and fat lips. She told me that if my dad asked me what happened, to tell him that I was playing baseball with the neighbor kids and the ball hit me in the face. Funny thing was, he never asked. To my knowledge, he never investigated why I always had cuts and bruises. I don't think he wanted to know. You'd think that would be second nature to a cop, but he only protected and served outside the home.

As my mother's rage escalated, I became more and more terrified. By the time I was in high school, I was afraid to go to sleep. Sometimes, when my dad was working graveyard, she'd get me up from my half-awake slumber and drag me by my hair down the long hallway, to beat me or force me to scrub walls. Sometimes during her attacks on me she'd say things like, "I wish you were dead." I became aware of her every mood and location in the house. I was always tense and on high alert. She would beat me in front of my brothers and sometimes in the garage when neighbor kids were out playing. I would be mortified. I felt so ashamed and miserable that I hated myself *and* her. I wished that my dad would divorce her. Either she was a great actress or he was in big time denial, forever the ostrich with his head in the sand.

I had no one to talk to about what was happening at home. I was afraid of what would happen to me if I did tell someone. Matthew was being physically and emotionally abused by her as well, but finally had the guts to grab her hands one time, when she had them around his neck. He told her not to touch him again. She didn't. My little brothers were often yelled at and slapped, but not beaten; however, were witness to Matthew and me as we cried and moaned under the barrage of her punches and thrashings of the belt.

"Stand up straight! Pull your shoulders back," was a regular demand made by my mom. I began slumping my shoulders, without realizing I was doing so. I now attribute that to extremely low self-esteem. I was also a tall girl. Being tall made me more visible and I would have preferred being invisible. My mom was going to make me wear a back brace; luckily, I talked her out of it. It was bad enough that I had to dress down for gym class with my legs full of bruises. I didn't need the added humiliation.

I had chores to do during the week like mopping, vacuuming, dusting the furniture, and folding and ironing the clothes. I also helped with dinner preparation and washed all the dishes. I still loved to sing and would do so in private or at school. But when I did my chores I was *expected* to sing, and it felt too much like punishment. Especially when my mom would hit me for not singing, or yell at me from another room saying things like, "I don't hear you singing. Are you dead back there?"

By the time I started high school, I had a lot of responsibilities where my brothers were concerned. I woke them up in the morning, fixed their breakfast, made their sack lunches, and made sure they were dressed and ready for school. Somehow I managed to get myself dressed as well. Once everyone was ready, I'd wake my mom up. Before she drove us to school, she'd fix my hair in a 50's style hairdo, which I hated, and make me put on the red lipstick that she wore. As soon as I got to school I'd head for the bathroom, hike up my uniform skirt, redo my hair, and replace the red lipstick with a frosted pink color that the girls were wearing at that time.

Our Lady of Mercy High School had 120 students. Only about 20 of them were males, who were most likely, bound for the priesthood, as very few of them seemed interested in us girls. Matthew was allowed to go to public high school. By then, I was getting tired of wearing a uniform and the ugly white saddle shoes. The classes were all college prep. They were tougher than those at the public school, and I had to work hard for my grades. I was as intelligent as my brother Matthew, but his good grades came easier for him.

When I was 15, I had several more survival mechanisms set in place. I was a habitual liar and a compulsive thief. I'd walk into the local drug store and steal notebooks, pens, and assorted school supplies, just for the sake of stealing. I hid my goods in my school locker. I stole change from my mom's purse to buy candy. I also began running away from home again, but I was always found. At 15, I also began having thoughts of suicide, but was too afraid of going to hell.

My dad had initially transferred from L.A. to the small town of Red Bluff, because he wanted to raise his family in a safer environment, and I'm sure he felt it would be safer for him as a highway patrolman. It's a good thing too, because not long after we moved, the Watts riots broke out and that had been my dad's beat.

Well, one morning I woke up at the usual time and headed for the boys room to wake them up for school, and I heard my parents talking in the kitchen. I was surprised to see my dad there, in his uniform, because he should have been in bed asleep after working the graveyard shift. There was a tension in the air. I asked my dad what was going on and my mom told me to bring the boys to the living room; they wanted to talk to us. The story that followed was incredible.

Apparently, my dad and his partner, Officer Carson, had been in a high speed chase a few hours before with two juveniles, who had robbed, and then tied up an old man in his home. My dad and Carson spotted the young men as they sped past them on the freeway. They proceeded to chase them at speeds in excess of 100 miles an hour, all the while, were being shot at by the passenger in the suspect's vehicle. My dad's partner, Carson, was riding shotgun, and was shot in the hand as he had his arm out of the window, shooting back at the suspects.

The young men were eventually apprehended and taken into custody by my dad and Carson. When I got to school that day, everyone was talking about it. Then I saw the picture in the paper. It showed the patrol car that my dad was driving, with a large bullet hole on the driver's side of the windshield. Miraculously, the bullet hadn't completely penetrated the glass, if it had, my dad would have been killed.

After that, we were afraid of something terrible happening to my dad when he went to work. There was another incident that occurred around that time too. My dad had been one of the first officers on the scene at the home of a family, whereby, the father had shot and killed his wife and all of his small children, before fatally wounding himself.

Because my dad was a highway patrolman, he witnessed a lot of car accidents and a lot of deaths. He was also the one who often had to go to the homes of the deceased and inform them of their loss. I came to understand much later, the effect that can have on someone. No wonder my dad seemed distant at times and emotionally unavailable. He was also a WWII vet, which is where his psychological numbing probably began.

Once in a while, on Saturday afternoons, when the boys were napping and my dad was at work, my mom would have me sit at the kitchen table with her as she drank her coffee, and she'd tell me about her childhood.

As is common in many Native American families, she was raised by her grandmother. My mother would talk about the house she lived in with the dirt floor and the outhouse, and about the closeness she shared with her grandma, who she called mom. Once, she brought out pictures of herself as a child with long black braids, smiling. When she was 12 years old, she said her real mother wanted her back, so she left the love of her grandma and went to live with her mom in Los Angeles. She talked about the abusiveness of her mother and how she felt unwanted and unloved by her.

Other times, she'd tell me funny stories about her teenage years or about how she met my dad. At those times she was no longer the woman that I feared, but a human being, with her own tragic story. It was during one of our times at the kitchen table when I felt comfortable enough to share something very personal with her.

I was 16 years old. I began by asking her what a "sex fiend" was, as I'd heard that expression used by girls at school. When she thoughtfully responded, I felt safe enough to tell her about the molestation by my foster father. I don't remember her response, but I knew she took me seriously. Years later, she told me that when she told my dad about it, he felt guilty and cried. "You *should* feel guilty," she told him. "How could you not know what kind of people they were?" After I told my mom about it, I would have appreciated some validation from my dad like, "Yes, that was horrible and wrong and it wasn't your fault. I'm sorry that I didn't protect you like I should have." But once again, there was no acknowledgement that it even happened.

Not long after that, my mom took me to a gynecologist to find out why I hadn't started my period. I think my folks wanted to know if it had something to do with my sexual abuse. That's why I think that I must've told my mom that there was more that my foster father did to me, but I've never asked her about it, and I no longer remember or need to know.

The doctor gave my mom birth control pills for me to take. A couple of days later, I started my period. When my dad found out, he had tears in his eyes. I don't know whether it was because his little girl was growing up, or because he was relieved that Mr. Howley hadn't physically injured me. But my injuries were far worse than anything physical.

I had my first paying job when I was 15 and a half years old. I started out by volunteering as a candy striper, handing out magazines to the hospital patients, delivering them their flowers, and chatting with them. The nuns at the Catholic hospital where I volunteered, noticed how much I enjoyed helping the patients, and took a liking to me. I was hired at $1.35 an hour and trained to be a nurse's aide. My parents were very proud of me.

The money I made went into my own bank account and was to be used for my college education. The job gave my self-confidence a boost and I enjoyed working one-on-one with the nurses.

Initially, I worked on the general medical floor, where the patients there were adults and kids, some were accident victims. Then I was transferred to another wing of the hospital to work with the elderly. That was depressing for me; most of them died there. I got tired of bedpans and having to feed them and treat their bed sores. When a patient died, I was often asked by another nurse to sit in the room with the body and wait for the morticians to come. I'd feel scared as I sat with the corpses, and watched the skin changing color. I'd half expect to see their spirit float up to the ceiling and leave through the window. Whenever one of my patients died, I had to clean the corpse, but never by myself. The nurses were protective of me because I was so young. I got tired of watching people die.

During the next three years, I worked on several other wards. I worked with surgical patients too, but liked the OB ward the best; I enjoyed being around the newborns. Once, I had the priviledge of witnessing a mother giving birth.

I was allowed to start going to dances when I was 16 years old. My friend, Kathy, asked me if I wanted to go to a dance with her on a Friday night. It was being held at the public high school. She said her mom would take us and pick us up when it was over.

I was very shy with boys. I'd get tongue-tied when it came to talking with them. But I had my good looks going for me and I definitely got noticed; although, I felt anything but attractive when I was younger. Because I felt so ugly on the inside, I naturally felt ugly on the outside.

When Kathy and I got to the dance that night, we were asked to dance right away, by two boys who were friends, Brian and Allen. We ended up dancing with them for the entire night. When it was time for us to leave, the boys asked Kathy and me out on a double date for the following Saturday night. I hadn't been on a date before and I really wanted to go. When I got home that evening, I asked my parents if I could go out with the boy named Brian. After a couple of days of deliberation, they said yes, but with conditions. I was elated! In those days, and in that small town, dating consisted of going out for a soda, to a dance, to a sports event, to the show, or to the bowling alley.

When Brian came to the door that night, he was ushered in by my mom. Since I was still getting ready, he had to sit in the living room, answering my father's questions about himself, his family, where he was taking me, and so on. My mom gave me a dime to call home in case I was in trouble. After that, she always gave me a dime when I went out on a date.

Brian and I met up with Kathy and Allen, but then we split up. Before Brian brought me home that night, he parked his 1964 Chevy Impala and started kissing me. I didn't care for it, but thought it was expected, and so I faked it.

My mom's favorite alcoholic beverage was scotch. She kept a bottle, high up in the kitchen cupboard. I rarely remember seeing her drinking it, though. My dad preferred beer. He'd drink a couple of beers, once or twice a week. Sometimes, my dad would go out drinking with his cop partner, Carson. Once, he walked home from the bar, drunk.

He ended up pissing in his bedroom closet. Other than that, I never saw my dad drunk. I never saw my mom drunk, either. Her addiction was to rage.

It was Brian who introduced me to getting drunk. We'd tell my parents we were going to a basketball game, and end up at one of his friend's houses, drinking beer. The parents were always gone for the evening. After two beers, I'd often have to go lie down in one of the bedrooms and pass out. When it was close to my curfew time, one of the girls would come wake me up. On our way home, Brian would turn on his car radio so we could find out the score of the game we said we were going to, because I knew my folks would ask me. I'd be chewing gum like crazy to get rid of the smell of beer. It seemed to work because when I kissed my parents good night, they didn't catch it.

My dad wanted to make sergeant. After passing the written test, he had to go to Sacramento to take the oral exam. It was a Saturday, and everyone was going to Sacramento. My mom said that I could stay home with my little brother, Kevin, who was about five years old at the time. They left in the morning and wouldn't be returning until late that evening.

My little brother and I were very close. He slept in my bed until he was old enough to sleep in a bunk bed. There wasn't enough room in my bedroom for a crib. I bathed him every night and rocked him to sleep while I sang to him, until he was about three years old.

It was early afternoon of that day, when I started drinking my mom's scotch. I don't recall what made me do that. Kevin was young enough that I knew he wouldn't tell on me. I don't remember how much I drank, but I was pretty drunk. It was the first time I got drunk on hard liquor and I liked the way it made me feel. I added water to the bottle of scotch, and managed to sober up by the time my family returned. No one suspected a thing.

Brian gave me his school ring after we'd been dating for a few months. That was a big deal. I had a boyfriend who cared about me and I felt special. It was a buffer to the abuse I was still receiving, and made life bearable.

I had three girlfriends when I was in high school: Kathy, Andrea, and Janis. Kathy always made the honor roll and later became an R.N. Andrea came from the only Mexican family that lived in Red Bluff. When we were sophomores, Andrea's mom died suddenly. She ended up marrying and having lots of kids. The last I heard, she was living in Mexico with her family. Janis had horses. Riding horses with Janis was one of the best memories I have of my childhood. I don't know what became of Janis. In 1970, her parents were killed in a head on collision. She was only 20 years old. But those three girls were true friends. I wish I'd stayed in touch with them.

One day, I was sitting in Chemistry class. It was during my junior year. All of a sudden, I became overwhelmed with emotion. I was afraid I'd break down right there in front of everyone, so I got up from my desk and left the classroom, very abruptly. My friend, Kathy, came after me and found me in the girl's bathroom, in tears. I'd reached a point where I couldn't hold my feelings back. When Kathy asked me what was wrong, I told her that I hated myself and that I wished I was dead. I'd never mentioned a word to my three friends about what I was going through at home. I was too ashamed to tell them. Kathy hadn't known I was in so much pain. She pointed out the things that she saw in me, "You're such a good person. You're smart and funny, and you always make me laugh," she said. I felt better after having a good cry and for being validated by my friend.

One summer night, Brian took me to an outdoor dance at the fairgrounds. I was in good spirits, but noticed that Brian seemed distracted. He said he had to talk to me about something, so we went to the bleachers and sat down. He told me that he wanted his ring back. When I asked him why, he said that he'd met someone else who liked "making out." That night, I used the dime my mom had given me.

I was devastated. My mom was extremely sensitive to how bad I was hurting. That was my first heartbreak. It took me a long time to get over Brian. Sadly, after that, I realized what I had to do to keep a boy interested in me, although, I never let a boy go too far.

High school was a tough time for me. Doing homework wasn't easy because I had difficulty concentrating and remembering what I'd read. I often found myself just spacing out and staring at my textbook, or daydreaming about boys. After my freshman year, my mom was determined to help me increase my grade point average from a C to a B, because she knew I could do better. She worked diligently with me every school night, and in my sophomore year, I made the honor roll with a B+ average.

After I finished the tenth grade, my mom decided that Matthew and I needed some volunteer experience. She had us sign up as activity counselors with a program for the mentally disabled. The only activity I remember was a camping trip at a lake. What a disaster *that* turned out to be. I loved camping and swimming, so I was really looking forward to it.

We arrived at the lake in the early afternoon. We supervised the handicapped people as they got off the bus and shepherded them to their tents. Then the other girl counselors and I located our lodgings and settled in. After the evening meal, I went back to our tent. Bobbie, one of the counselors, produced a fifth of whiskey, and asked if anyone wanted a drink. I was the only volunteer. That night, we were supposed to be in the dining room, supervising a dance. After having a few drinks with Bobbie, I staggered into the dining hall, drunk on my ass, making a complete fool of myself. Matthew knew I was drunk, but didn't say anything to me. I think he was too embarrassed.

The next day, I was horribly hung-over. I'd been assigned to take some of the disabled folks out on the lake, in a raft. I paddled us out into the lake, using an oar, and proceeded to get us stuck in some tall weeds. I was in a foul mood and started yelling at my passengers to help me get us the hell out of there and back to shore. I didn't care if they *were* retarded. When we made it back, I was informed that the trip was over; we were returning to Red Bluff.

Nothing was said to me directly, but I knew it was because of my drunken behavior the night before. On the bus ride back, I told my brother that if he ratted on me, I would tell our parents that I'd seen him kissing a girl—which I did—and he didn't. Phew!

During my junior year, I began to experience more depression than usual; as a result, I dropped back down into a 2.0 grade point average. At the end of that school year, my parents wanted me to repeat the 11th grade. I begged them to allow me to move on with my class, but they wanted me to improve my chances of getting into nursing school. I no longer had an interest in becoming a nurse, but didn't have the guts to tell them. I just knew how ashamed I'd feel, watching my classmates graduate ahead of me. I asked them if I could go to public school as a senior, instead. Eventually, they relented, much to my relief.

My mom ordered my school clothes from the Sears catalog. It was 1968 and styles were changing in a most dramatic way, and I loved it. The "Mod" style was replacing the large-striped surfer shirts and canvas tennis shoes. Mod clothing was brightly colored. Miniskirts and go-go boots were all the rave. My mom was cool in a lot of ways, especially when it came to my clothes, some of which she made herself. She even bought me a pair of white go-go boots. She made me a pair of long, white, bell bottoms and a matching top of a Native American print, with fringes on the bottom.

I had lots of compliments from the girls at school about my homemade clothes. But before I went on a date, I had to stand in front of my dad for inspection, making sure my skirts and dresses weren't too far above my knees. My dad was more old-fashioned than my mom.

My favorite class in senior year was speech. I loved creative writing, and received a lot of compliments from my teacher, Mr. Gleason. He was impressed with my writing and public speaking abilities. My mom would help me with my speeches. She was creative and clever and enjoyed helping me with my homework, as long as it wasn't math. Her abusiveness had slowed down a lot in my senior year.

I signed up for the school talent show. I wanted to sing. I chose the song, *You Keep Me Hangin' On,* by a group called Vanilla Fudge, originally sung by the Supremes. A group of rock musicians from the school agreed to accompany me. I had a new friend, Sheri, who was going to sing harmony. I was terrified of getting in front of the entire student body, but I also knew I had a good singing voice. My desire to sing outweighed any possible risk of me looking like a fool.

I stood behind the curtain, waiting to go on. The announcer introduced me. I very gingerly walked onto the stage with Sheri, legs shaking. As the curtain opened up, I couldn't look out at the audience; instead, I glanced over at the band and at Sheri, with a look that said, "Please, don't screw this up." I waited for my intro. Then, in my husky voice I sang..."Set me free...why don't ya babe." As the guitars, drums, and mine and Sheri's voices melded together, I felt alive and powerful.

I had lots of compliments afterwards. Matthew told me that one of his buddies said I sounded like a guy. What was funny was that as Matthew's voice started cracking, mine was getting deeper.

The Kiwanis Club of Red Bluff was sponsoring a speech contest. They wanted three seniors from the high school to participate in their contest. I was chosen as one of the three, by my speech teacher, Mr. Gleason. The topic was, "The Youth of Today." It was 1969, and boy, was I ever going to have fun with *that* topic. By then, I had developed some very definite views regarding the war in Southeast Asia and the so called "establishment." My mom was of the same mindset as I. We had fun writing my speech. With my mom's help, I decided to write about the revolting by students at a college in San Francisco. I titled it, "The Unrest at San Francisco State." I also included a piece on the S.D.S: Students for a Democratic Society.

The night of the speech, I met the two other student speakers. I didn't know them very well, but sensed that their views would be more to the liking of the panel of old, right-winged, white guys. I wasn't surprised when I came in at 3rd place, yet I didn't feel as though I had lost.

Hubert Gronin was an exchange student from Germany. He was enrolled at our high school for his senior year. He was tall and lanky, with very long fingernails. I was surprised when he asked me on a date. Of all the girls in the school, he seemed to be interested in me. I was quiet and kept to myself, so I couldn't figure it out. The first time he came to pick me up, he sat in our living room with my dad and my brothers while I finished getting ready. Many years later my brother, Frankie, who was about eight years old at the time, told me about that night. My dad was watching one of his favorite WWII combat shows. He had a dry wit that would often have my mom in tears; she'd be laughing so hard. So, as my dad and Hubert were watching the Americans blasting the Germans, my dad asked, "So Hubert, do you like American television?" "Not really," Hubert replied.

Hubert asked me to the senior prom. I'd never been asked to a prom before and I was really excited about it. My folks couldn't afford to buy me a gown, but I looked nice in my new dress just the same. My mom drove me to the dance because Hubert wasn't able to get a car for the night. He was meeting me outside the gym. When we got there, he was sitting alone on the steps, crying. That was a turn off in itself. He said that one of the guys had punched him. He had a shiner all right. My mom told him to get in the car and back home we went. She gave him an ice pack for his eye and he was still crying. *Shit*, I thought, *what a wimp. It's my last chance to go to a prom and this guy has to go get a black eye*. I don't think we dated after that.

There was only one other boy I dated in high school. His name was Delbert and I believe he later became a cop. My husband to be, who also went to Red Bluff High, said that he noticed me at school, but didn't bother trying to talk to me because he thought I was stuck up. Stuck up? That wasn't it at all. I wore a mask of aloofness because I was terribly self-conscious and not the least bit flirty.

There was one young man, Stan, who liked me as a friend. He'd wait for me outside my civics class and walk me to our speech class. He even carried my books. We hung out together at school and got along well. One day, I was standing outside of civics class, waiting for Stan. He didn't come. I went to my speech class and he wasn't there. When I asked about him one of the girls said, "You didn't hear?" "Hear what?" I said. "Last night Stan killed himself with a sawed-off shot gun." "Oh my God," I exclaimed.

I was allowed to attend the Catholic Rosary for Stan. The casket was closed for obvious reasons. The room was heavy with grief. I didn't approach his family because I didn't know what to say, I was so shocked. I never found out why he killed himself. He probably felt comfortable being in my company because he sensed that same feeling of desperation in *me*: wanting to escape the pain.

During 1969, the hippie movement had really gathered momentum. These were the free spirited youth who abhorred anything and everything that was conventional or of the norm. LSD and pot were the drugs of choice for many of the youth who called themselves hippies. Their spiritual and philosophical beliefs leaned toward the Eastern religions and those of Native Americans. They were searching for truth and a way of life that had meaning; they were fed up with the lies that were being told in newspapers, on television, and by the government. It was a very exciting time in my life.

At our high school, there was a ban on guys wearing bell bottom pants and the girls still couldn't wear pants of any kind. The boys who had longer hair, were the ones smoking dope and dropping acid. I longed to be a part of that group, because I'd always felt different from everyone.

The day I graduated from high school, June 10th, 1969, was also my birthday. My grandmother, Lela, came up on the train from Los Angeles for my graduation. After the ceremony was over, we went home to celebrate my birthday. I opened my presents and then I dressed for the senior party that was being held at the bowling alley.

That night I saw Brian. He asked me if I wanted to party with him and some other kids. I should've told him to fuck off; instead, I was thrilled by his attention and left with him and his friends. We drove around and then parked to drink beer and smoke pot. I took a puff, but didn't get anything out of it. Around 12:00am, they took me home. My mom was waiting up for me. She did something totally out of character and asked me if I wanted to go back with Brian and his friends to party some more. I had to have smelled like a brewery, but it wasn't a problem with her. My dad was at work. If he'd been there he wouldn't have allowed it. I had a blast that night and Brian brought me home just as the sun was coming up. Brian and I were on again, because I'd since learned how to kiss. When I got home that morning, I was allowed to sleep all day. I liked being 18.

After graduation I was expected to go to college, and since my GPA and SAT scores weren't high enough to get into nursing school, I'd have to go to a community college. The plan was that I'd go to Shasta College in Redding, about 20 miles away. I wasn't looking forward to any more school—period!

During my senior year I'd taken a water safety class. I learned CPR and lifesaving skills. My mom knew that I loved swimming. She told me about a job opening for a lifeguard at the city pool. I applied for the job and was hired to lifeguard for the summer.

For some reason, Brian and I broke up again and I started dating his friend, Allen. Allen turned me on to "downers." There were red ones, yellow ones, and rainbow ones. One night, I came home from a date, went into my room, and stumbled, falling into my dresser. My mom was in bed, but she yelled, "What's the matter with you? Are you drunk?" "No," I answered, truthfully. After that, my dad said I couldn't go out with Allen anymore.

Sometimes in the evening, my dad came to the city pool and I'd practice my lifesaving techniques on him. One such evening, I saw a boy that I vaguely recognized from high school, standing at the chain link fence, near the shallow end of the pool. He motioned for me to go talk to him. Earnie was a handsome boy, about 5'10, with dark hair and brown eyes. He asked me out on a date. It was a little weird because my dad was in the pool watching us. My dad was very protective of me when it came to boys. I learned later, that he always checked to see if my dates had criminal records.

Earnie and I hit it off right away. I wasn't shy with him and we had a mutual attraction for one another. I'd only known Earnie for two weeks when one day, he drove us to the Sacramento River. We were sitting on the grassy riverbank, when he told me that he loved me and wanted to marry me. I couldn't believe it. I was thrilled because I felt the same way about him.

My parents didn't like Earnie, but they didn't stop me from going out with him. I'd met his mom, Laverne, and his three brothers. Earnie was the eldest, so we had that in common. His parents were divorced and his dad lived in Michigan, which was where Earnie was originally from.

One day, soon after he'd proposed, Earnie called me and said he had something important to talk about. He picked me up and drove us to a cemetery. It was a strange place to go, I thought, to discuss a serious matter. The irony in that—is this. Earnie took me there to talk about our future, and that's where he ended up, much too early.

We both knew that his mother didn't care for me and didn't want her son getting too serious about me. Earnie's solution was to run away and get married, since our parents would never approve. I'd run away from home about four times in high school, and didn't want to cause my family any more grief, and I told him so. He gave me an ultimatum. Either I take off with him, or he would leave without me. I didn't want to lose him, yet I hoped that in time he'd change his mind.

About a week later, Earnie picked me up and we went for a drive to talk, and did some light making out. Afterwards, he dropped me off at home. As soon as I walked in the house, my mom cornered me in the kitchen and slammed me up against the wall, calling me a whore, accusing me of going to a motel room with Earnie. Well, she started calling me a whore before I even knew what it meant, so it was nothing new. It's a wonder I'd never acted on her accusations. And then, for the first time in my life, my dad stepped in and told my mother, "Don't touch my daughter!" That was the last time she put her hands on me. But it was too little, too late, for my dad to finally stand up for me. The damage had already been done. A few days later I told my mom, "I don't want to live here anymore." She didn't get angry; instead, plans were made for me to live in the college dorm in Redding.

Earnie was getting restless and kept pressuring me about leaving. I finally gave in, and we set a date to split. The plan was to go to Reno, get married, and from there, go to

San Francisco to check out the hippies. We were both tired of living in a one horse town. We wanted more excitement than what Red Bluff had to offer. I was to leave first and go to Redding and wait for him there. He was a fry cook at Denny's and had to collect his last check. I'd recently been fired from a restaurant job I had as a dishwasher. On the day I was to leave, Earnie said he'd call at a certain time, pretending to be my old boss from the restaurant.

On that day in late August, I was right there to answer the phone. When I hung up, I told my parents that I was needed to fill in for someone at the restaurant, who hadn't come in to work. They were both surprised, thinking it a bit odd, since I'd been fired. But I got dressed and kissed my dad goodbye, which he later called, "the kiss of Judas." My mom drove me to the restaurant. On the way there she sensed my uneasiness and asked, "What's the matter with you?" I told her nothing was the matter, but I was scared and feeling guilty for what I was about to do. After she dropped me off, I went inside the restaurant and used their pay phone to call a cab. I had the driver take me to my bank and wait for me. I withdrew all my money, about $500.00. Then he dropped me off at the Greyhound bus depot, where I caught the next bus to Redding.

Part Two
Naïve Wife and Child Mother

I was finally free! For years, I'd had to put up with my mother's control over me. I had to think the way she wanted me to think, feel the way she wanted me to feel, and act the way she wanted me to act. I was rarely allowed to make my own decisions about anything. This included everything from how I fixed my hair, to the clothing I wore. So the first thing I did, after checking into a motel room, was to go shopping. I purchased a set of huge rollers for my hair, a pair of Levis, sandals, and some long hippie dresses, and tops. Next, I bought a small record player, and albums by three groups that were popular at the time: The Box Tops, Led Zeppelin, and Cream. I also bought cigarettes and makeup. That night, I called Denny's Restaurant to let Earnie know I'd arrived.

The night before Earnie was to meet up with me, I met a guy at a concert, selling LSD. I bought $50.00 worth of acid. Since I had absolutely no boundaries when it came to my body, I thought nothing of taking a drug that could potentially, "blow my mind."

The guy that sold me the acid took me to a hippie "pad," where there were several other young people who were already "tripping." They welcomed me with open arms. I felt accepted, instead of different and unwanted, as I'd always felt. Acid was the drug I'd been waiting for. I thought I'd found the answers to all my questions. I had no fear, no anxiety, and no depression; only a feeling that everything was all right. I felt totally alive and beautiful for the first time in my life. We all talked until the sun came up, philosophizing about the meaning of life, with *acid rock* music playing in the background. I saw the most amazing colors and patterns of energy, and I merged with it all.

Around 7:00am, I knew I had to get back to the motel room; Earnie would be coming for me. A couple of the guys drove me back. Earnie arrived shortly thereafter. When he saw the young men in the motel room, he seemed suspicious; as well he should have been, although nothing of a sexual nature had occurred. He told the men to leave, and we loaded my things into his little, blue, Austen Healy sports car, and took off for Reno.

We stopped at the first wedding chapel we saw, and were informed that we couldn't get married without *his* parents' consent. I was of a legal age, but Earnie had to be 21. We had no idea! "Well," I told Earnie, "I guess we'll have to live together until we're 21." He seemed pleasantly surprised by that. We checked into a motel and then decided to go to the show. I took a hit of acid before we got to the movie. Earnie didn't want one. As we sat down to watch Bette Davis in *Whatever Happened to Baby Jane,* I began to freak out and we had to leave.

That night, I was afraid that Earnie would want to have sex with me. I was still a virgin and Earnie had always been appropriate with me, never trying to do anything more than kiss me. I knew that if we were going to live together, we would be having sex eventually, I just didn't want it to be that night. So I set my hair with the huge rollers, hoping that they would be a turn off. Then I got in bed and just lay there on my back, eyes closed, still high from the acid. He leaned over and kissed me on the cheek, before rolling over to go to sleep.

The next morning we hit the road, bound for San Francisco. We arrived in the early evening and got a room in a cheap hotel. Earnie agreed to take some acid with me that night, and we took the trolley car to the Fisherman's Wharf.

Afterwards, when we returned to the hotel room, I knew that we'd have sex. We were both high and I don't remember much about it.

We hung out in San Francisco for a couple more days, tripping on acid, marveling at all the "flower children" and hippie venders, selling tie-dyed tee-shirts, marijuana paraphernalia, protest buttons, and black light posters. All the young people seemed so friendly. We sat in Union Square, eating the bread and cheese they offered, while listening to guitar playing and singing.

We knew that we had to find a place to live. San Francisco was just too big. We settled on Santa Rosa, a town not far from San Francisco. We found a little furnished house to rent for $125.00 a month, right on Santa Rosa Blvd. It was well off the road, surrounded by trees, with a generous yard.

Earnie soon found a job as a fry cook at the Denny's Restaurant there. We didn't have a TV and I was bored while Earnie was at work. I knew about hitchhiking and started hitching rides to town and hanging out at a local park that was frequented by hippies. Sometimes Earnie would have me drive him to work so I could have the car. He didn't like me to hitchhike.

I felt bad about not being able to contact my family. I was afraid of them finding us though, because I was sure they still wouldn't allow us to be together. I was really attached to Earnie, but was filled with guilt, yet he was adamant about us not calling home.

About two months after we'd been together, Earnie went with me to a doctor because I hadn't had my period; I thought I may be pregnant. And I was. It must have happened the first night we had sex, because my child was born practically nine months to the day that we first made love. We were both hoping that I was pregnant and happy that I really was. I was eighteen, but still such a child myself.

One day, Earnie came home from work and told me that our families knew where we were. Apparently, a waitress at his job there in Santa Rosa, had a friend who waitressed at the Denny's in Red Bluff. What were the odds of that happening? In a way, it was a relief. I didn't like the fact that my family had been worrying all that time about where I was.

We contacted our folks and told them that we were married and that I was pregnant. A week or so later, I received a letter from my dad, saying how disappointed he was in me for what I'd done. Since I was pregnant, we decided to return home.

The night we got back to Red Bluff, my folks told us that we'd have to stay at our own houses. My mom wasn't angry and my dad didn't say much to us at all, but I knew he was upset. We thought we were so slick, and were sure our folks would believe we were married.

The next day, Earnie came to our house. My mom and I were in the kitchen. She asked to see the marriage certificate. I told her we'd lost it. She kept asking us if we were really married, and we kept telling her that we were. She knew we were lying. I finally broke down and told her the truth. She didn't get mad. She'd known all along. I wasn't there when she told my dad. But they decided that we'd *have* to get married since I was pregnant.

About a week before we were to be married, Earnie came to the house to talk to my parents and me. He was upset, saying that his mother, who had initially agreed to sign the consent papers, had changed her mind, refusing to allow her son to marry me. Then he left. I was blown away! I told my dad to take me to Earnie's house. I was desperate. I couldn't lose him. When we got there, I walked right past Earnie, who was sitting outside on the porch, and into the house, where I confronted his mother. I didn't like Laverne, and she regarded me as a threat. She said she didn't want her son trapped in a marriage when he was so young. Then I went outside to talk to Earnie. I begged him to make his mother change her mind. He just stared ahead, saying nothing. I couldn't believe this was happening. I went back to my dad who was sitting in his truck and said, "Dad, do something!" He just sat there. I was sure he was relieved that I wouldn't be marrying that boy. I went back to the porch and told Earnie, "You will never get to see this baby!" and I left with my dad.

When we got home I went to the bedroom, threw myself down on the bed, and sobbed from the depths of my being. My mom came in the room and sat down on the bed next to me. She said that I could go live with her sister, my aunt Gina, who lived in L.A., until I gave birth to the baby, and then give it up for adoption. I was desolate. I didn't want to give up my baby, but in those times, under those circumstances, that's what usually happened. I could tell my mom really felt for me. She knew how bad I was hurting and tried to comfort me, but I was inconsolable. I realized that she had always been there for me, when it really counted. My dad was sitting in his chair in the living room, quietly pondering the night's events.

About an hour later, Earnie returned. I could hear him in the living room, talking to my folks. He said that he'd convinced his mom to sign the papers. All of a sudden, the pain in my chest was lifted completely, as if it had never been there. Then my mom got mad and she let Earnie have it. "I love that girl. If you marry her, you better not hurt her." When she was through confronting him, again I thought, *She really does love me.*

My dad, I later learned, had seen Laverne's refusal to sign the consent papers as an opportunity to have Earnie arrested, for taking me across the state line into Nevada. Now his plans for me making a success out of my life and going to college were not to be. I knew that I'd hurt him deeply. I went into the living room, just as Earnie was getting ready to leave, and we talked. After he left, my dad said to me, "What happened to the sweet little girl I used to have?" At that moment, I felt like a complete failure in his eyes. It was the first time he had said anything that hurtful to me. "Yeah dad," I should have said, "I know I really messed up, but I didn't get to this point all by myself. Maybe if you'd paid more attention to what was happening to your sweet little girl, and had protected me more, I wouldn't have fallen for the first guy who said he loved me and wanted to marry me. I needed *you* dad—you weren't there!" Instead, I said, "I'm sorry dad."

During the next few days, Earnie was busy working at Denny's restaurant again, and I was busy preparing to get married. As a wedding present, my parents gave us enough money for our rings and for our first month's rent on a little house in Red Bluff. We got nothing from Earnie's mother, Laverne, except her notarized signature on a piece of paper, and that was enough for me. She even made him give up his car, since the registration was in her name.

It was a cold day in late November, when I put on a white and brown dress, with a pleated skirt. I was three months pregnant, and it showed. Earnie looked nice in his blue suit, as he climbed into the back seat of my parent's car, to sit next to me. On the way to Reno, we hardly spoke, except to make small talk. It wasn't a happy occasion for my parents, and it felt awkward and uncomfortable.

Earnie and I stood before the minister, repeated words of promises to one another, and it was done. No fanfare. No feeling of celebration. No wedding pictures. As I turned around to face my parents, I looked at my mother and could see that she was just going through the motions, hiding her feelings well. My dad had tears in his eyes. I felt badly for both of them, I knew that this was not what they had wanted for their only daughter.

That night, as we lay in bed in our little house, Earnie said to me, "I always knew I'd marry a pretty girl, but I didn't think she'd be as beautiful as you." I was about as happy as I knew how to be. I was relieved that we were married. I didn't feel alone anymore.

While Earnie was at work, I concentrated on making our house a home. My mom gave me some pots, pans, and dishes and I tried my luck at cooking, which was no easy task. Earnie was a better cook than I was. We lived just yards away from the railroad tracks, and whenever the train went by, the whole house shook. *No wonder the rent was cheap*, I thought.

After the first month, Earnie realized that we wouldn't be able to make it on his meager salary, and was concerned about how we would survive when the baby came. His answer to our dilemma was to join the Army. When he informed me of his decision, I was floored! It was late 1969, and the end to the Vietnam War was nowhere in sight. I hated that war. Every night for years that damn war was broadcasted on TV news. The casualty and mortality rate was continuing to take its toll on the young men of my generation. I tried talking Earnie out of joining the Army, I was afraid he'd end up going to Nam, but his mind was made up.

We moved out of our rented house and in with Earnie's family. You can imagine how thrilled I was about that! A couple of weeks later, I took the bus with my new husband to Oakland, California, for his induction into the Army. The following morning, he got on the bus with all the other recruits, and shipped out to Fort Lewis, Washington for basic training.

After Earnie was gone, I was filled with a terrible sense of loss. I knew that after basic training, he'd be sent to another Army base, or even Vietnam. I wondered if he'd joined the Army because he wanted to get away from me. That's how insecure I was.

During his absence, I had an argument with his mother and moved in with Hazel, a friend of our family's, who lived a few houses down from my parents' house. Hazel was divorced, with two small boys, and needed someone to live there and look after them while she worked.

Earnie called me after he finished basic training, saying that he was being shipped out to Fort Rucker, Alabama. He'd requested training in helicopter mechanics and got his wish. He would learn all about how to fix *and* fly a Huey chopper. He said he'd send for me once he was settled and had found us housing. I was miserable not being able to be with him and knowing he was so far away.

I told my folks that I was going to Alabama. It had been two weeks and I wasn't about to wait any longer for Earnie to find us housing. I missed him and felt out of control, not knowing how long it would be before he sent for me. So I purchased a one way Greyhound ticket to the town of Daleville, which was just outside the Army base. My parents were concerned about me taking the long trip because of my pregnancy, and thought I should wait to hear from Earnie. But I wouldn't listen. The day I left, my dad had tears in his eyes again. As I boarded the bus, I promised my parents that I'd take care of myself.

The trip took several days and I was nauseous the whole time. When I finally got to Daleville, I took a cab to my husband's barracks, and was met by a very surprised and concerned Earnie. He wished that I'd waited for him to find us a place, but nonetheless, was happy to see his very pregnant wife.

It was March, 1970. Daleville was quite the culture shock for me. The people talked funny and so slow, I thought. We found a place to live in a mobile home park. I'd never been exposed to cockroaches before and they were huge and plentiful in Alabama. I'd be horrified after turning on the kitchen light, and see them scurrying about. It was disgusting! And the humidity! We were dirt poor. Earnie was receiving $200.00 a month, and I was getting an allotment check of $100.00. Many nights we had popcorn and kool-aide for dinner, because it was inexpensive and it filled us up. We had no TV, so we played cards a lot or took walks.

May 26th was a very muggy day. It was around dusk of that evening, soon after Earnie had come home from the base, when I went into labor. He called a cab, and we were off to the Army hospital to have our child. I was put in a room alone. Earnie spent the night in the waiting room. At that time, husbands weren't allowed in the labor, or delivery rooms.

I was terrified with every contraction; I'd never known pain like that before. I screamed and cried, I cursed

God and my husband. After about 12 hours, I was rolled into the delivery room. I was told to sit up because they were going to give me a spinal tap. I saw that huge needle about to go into my back and nearly lost it. The Army nurse was a mean old bitch. She told me to shut up, and not to move, as she stuck it in. Jesus, it hurt! Then, I felt no pain at all. I was finally able to push, and my baby daughter came into the world.

When Earnie walked into my hospital room, despite the fact that he'd been up all night, he was beaming with joy. We were both ecstatic about our little girl. We named her Lisa Anne.

We knew that when Earnie completed his helicopter mechanics school, he'd be getting orders for wherever he was to be stationed next. We'd only had our baby home for a week, when he walked in from the base—and I knew. He said he had a two week leave before he had to be in San Francisco, to ship out to Vietnam. I was in shock. I hadn't allowed myself to think of that possibility, although I'd feared it all along.

Earnie had a of couple buddies on base that had gotten their orders for Nam as well, and they were both from California. We got a ride with them. Earnie, myself, and our baby, spent the entire trip in the backseat of their car. It was a long and lonely ride home for me.

When we reached Red Bluff, we went to stay with Earnie's family for a couple of days. I can't remember why, but I'd decided that I wanted to live in Redding while Earnie was overseas. We found an upstairs furnished apartment, in a two-story Victorian-style house, for me and the baby to live in. The rent was $90.00 a month. I'd be able to just about manage, between my allotment check and the one I would receive for the baby.

The day before he was to leave for San Francisco to ship out for overseas, Earnie said he wanted to go to Red Bluff to visit his family, and that he'd return that evening. I was hurt. How could he not want to be with his wife and child the day before he was going to war? One of his brothers, Michael, came to pick Earnie up, and they headed back to Red Bluff. I waited and waited, watching the clock and getting more anxious by the hour. What I've learned since is that it's a common ritual for soldiers to want to get "plastered" with their brothers and buddies before shipping off to war.

I was still up when Earnie's brother dropped him off at the apartment. It was around 4:00am. Earnie was still a bit "buzzed." His bus was due to leave in an hour or so. I was upset because that didn't leave us much time together. He put on his uniform, the dress greens, and then came to sit next to me on the sofa. He began to cry. It was then that I realized how afraid he was. We talked and cried for an hour. Lisa was asleep in her bassinet in the bedroom. He kissed her goodbye, and then we held each other once more, before he walked out the door. I watched him as he descended the flight of stairs, his duffel bag slung over his shoulder. I went to the window and watched as my 18 year old husband faded into the still, darkness of the morning, and wept all over again.

I don't know how I managed those first few days. I went through the motions of living. I took care of Lisa, fed her, washed her diapers out by hand, and sometimes I'd put her in the stroller and we'd go for walks. I had no appetite, and lost weight that I couldn't afford to lose. I lived on chocolate peanut clusters and soda.

I started seeing a psychiatrist. He prescribed an antidepressant, but it didn't seem to work, so I stopped taking it. I asked my psychiatrist to help me get my husband back on a hardship discharge. I told him I couldn't live without him. And I believed it. He said he'd try.

I wrote letters to Earnie every day about the baby and about our daily activity. And every day, I eagerly awaited the mailman, for some word from my husband. But there was none. Then, after about 30 days, I got a stack of letters all at once. I was extremely relieved to hear from him and to know that he was alive. But I'd scare myself by thinking, *What if he was killed after he wrote his last letter?*

The Army informed me that my husband had been granted leave, due to my mental state. After having been overseas for two months, my husband was coming home.

I was so excited the day Earnie was due to arrive. I put Lisa in her stroller, and walked the short distance to the bus station.

He was smiling as he stepped off of the bus. Then after a couple of days, he seemed distant. Something had changed and it scared me. I became even more anxious. But the more I pushed and demanded for validation of his love for me, the more withdrawn he became.

About four weeks after Earnie had been back, the letter came. He was being ordered back to Vietnam. It didn't come as a surprise, but I had hoped that by some miracle, he wouldn't have to return. Before Earnie left, I told him I wanted to live with my family, so we packed up everything and I moved in with my parents.

Earnie wrote to me saying that when he completed his tour in Vietnam, there was a good chance he'd be stationed at Fort Ord, CA, which is near Monterey, just a few hours drive south of Red Bluff. Well, that was all I needed to know. I decided that I'd hurry that process up by moving there.

Once again, my parents feared my impulsive decision to move. I didn't have a place to live, or know for sure if Earnie would even be stationed at Fort Ord. I thought that somehow I had the power to make it happen, though. I was 19 years old with a baby. In many ways, I was as naïve as they come, but on the other hand, I had a way with working the system and by God, I was going to work it.

As soon as I got to the Army Base at Fort Ord, I checked into the base guest house. I had no long-term plans, as I hadn't thought ahead. I just figured this was one step closer to getting my husband home for good. I wore out my welcome at the guest house though, because I didn't hide the fact that I was a war protestor.

One day, some sergeant major told me, "I know you and your kind. You have to leave." So I took Lisa and checked us into a motel in Monterey, across from the fairgrounds. The first night we were there, I heard what sounded like a rock concert going on. I found out that the concert was a tribute to Janis Joplin and Jimi Hendrix, who had played there at the Monterey pop festival, a few short years before.

My baby and I were at the motel for about two weeks, when I ran out of money. I was given notice to vacate. I felt desperate and decided to call the Catholic church for help. I spoke to a priest named Father Larry. I told him all about my situation, that I had a new baby, and that I was broke and had nowhere to go. Father Larry said he would see what he could do to help. When he called again, he said he'd found an older couple from the church parish who would be willing to take us in.

The Canons were wonderful people. They had an extra bedroom for Lisa and me. They just adored the baby. They took care of our every need. I wrote to Earnie, letting him know where we were. He was relieved to know we were safe. Once we were settled into our new home, I went to see the psychiatrist on base about my depression, and to work again on getting my husband home. He promptly filed the paperwork needed to get Earnie back on a hardship discharge.

It was December of 1970. Lisa was seven months old and her daddy was finally coming home. The Canons helped us find an apartment, at my husband's request. We found a two-bedroom furnished apartment in the town of Seaside, which was about five miles from the base. Earnie and I and our baby moved into our new home, and I was feeling very blessed. But my happiness was short-lived. Earnie got his orders to return to Vietnam a month later. He'd already spent five months in Vietnam at that point.

For the days and weeks that followed, I went through the motions of displaying somewhat of a semblance of stability. After a while though, my depression began to lift, and I came to accept the fact that my husband would not be returning anytime soon. I'd just have to deal with it the best way I could.

I made friends with the other Army wives and military couples who lived in the apartment complex. I played my rock and roll music on the record player, and watched TV on an old black and white console that I'd acquired. In the evenings, after I'd put Lisa down to sleep, I'd write poetry. I wrote about my feelings concerning the war and about the government. I had protest posters hanging on the walls and loved flashing people the peace sign, especially the young soldiers at the Army base, most of whom gave it back to me.

In February, I knew I was pregnant again. I was excited and hoped it would be a boy, and then our family would be complete. Lisa was crawling everywhere and getting into everything. She was a happy baby. We couldn't afford taxis. Whenever I had to go to the base, I had to hitchhike. Those were the days when it was still a safe thing to do. I bought a carrier for Lisa that I wore like a backpack. I never had a problem getting a ride with a baby on my back and a big belly.

One evening in March, my mom called and told me that my dad had had a heart attack a couple of months earlier. I was upset and asked her why she hadn't told me before. "You're pregnant, and I didn't want you to worry," she said. "How's he feeling now?" I asked anxiously. "Oh, he's fine," she said.

It was nearing Easter and I wanted to see my family. I boarded a Greyhound with ten month old Lisa and went to Red Bluff. My brother Matthew had a friend named Juan, from South America, who was visiting the family for a few days. Part of the reason for my visit was my dad's heart attack. I was planning on having a heart-to-heart talk with him. We'd never really had one before.

One day, my dad left for a doctor's appointment. He was never one to initiate a visit to the doctor, but since his heart attack three months earlier, my mom made sure he made it to his appointments. Later that afternoon, I heard the car pulling into the garage and went out to meet my dad. I asked him what the doctor said. He was nonchalant as he told me that his tests were fine. I felt relieved as we went into the house.

It was the night before Easter. My parents, my brothers, and Lisa and I, had all gone to bed. At about 2:00am, I awoke with a start to hear my mom yelling, "Sheila, there's something wrong with your dad!" I jumped out of bed and ran to the living room, where she stood, frantic, in front of him.

My dad was seated in his chair, making some awful guttural sounds from his throat. I ran outside to the trailer where Matthew and Juan were sleeping and banged on the door shouting, "Matthew, wake up, it's dad!"

I ran back into the house to where my dad was still sitting. His eyes were open, but he had a fixed stare. I was pleading with him to wake up. I lacked the presence of mind to realize the gravity of the situation; to do that would have been too much to take in. I didn't know what to do.

It seemed as if time stood still, but by the same token, it was all happening so fast. When my brother and Juan got there, they lay my dad out on the floor, and then carried him to the car, where my mother had the motor running, ready to rush him to the emergency room. I later learned that Matthew performed CPR on my dad, all the way to the hospital.

I waited for what seemed an eternity, for the phone call that said my dad was okay. Finally, I couldn't stand it anymore. I called the hospital. This was the same hospital where I'd worked, and where I'd seen my dad on numerous occasions, getting statements from accident victims.

I had Matthew paged. When he got on the line, he spoke in a voice that sounded far away, telling me that my dad was in the ER; they were still working on him, he said. I hung up. *Oh, no! Still working on him !?* I went to the bedroom where my younger brothers were. They were all awake. Donald was 12, Frankie was 11, and Kevin was 8. They knew something was terribly wrong with my dad, but were just lying there quietly on their bunks. "We have to pray for dad," I said. I started praying out loud.

Then I heard the car pull into the garage. I heard the garage door shut. I went into the dining room and stood there. My heart was racing and I could hardly breathe. The dining room door that led to the garage, opened. My mom walked in, my brother and Juan, right behind her. I looked at my mom, waiting to hear her say they were keeping my dad overnight for observation. Instead, she said the words no child ever wants to hear…"Your father died." "Oh, no!" I moaned. "Stay with her Matthew, I have to tell the boys," she said. I grabbed a hold of Matthew and pleaded with him to tell me the truth. I knew it couldn't be true. "It's true," he said. Then I heard my younger brother's cries all at once.

My father had suffered a massive heart attack due to blockage of the arteries. He was only 49 years old. It was 1971, long before by-passes were being performed.

What we later learned was that earlier that day, he had been in a foot pursuit of three suspects and had caught them all. He then finished his shift and came home. My mom said that he went to bed early because he didn't feel well; he'd then gotten up around 1:00am, complaining of chest pains, and thought it was heartburn, she said. She decided to check on him, and that's when she found him sitting in his chair, having his heart attack.

****

On May 8, 2012, my father was finally officially honored as a fallen officer in the line of duty. My brother, Kevin, a sergeant with the sheriff's department in the Reno area, set that in motion and saw it to fruition. The ceremony took place at the CHP Academy in Sacramento, California. It was a beautifully orchestrated memorial. Gov. Jerry Brown was present and shook our hands. It was the first time in 41 years, since my father's death, that my four brothers and I were together at the same time. My mom was also present. It was very emotional for us all. My dad's partner, the one he had at the time of his death, was there too. He called my dad "a cop's cop."

****

The hours that followed my dad's death, seemed unreal. My mom was on the phone to her family in L.A. and to my dad's sister, Marion, in Chicago.

We went through hours of numbness and disbelief as the relatives arrived by plane later that day. My mom sat at the kitchen table with the funeral director, making arrangements for a funeral she hadn't planned on having quite so soon. I watched her through it all and was amazed at how well she held up. She was never one to solicit pity. She wasn't comfortable with anyone being overly concerned about her, and this was no different. She was more concerned for me, because I was pregnant.

There was a constant parade of friends and neighbors as they brought casseroles and other food dishes. My mom wouldn't eat. She couldn't. I, on the other hand, couldn't stop eating. It was Easter Sunday, and our Easters would never be the same. A neighbor lady came to take my younger brothers on an Easter egg hunt. They came back with their baskets full of goodies and sad little faces.

The night of the Rosary, my three younger brothers stayed at home with a family friend. As I sat there in the pews with my mom, Matthew, and my aunts, I could see my dad's coffin, several yards away. My mom told me to go up and pay my respects. I'd seen many corpses, but this was my dad's. "I can't," I said. I was too afraid of seeing what had once been my father. But she insisted.

The funeral Mass was surreal as our priest, Father Reilly, spoke about my dad from personal experience. The funeral procession was amazing. There were about a hundred cop cars: city cops, sheriffs, and highway patrolmen all there to honor my dad, who'd been a good cop. There were many other cars that followed who were friends and acquaintances of our family. An American flag was draped on my dad's coffin during the ceremony at the cemetery, which was later folded and presented to my mom. It was a cop's funeral.

The whole thing is like a blur to me now, just as it was then. What was especially sad was that my mom was only 35 years old, with three young boys to raise. Matthew was almost 19, and in college, but he would be able to help out with our younger brothers.

We went to a reception afterwards at the home of another highway patrolman. Family and friends were telling funny stories about my dad. I just sat in their living room with my brothers, in a daze, unable to even smile, and stared out the window.

For the next few days, we still had a lot of family around. But eventually, relatives were taken back to the airport, one by one. As each one left, the reality of it all began to set in.

The day came when I was to return home to Monterey. My mom took me to the Greyhound station, where my daughter and I boarded. She handed me some money, saying that my dad would want me to have it.

After I got home, the shock began to wear off, and I fell into a deep, dark, hole of despair. I desperately needed my husband, who'd by this time, completed his nine month tour in Nam. Now all I had to do was wait.

Five weeks later, around 2:00am, there was a loud knocking at the front door. I opened it to see an emaciated version of the nicely muscled man I had last seen. "What the hell happened to you?!" I exclaimed. Once inside, he explained to me that he'd been in a hospital in Okinawa, Japan, detoxing from heroin. At first I was shocked, and then I was angry. So that's what he'd been doing with his combat pay. I'd wondered why he hadn't been sending much money back to me.

He said he was sorry to hear about my dad. We talked until dawn, and eventually, I realized it was enough that he was alive and back home with us for good.

Earnie was assigned to the ammo dump at Fort Ord. As one day followed another, we got back into our routine. Earnie was hitchhiking to and from the base and I was getting bigger as my pregnancy progressed.

I was always looking for ways to save money, especially now that we had another baby on the way. I noticed a little two-bedroom house for rent, just down the street from us. The landlady lived in the front house. She walked me to the back and showed me the inside of her rental. It was small, but the rent was much cheaper, and it had a yard. "I'll take it," I told her, and went back to the apartment to plan the move. A friend with a truck helped me move all our belongings that same day.

I called Earnie at the base and told him not to come home to the apartment because we didn't live there anymore. I thought nothing of making a decision like that on my own, and couldn't understand why he was angry.

Despite the decrease in rent, we still struggled. Toward the end of the month, we always pawned the record player, and on the first, we'd get it back out again. We never had a car, we couldn't afford one. I learned how to make yeast bread. I'd cook a pot of pinto beans, and serve it with the bread. That was dinner for many a night. Lisa was still eating her baby food, of course. We didn't have a bank account, so when I paid the bills, I'd put the exact cash and change into the return envelopes. That was acceptable payment in those days.

May the 26th, 1971, was Lisa's birthday. She was one year old. I invited a woman from the apartments we previously lived in, to come and bring her year-old toddler. There were party favors, presents and birthday cake. Lisa was too young, though, to understand what the festivities were all about.

While Earnie was at work, I'd play records, and Lisa loved to dance. She looked so cute, wriggling her diapered behind to the rock and roll songs. There was one song by the Beatles that she liked and would try to sing the words. I was always singing. When it was her bedtime, I'd rock Lisa to sleep with lullabies.

When I was pregnant with Lisa, I had morning sickness, but no food cravings. During my second pregnancy, I had no morning sickness, but had cravings for peppermint lifesavers.

My second child was due toward the end of August. But the baby didn't come in August. Finally, on the 8th of September, the pains came. They started right after Earnie had left for the base that morning. A friend of ours took me to the hospital at Fort Ord, and agreed to keep Lisa for a few days. When we got to the hospital, Earnie was there to meet me. He was able to stay in the labor room with me for a little while, then said he had to return to work.

Travis only took eight hours to come into the world. I was excited about having a boy and couldn't wait to tell Earnie. We'd both agreed on Robert as a middle name, because that was the first name of both of our fathers. Travis had black hair, and favored his dad. He was a cute, pudgy, eight pound baby, unlike his sister, who had my long legs.

I was in post-partum depression for several weeks. One night, Earnie came home from the base with these little white pills. They were called "cross-tops" or "bennies," and were a form of Benzedrine. He told me they would make me feel better and give me more energy. Wow! Did they ever! Those little magic pills made it possible for me to do the housework I'd been neglecting, and my depression vanished completely. At that time, I knew nothing about addiction, or tolerance to a drug. I soon found that one pill was not enough and progressed to 20 bennies a day. It wasn't long before my use of speed caused me to become paranoid, edgy, and delusional. When I ran out of them I'd fall into an even deeper depression than the one I was normally in.

I was 20 years old the first time I was admitted to the Monterey hospital psychiatric ward. I'd become suicidal. Over the course of a year, I was to return four or five more times. During my first stay, I was diagnosed with major depression, and prescribed an antidepressant. All it did was make me drowsy, so I stopped taking it. Of course, I never said a thing to the psychiatrist about my intermittent use of speed.

In between hospitalizations I continued to take the bennies that Earnie brought me. He was taking them too. I was sure that the pills were the only thing holding me together. Earnie was also smoking a lot of pot during that time, but pot only made me paranoid.

I finally quit taking the bennies and tried to be the mother that my kids needed. I went through the motions by taking care of their basic needs, but because of my depression, I was neglecting them in ways that were damaging to their emotional well-being. There were times when I was so overcome with grief over the loss of my dad, I was barely able to function. I couldn't even get out of bed.

I was getting fed up with Earnie and his pot smoking. Once, I flushed his precious marijuana down the toilet. Another time, I scattered it outside in the yard. He went out there with a flashlight, salvaging what he could.

One Saturday, I found Earnie sitting at the kitchen table, cooking up something in a spoon. It was heroin! After he finished fixing himself, he wanted me to try it. I don't remember how I made the decision to try heroin that day. I remember that I was shocked at seeing my husband shooting up, and stunned that he would want me to use that drug. After he injected the stuff into my arm, I spent the next few hours vomiting, and wondered how anyone could get pleasure out of using a drug like that.

A lot changed for me after that day. How could my husband love me and do that to me? And I hated myself for letting him. That's when my panic attacks began. An extreme anxiety reaction would come out of nowhere. It would feel as if I were going to die. I wouldn't be able to breathe because my throat would close up. I had a feeling of impending doom. My subsequent trips to the psych ward had me diagnosed as having a panic disorder. I was prescribed Valium.

I was the typical wife of a combat veteran. I couldn't understand why my husband was pulling away from me, why he would no longer communicate with me. I didn't realize then, the impact that war can have on a soldier. But at the same time, I'd just lost my father and I needed the security of knowing that my husband was still there for me, emotionally. But he wasn't. He couldn't be.

Yet, I didn't give up. I tried to be a good wife to Earnie, until I couldn't stand it anymore. I'd end up yelling at him for avoiding any kind of emotional connection with me. I tried on numerous occasions to get him to talk about what he was feeling. He'd just say, "There's nothing to talk about," and continue to shut me out and smoke his pot. I didn't know how else to reach him, to get his attention. I was losing him and I was scared. Once he actually agreed to attend couples counseling. I was hoping that it would help him to open up, but all he did was blame me for the problems in our marriage.

When my anger began to escalate, Earnie would leave and not come home for hours, or he'd call the police and have them take me to the psych ward. My kids were being shuffled around, staying with different families when I was in the hospital, and I know they suffered dearly because of it.

In the beginning of 1972, Earnie met a group of hippies and started bringing them to the house. They'd all smoke pot in my living room all night. I got fed up with it. I didn't want my children around that scene. I'd yell at them all to get out of my house, Earnie included. He no longer resembled the man I'd married. I felt helpless as I watched him self-destruct, and he was taking me with him.

A couple of times, I got a neighbor to babysit the kids for the evening, so I could accompany Earnie to the house where his hippie friends lived. One night, when we were at the hippie "pad," I looked around for Earnie and couldn't find him. I went outside and saw him walking away from the house with some hippie "chic." Earnie had been talking to that woman the whole evening, and I sensed that there was something between them. Feeling very hurt, I decided to hitchhike back home.

A guy picked me up right away, but instead of taking me home, he forced me into his house at gun point. He held me captive for a couple of hours, raping me, before I was finally able to escape.

Earnie wasn't home when I got there, so I got my kids from the sitter and waited. He finally returned the next morning. When I told him about the rape, he showed no emotion. As traumatized as I was about being raped, I was even more devastated by Earnie's lack of concern for what had happened to me. I collapsed into a state of complete and utter despair.

A couple of months after that incident, I was waiting up for Earnie, as I always did, unable to go to sleep until he returned home. About 6:00am, the front door opened and in he strode. He looked like he was on a mission, as he headed straight for the bedroom. I followed him. He got his duffel bag out and began filling it with his clothes. "What are you doing?" I gasped. "I'm leaving." "Please don't leave us Earnie," I pleaded and began to cry. "I can't do this anymore," was all he said, as he rushed past me and out the door.

I just sat there in the living room. I couldn't believe it. It had never occurred to me that he would actually leave us. I thought about our children in the next room, sleeping. How would I take care of them when I was having trouble taking care of myself? He hadn't even left me any money. I'd just lost my dad and now this. I didn't know how I was going to go on.

About 7:00am, the kids woke up. After changing their diapers and feeding them, I took them to my neighbor and asked her to watch them for a while. I hitchhiked to where Earnie's hippie friends lived, figuring that's where he'd be. I arrived there just as they were all piling into a van with their gear, ready to leave. Earnie was sitting in the middle seat, and I pleaded with him again to come home. He didn't even look at me, just told me to take care of the kids. The hippie chic, the one Earnie had left with that night, was sitting in the front seat. She had the nerve to tell me that I had to let go of Earnie. I later found out that Earnie had been sleeping with her all along.

For the next few hours, I functioned as if in a fog. I was fluctuating between panic and despair. Lisa was standing up on the couch, looking out the living room window and asked, "Mommy, where daddy go?" It broke my heart and reminded me of a time long ago, when another little girl would stare out the window, waiting for her daddy. In the span of a year, my kids and I had both lost our fathers. I didn't know how to answer my daughter.

Later that afternoon, I put Travis in his high chair and was feeding him his baby food. All of a sudden, I knew what I had to do. I called the police.

When the two officers showed up, I told them my husband had deserted us and that he was AWOL from the Army. "Please take my kids," I said. "I can't take care of them and I'm afraid I'll hurt them." The cops wanted my name and the name of my husband. When I gave them Earnie's name, one of the officers said, "Earnie Davis? I was his juvenile probation officer in Red Bluff." I hadn't even known that Earnie had been in trouble with the law when I'd met him, but I'll bet my dad knew.

My plan was to find my husband, convince him to come home, and then pick up our kids. I don't know how I imagined I'd have that kind of power over Earnie, or that I had the ability to find him. Yet, in order for me to stay focused and sane, I had to believe it was possible, because I knew I couldn't function without him.

I told the officers to take my kids to the woman who had cared for them when I'd been in the psych ward. Then I watched as the policemen took my children and headed for the squad car. One of the officers carried my nine-month-old baby boy; my two-year-old daughter was trustingly led by the other officer, as he held her little hand.

The next three days were spent hitchhiking around Monterey, frantically looking for Earnie. On the third day, I went to a medical clinic and was given tranquilizers for my anxiety. Throughout that day, I took about eight of those pills, but not all at once, which makes what happened later, seem very strange.

I was all over Monterey that day, and would return home intermittently, to see if Earnie had returned. Finally, it was getting dark, and I went back to the house. I began feeling very strange, and it scared me. I walked the few blocks to the police station, and told an officer that I didn't feel right. I told him about the tranquilizers I'd taken. He led me to a squad car and had me get in the front seat. As he was driving me to the hospital, he kept asking me questions, probably to keep me from closing my eyes. I told him I was afraid I was going to die. Then, all of a sudden, he must have noticed a change in me because he put on the siren and was speeding to the hospital.

When we got there, I had no problem walking into the emergency room un-assisted. As the officer was talking to the desk nurse, I stood up against a wall to steady myself. Then, I began sliding down the wall to the floor. Attendants raced over, put me on a gurney, and wheeled me into a room. There were nurses and a doctor present. I felt myself getting very cold and I was unable to move my body, but my eyes were wide open and I was cognizant of what was going on around me. The mood was intensely serious in that room; there was a lot of rushing about and orders being ushered from the doctor. I felt myself dying. I thought about my kids. I didn't want to leave them. I began to pray out loud. The doctor told me to pray to myself. I asked for a priest and was told, "It's too late for that." At one point, I heard a nurse's voice yelling, "Breathe, God damn it!" After what seemed like a very long time, there was a sense of relief in the air as things began to wind down, and some of the attendants left. I asked the doctor if I was going to live and he said that I was. To say I was relieved would be an understatement. The doctor informed me that I had been clinically dead for a time, and that if I'd gotten there a few minutes later, I wouldn't have made it. He said it was a miracle. If I hadn't paid attention to that strange feeling that I had, before going to the police station, I'd have died in that house. That was the first time the Creator nudged me, and saved my life.

Once I realized I was going to live, I was nearly elated. I was transported to the psych ward upstairs. When I was able to move my body, I got up and went to the bathroom to look at myself in the mirror. I remembered what people looked like when they were dead, and that's what I saw as my death face stared back at me. My chest felt like a truck had run over it, as a result of them trying to get my heart started.

Later that day, my psychiatrist came in to see me. I asked him why I almost died after taking only a few pills. He asked me if I'd been feeling suicidal lately. I told him I had been. "Then that's why," he said. After I told him that my husband had left me he said, "Well, I've got more bad news. Your children have been taken from you on the grounds that you're emotionally unstable. They're now wards of the court." Prior to hearing that, I hadn't wanted to even close my eyes, afraid I wouldn't wake up again. But I told the doctor, "I just want to go to sleep." "That," he said, "can be arranged." He left and a few minutes later, a nurse came into my room. She gave me an injection and I slipped into a dark oblivion.

Part Three
Temporary Band-Aids and Mind-Altering Men

"What's a nice girl like you doing in a place like this?" That was the question I heard on a regular basis; or, "You don't look like you belong here," as I sat huddled with my wino buddies, on the ground next to the train tracks, drinking Thunderbird wine. The truth was, I didn't feel like I belonged anywhere else. I couldn't see myself functioning in the straight world; besides, living on the streets had its advantages: free rent, no utility bills, no car payments, and no unpleasant feelings to deal with. My one and only mission was to stay as drunk and high as possible. I didn't worry about where I'd sleep or what I'd eat. I slept in abandoned cars, abandoned houses, and on flattened cardboard.

Most of the time the other bums, many of whom were old enough to be my father, came back with food they found in dumpsters. I'd hit a new "rock bottom" when I left Monterey for the railroad tracks of Salinas. So before I take you any further, allow me to catch you up.

After my subconscious suicide attempt, and while still a patient in the psych ward of the Monterey hospital, I turned 21 years old. I asked for a pass on my birthday and went to my first bar. I came back to the ward, drunk, but managed to play it off.

A week or so later, I acquired some LSD from another patient. I took it just before our weekly outing to the beach. When we returned, I felt so guilty about it that I told one of the nurses what I'd done. Needless to say, I was given my walking papers, yep, kicked out of the psych ward. I was told that if I had it together enough to function while under the influence of acid, I was together enough to be out on my own. Wow! I didn't understand that bit of rationale.

I had no home to go back to. I found out that my landlady had put all our family's belongings in the street, and that people were coming by and taking everything. So I left the hospital with just a few clothes, and went to live with an older woman named Sharon. Sharon had recently been released from the psych ward. She lived in Salinas, a small farming community, not far from Monterey. Living in Salinas sounded like a good idea because that's where my children lived with their foster family.

I went to juvenile court to find out what the requirements were for regaining custody of my kids. I was informed that I had to have a residence and a means of supporting them. The judge deemed me to be mentally unstable, yet didn't require me to seek therapy, nor did he suggest where I could get any kind of assistance. I left the hearing not having any idea how to even begin to put my life back together. I was completely overwhelmed with my situation.

I was too depressed to remain at Sharon's house and went back to Monterey. I ended up hanging out with a group of outcasts and hippies, some of which were part of the bunch I'd known when I was still with Earnie. I found out that the ones I'd seen leaving in the van that day, had gone to Oregon to live in some commune, and that Earnie and the hippie chic were with them.

The year was 1972, and The Vietnam war was still going on. There was one main crash pad where my group would congregate. Whatever anyone had, be it food, drugs, or alcohol, was all shared. There was always a pot of stew on the stove that the women cooked up. On any given night, we'd be hanging out in the living room, spinning rock music on the record player like Jimi Hendrix, the Doors, Deep Purple, and Led Zeppelin. We'd be passing joints around, dropping acid, guzzling Red Mountain wine, and spacing out on the throw pillows in the half-dark of the room.

I fell right into the hippie lifestyle like a warm blanket. We had our own lingo: "far out," "right on," "outa sight," "heavy," "what's happening," "that's bitchin," "dig it," "bread" (money), "that's cool," and "wow man," to name a few.

We all had nicknames too. The one I was given was *Sheba*, queen of the jungle.

Many of the hippies in that family were from out of state. There were also a couple of AWOL GI's among us.

Everyone said, "I love you man," and called each other brother or sister. We were like a family should be. I was accepted for who I was; whoever that was. I'd lost my previous roles of wife and mother and desperately needed to fit in somewhere.

The guys wore Levis that were loaded down with patches of leather, embroidered flowers and peace signs. Some of us women wore long "granny" dresses and cut-off jeans with halter tops. Everyone had long hair.

We were a bunch of freaks, anti-government, and anti-doing-anything-constructive-about-it. We were society's dropouts and just wanted to be free and expand our minds with mind-altering substances. No one did the harder drugs like heroin or cocaine; that would have changed the whole dynamics of the "family."

No one had a job, because that was just too "establishment," so during the day we'd hitchhike to the Fisherman's Wharf and panhandle. Some of the guys sold pot and acid to the soldiers. We didn't cause trouble and weren't hassled by the cops.

After about a month, the pseudo-bliss I got from alcohol and LSD wasn't cuttin' it. Pot made me paranoid, and the acid trips were getting scary. When the high wore off, it seemed that all the grief of a lifetime would hit me like a ton of bricks; the loss of my father, my husband and my kids would come crashing into my consciousness with such a force, that I wished I were dead.

Now, for those of us who've been down this road, I know with certainty that none of us ever said, "When I grow up, I'm going to be a heroin addict." In fact, when I was in Catholic school, I remember fantasizing about being a nun. So you get the point. But becoming a junkie was to be the next stop for me on my trip to self-destruction. Instead of wanting to expand my mind through LSD and experience the beauty and truth of all living things, I wanted to be forget, to numb out, and heroin was a great painkiller.

I was the first to break the strict code of the family, the no hard drug rule. It started when I was out and about on my own at the Wharf. I'd run into soldiers who were looking for heroin. I'd score for them and would get a free fix out of it. When the family found out, some of them gave me a hard time. So I spent less time there, and more time crashing wherever I could. I quit taking all drugs, except heroin and pain pills, and was soon becoming a pass out drunk. Up until then there was always someone willing to supply me with free booze, drugs, food and a place to crash. But the time came when there was no more free lunch for me. So I went to Plan B.

Before my overdose, and during my hitchhiking around to try and find Earnie, I'd met a guy named David. He'd taken me to his house one night after he picked me up hitchhiking. He knew I was really hurting and gave me some wine. We drank and talked all night. He seemed to care about me, in fact, I called him when I was in the psych ward, and he came to visit me and brought me flowers.

David had also been in the Army and worked at a gas station. He was Japanese and Mexican and looked like a samurai warrior, with his stocky build, and his long black hair in a ponytail, high on his head. So I went to David's house. He'd told me that if I ever needed a place to stay, to come by.

David was happy to see me again. He had a two-bedroom house and he let me have one of the bedrooms. His wife had divorced him not long before, and had taken his two boys with her and left the state. I believe that David just wanted someone to take care of, and he either saw me as a *damsel in distress,* or his project.

David was my plan B. He didn't have heroin but he had a pretty good substitute. As a result of a back injury, David had a standing prescription for codeine and he didn't mind sharing. I'd stay with David for a few days, drinking his wine and popping his codeine, and then get itchy feet and have to hit the streets. I had to check out the old haunts for my hippie friends. And yes, I was still hoping to run into Earnie, or at least to hear some news of him.

One night, I was at the hippie pad. I was in the living room, drinking beer with the others, and guess who walks in? Our eyes locked for a half a second, and then he quickly looked away. I couldn't read him, but felt an enormous relief at seeing my husband standing there in the flesh.

Earnie didn't acknowledge me, just sat down and cracked a beer open and began talking to the guys that were hanging out. I finished my beer and got up to leave, hoping Earnie would follow me. He did. We stood outside the house and made small talk. We started walking and were both a little buzzed. He apologized for what he did. He asked about the kids, and I told him what happened with my near-death experience and how the county had taken the kids. He started to cry and vowed to make it right. I couldn't have been happier as we walked back to where Earnie was staying.

Earnie and I went to the social services department, stating that we wanted to get our kids back. We were told that the same requirements applied. Earnie was still AWOL, but he got a job as a fry cook. When he realized we couldn't get the kids back as long as he was AWOL, instead of turning himself in to Fort Ord, he quit his job and started dealing weed. What a man! My hero, come back to save the day.

We were both drinking daily, and it wasn't long before he was back on heroin, and so was I. We were quite the pair. After a while, I needed to be high on heroin to even be around him. We spent most of our time together, and eventually, I realized that he had no intention of getting the kids back. The anger that I had toward him for leaving us; that I had managed to bury for so long, began to rear its ugly head.

Sometimes I'd watch Earnie after he'd shot up his heroin, drooling, with his head in his chest, and I'd feel disgusted. I could hardly stand the sight of him anymore.

One day, out of all the rage I felt for him, I called the police and turned him in for being AWOL. He was picked up and confined to the base, to finish out the last few months of his term.

I ended up returning to David, who readily took me back. Good ole' Dave and his codeine. Poor ole' Dave for me using him. I didn't intentionally set out to "play" him, but he had something that I needed. He knew about my love for opiates and was only too happy to oblige. He would dole the pills out as he saw fit, usually four pills a day. When he got too controlling with them, I'd split and go find some free drugs on my own.

Dave knew about Earnie and the situation with my kids. He said he'd help me get them back and then take care of all of us. I liked Dave, but I couldn't see bringing my kids into that situation. I appreciated the fact that he took care of me, but only to a point. I didn't want to feel obligated or controlled. I wanted to come and go as I pleased. I wanted it both ways.

Dave was a functioning alcoholic. When he got home from work, we'd have dinner, and then he'd get drunk on his beer or wine. He'd go to sleep at a reasonable hour in order to get up for work, unlike myself, who drank most of the night. He kept me in booze, food, and pain pills. But there was something about the streets that appealed to me. I felt freer there and was with people who I thought were my own kind. Living with Dave was too normal and a constant reminder of what I'd lost.

I remember the first time I needed a fix and wasn't able to get a free-be. One GI told me, "Do what other women do and become a prostitute." That thought appalled me, so I just continued to drink. But I needed relief from the nagging pain and panic, and booze alone, just made me feel more depressed. I didn't know that there was a way out, and if there was, I wasn't willing to face the despair and terror that was underneath it all. By now I hated myself. I'd never really liked myself anyway, not really.

The self-loathing was becoming unbearable, and it was about to get even worse. Yes, I remember the night that I stood alone at the wharf, thinking about what to say to the soldiers who might be looking for a "date." I was about to embark on a journey to the dark side, as I had never known it.

It was a Friday night and I was halfway drunk. There was no way I could do what I had to do, if I was sober. I wasn't one of those free-love hippie chicks, hell; I hadn't even slept with Dave.

I stood near an entrance to the wharf and watched as GIs walked past me. Most of them were in groups of two's and three's. I don't remember how long I stood there before I decided to take the plunge and get it over with. Three GIs were approaching me. They looked like they'd just finished boot camp with their shaved heads. I blurted out, "Are you guys looking for a date?" "How much?" they asked. "$5.00 apiece and the price of a hotel room," I said, with a boldness I didn't quite feel. They agreed, and we walked to the cheap hotel a short distance away, on Alvarado Street.

I won't go into any details, let's just say that I went through the motions and when it was over, they split without paying me. I don't know what pissed me off more; the fact that I didn't have my heroin money, or that I had just committed an act of such profound disgust…for free! It was probably both. They must have known I was new at "hooking" and saw me as an easy target. I went right back out there to the wharf, and made damn sure that the next soldier paid me first.

I was oblivious to the fact that the narcotics agents were on to me. I'd been "hooking" for a couple of months, before I was finally busted. I thought for sure I'd get a break, since I'd never been arrested before, but that wasn't the case. I received 90 days in the Salinas County jail.

My first experience with jail was a shocker. I kicked alcohol and heroin in a cramped cell with five other women. One day, this young woman, another heroin addict, was put into our cell. She was from Monterey and knew all the junkies there. After I asked her if she knew Earnie, she was only too happy to tell me, that not only did she know him, but that he was shacking up with a woman named Sharon. It felt like a knife in my heart. It was one thing to know that he and I weren't together, but another to know that he'd moved on so quickly.

After a couple of months, I was thinking more clearly and my desire to get my kids back was renewed. I contacted my old friend, Father Larry, asking him to come visit me. When he came, I filled him in on all that had transpired since our last visit, when he'd come to see me at the psych ward after my overdose. He didn't judge me for what I'd done.

The day I was released from jail, Father Larry was there to pick me up. We went straight to the social services office in Salinas, where we met with a worker who was familiar with my case. The woman didn't mince words in letting me know how damaged my kids were, as a result of my actions. She said that when they first became wards of the court, my daughter would pull out strands of her hair to wrap around her thumb and suck it. My son, she said, would just sit quietly by himself, hardly ever crying. I was in tears, realizing what I'd done to them.

Father Larry agreed to help me get back on my feet so I could get the kids back. I don't remember what that plan looked like, just that I never followed through with his suggestions.

I returned to Monterey and to Dave's house. He took me back, despite the fact that I'd been busted for prostitution. He was willing to take me any way he could get me. It was easy for me to take advantage of a guy like that. Yet I stayed, and played at housekeeping, and tried staying sober.

I knew the last name of the foster family my kids lived with. I managed to find their phone number, and decided to call. I had to know how my kids were. I dialed the number. The foster mother, Beth, answered the phone. I could hear Lisa, who was about three at the time, crying in the background. When I told Beth who I was, she freaked out and demanded to know how I'd gotten their number. She then made it clear that I was never to call again, and hung up.

I loved my children and missed them terribly. I hurt for what I was putting them through. I took a hard look at the kind of person I'd become. I saw a young woman who was emotionally immature and psychologically incapable of being a good mother. I was too hell-bent on destroying my own life, and I was afraid of being the kind of mother that *I'd* had. So I made a decision. I would let my children go. I knew they were much better off where they were. If they were with *me*, they'd never have a chance. I'm glad, now, that I wasn't one of those women who selfishly refused to let their kids go, only to abuse and neglect them. My kids had had enough of that already. Yet, it would take me over thirty years to forgive myself for that decision.

There's a stigma attached to women who give their children up. Most people are quick to judge when they don't have all the facts. I wanted my kids to have a better childhood than I had. I knew that it would be hell not being there to see them grow up; not knowing how they were. The worst part was not being able to touch them, to hold them. It left an unbearable emptiness inside, as if something had been ripped from my being. And that pain would lead me down some very dark roads.

As soon as I began a physical relationship with David, he started hitting me. Well, that was a fine turn of events. I became afraid of him, especially when he was drunk. I'd leave him for a week or so at a time, and when I returned, he'd be so glad to see me that it would be great for a while. But the honeymoon period would soon be over, and it was back to his beating me up, and me running away.

Once, I was at one of the main crash pads, and Earnie showed up with his girlfriend, Sharon. He asked me if I wanted to go with them to their house and fix heroin, because he'd just scored some. Despite the jealousy I felt at seeing him with his new girlfriend, I accepted. I really needed a fix after seeing that picture.

We spent the night high on heroin, drunk on beer, and talked for hours. It was weird being at the home that Earnie shared with another woman. But because I was high, it buffered the incredulity of the situation. And because we were all high, we were able to get along quite amicably. Earnie told me I could spend the night. I accepted because he had more heroin for us to fix in the morning.

As I lay on the couch that night, I slept very little. I wasn't able to block out the sounds of lovemaking coming from the bedroom. The more sober I became, the more hurt I felt about how Earnie could do that to me. He now had a house and a job, and I would've left David in a flash, if Earnie wanted me back. I should have hated him for not getting *us* a house. After all, I was still his wife! We could have had a place for the kids. The next morning, I made sure I got my shot of dope, and then went back home to Dave's.

I met up with Earnie a second time. I was at the wharf one night, bumming around, and he'd come looking for me because he had some heroin. He invited me to his house again and Sharon was there.

The three of us were feeling no pain when Earnie decided to go down memory lane, reminiscing about how we first met—the highlights of our relationship—our kids. When he told me he still loved me, right in front of Sharon—that did it. Sharon had heard enough and told him she was leaving and going home to her mother. She packed a bag and left. With renewed hope that we'd be together again and would get the kids back, I slept peacefully that night in Earnie's arms.

The next morning, as we lay in bed together, the front door opened. A very distraught Sharon walked right into the bedroom and begged Earnie to take her back. Then she said to me, "What about Dave?" They'd never met him, but knew about our relationship. "Fuck Dave," I told her. She left the house crying. I can't recall Earnie saying anything to Sharon, although he did seem embarrassed about being in bed with his own wife.

Earnie got dressed and left for work. He was a cook at some bar and grill-type restaurant. I didn't feel like hanging around the house all day alone, so I went to his job and sat at the counter. I was drinking a beer when he noticed me there. He came out and told me that he'd changed his mind about us; he wanted to stay with Sharon. What a son of a bitch. I was heart-broken all over again, but I wasn't about to beg or plead. I was done with the man. That was the last time I ever saw my husband.

About a year into my relationship with Dave, I became so sick of drinking that I turned myself into a halfway house for alcoholics. It was in a nice Victorian-style home in Pacific Grove, near Monterey. That's when I found out how addicted I really was. For the first week, I had the shakes so bad I wasn't able to put my makeup on. I hadn't experienced withdrawal before and I was pretty sick. My body was screaming for booze, but I still had to attend lectures and AA meetings. I had no problem identifying myself as an alcoholic. I could relate to the personal stories I was hearing, to an extent, but my lifestyle had been much worse than theirs, even though they had a lot more years of drinking on me. It was suggested that I get a female sponsor.

So I chose a male, only because he seemed like a guy who would buy me cigarettes, which he did.

After about three weeks, I felt much better physically, and decided to leave. I told myself that I was still young and still had some partying left to do; besides, I rationalized, the residents there didn't look much worse for wear after 20 years of boozing. I had conveniently forgotten my rock bottom and wasn't ready to quit, not yet anyway. I still couldn't imagine a life of sobriety. Even though there was no fun in drinking, it was a means of coping with the feelings that I didn't know what to do with or control. It was a way to stay unconscious. So off I went on another bender, and eventually, back to Dave.

One night, Dave beat me up pretty bad, so I left to go live with Jennifer, one of the original members of the family. There were a few other hippies living there too. I was pleasantly surprised to find out they had all turned into junkies.

Word had gotten out that I was living at Jennifer's. One day, there was a knock on the door. I opened it and was surprised to see that it was Earnie's girlfriend, Sharon. She stood on the front porch, holding the hand of a toddler, with dark hair and brown eyes. Sharon was beaming as she stuck a piece of paper at me and said, "Here's your divorce paper. Earnie and I went to Mexico and he divorced you and married me." I just stood there, in shock, as she walked away with the little girl.

I went back inside and stared at the certificate. It looked authentic. What a gutless bastard Earnie was. And I was sure that Sharon thoroughly enjoyed humiliating me that way with their child. It had to be their child. She looked just like him. If there ever was an excuse to get totally fucked up, that was it. After a long, hard binge, I wore out my welcome and Jennifer asked me to leave.

So back to Dave I went crawling, to get back on his pain pills and to continue our sadistic game of, who's going to kill who, first. I'd been practicing knife throwing.

One night, when Dave started in on me, I threw my knife at him, aiming for his chest. The knife spun in the air and stuck in his foot, instead. David just sat there, shocked. I got scared and ran out of the house and then thought, *Hell no. I'm going to get some codeine out of this mishap.* I went back inside and drove a bewildered Dave to the hospital, telling him that he'd better ask the doctor for some pain pills. I got my codeine, and David was a bit nicer to me after that, but as usual, it didn't last. We were together for another year, repeating the same old cycles. He finally kicked me to the curb for good, for my "whoring around," and I never went back.

I was close to 23 years old and a full-fledged junkie and alcoholic. I was out on the streets day and night, prostituting myself. I made just enough money for my dope, booze, and a motel room for the night. Sometimes I had enough left over to buy myself an outfit.

I was far from being a high classed hooker. I survived any way I could. I didn't have a pimp and I didn't stand on street corners. A lot of the time I just acted as if I were hitchhiking when I picked up guys. I liked going to nightclubs. I'd sit at the counter with enough money to buy my first drink, and wait for a guy to offer me another. Then I'd hustle him, if it felt right. I had my own style, I wasn't flirty and I didn't dress sexy. I was still very attractive with my long dark hair and green eyes. It was never that difficult for me to get a date.

I went to my first heroin detox clinic when I was about 23 years old, in Monterey. There was a new drug out called Darvon N, for heroin withdrawal, and that's what we were being administered. While there, I met Tony, who was from Salinas. Tony was Chicano, which meant that he was a U.S. born Mexican. He was a "bad boy," just the type I was attracted to. He had tattoos and had been to prison. We became attracted to each other, and decided to leave the clinic and go live at the home he shared with his grandmother, in Salinas. We'd kicked our habit and were going to live happily ever after. Yeah, right.

Tony turned me on to a type of wine called MD 2020: Mad Dog, for short. But it didn't take long before we were back on heroin.

Although smaller than Monterey, Salinas had a very high heroin addict population, and Tony knew all the connections. Tony missed a court date, and the cops came to the house and took him to jail. There went *my* heroin connection.

I stayed at Tony's house with his grandmother, who spoke only Spanish, and at night I'd leave and hitchhike, hoping to find someone to buy me alcohol. One night, I caught a ride with three Chicano guys. I took a lot of very dangerous risks when I needed a drink or dope. These young men already had beer in their car, so we drove around, drinking and listening to oldies music. I just wanted to get a good buzz going, before I had them drop me off downtown.

See...here's the thing; I preferred the companionship of men to women. They were easier to get along with than were the females I encountered; not to mention, I'd grown up with four brothers, and was still a tomboy. Also, men were the ones who bought me booze, not women. And men were easier to hustle, to manipulate. I also liked the attention

I got from them. One thing was for sure though; I didn't choose to hang out with men because I wanted sex. I only desired sex with a man if I was emotionally involved with him. When I prostituted, it was for booze and heroin money, period! Yet, many men naturally assumed that because I liked hangin' with the fellas, I must also be a nymphomaniac. They assumed that because I was a hooker, I must *like* getting laid. On the contrary, I hated having sex with a stranger. But here's a statistical fact. Did you know that 99% of prostitutes have been sexually abused as children? Think about that one for a moment. Another assumption is that if a hooker gets raped, it's no big deal. Wrong!

Hell, there were a lot of times when *I* had money, and would invite a guy to drink with me, just for the company, and I never expected sex or anything else from him. So, sorry guys, but I have to say this, and I'm sure you'll agree—most men are dogs.

When the driver of the car I was in, started driving away from town and up some dark road, I knew I was in trouble. All of a sudden, the mood changed dramatically. The men weren't so friendly. The driver pulled off the road and stopped the car.

After they all had their turn, they forced me out of the car and took off. I had no idea where I was. I started walking back in the direction of town, though I was in the middle of nowhere. I saw the lights of the city and thought I'd just follow them.

It was late at night, and I couldn't see where the road was. I ended up walking through heavy foliage and then found myself walking in water. The longer I walked, the more sober I became. I was scared shitless. It was creepy and spooky and hardly any moon out. The harder I tried to get on solid, dry ground, the deeper I found myself in the swamp. At first, I was up to my ankles in water, and then I was in muddy water all the way up to my knees. I must've fought my way through the swamp for five hours or so, pushing my way through bushes and getting scratched up from running into branches. I freaked out every time I heard a sound, thinking it may be a wild boar or some other wild creature.

The sun started to come up. I felt relieved because I was able to see the main road. I must have been a sight, as I made my way down that road at the break of dawn; a skinny, mud-soaked waif with long tangled hair. I saw houses here and there. The countryside was farming land and Mexican families lived in those houses. Lights were coming on as men were getting ready to go to work in the fields. I thought, *There's no way I can walk into town in the shape I'm in.* I was pretty scary looking, I'm sure. So I stuck out my thumb and got a ride with a Mexican man who was kind enough to take me back to Tony's grandmother's house.

I knocked on the door and she opened it. She saw what a mess I was, but said nothing, as I headed straight for the bathroom to clean up. I knew I couldn't stay there anymore, because Tony was in jail and would probably be there for some time. Plus, I didn't feel right using the old woman's home for a crash pad. I put on clean clothes and left, with a grocery bag of my belongings.

I needed a drink real bad. I knew where skid row was so that's where I headed. I found some winos and they shared their wine with me. That was my introduction to cheap port wine. I found out that they always met up at the railroad tracks. There were a couple of abandoned warehouses, and one could easily hide there, undetected by the cops or other intruders.

Since I was out of a place to stay, the winos took care of me and treated me like a daughter. These were the men that Steinbeck wrote about: the hobos, the tramps, and the bums. They knew how to survive and taught me a lot. They had lots of stories about riding the rails, and about other skid rows they had frequented. They talked about buddies they had who'd lost legs and sometimes their lives, trying to jump on the fast moving freight trains. Many of them actually had good lives before they ended up in skid row. I met teachers and men who'd had highly paid jobs. Some had been married, and had families who loved them, and wanted them to return home. I watched sadly, as wives would come and plead with their men to come home. Sometimes, family members would come just to check up on their loved one, to make sure they were all right. Other times, the relative would give them money to buy more booze, because they knew they couldn't stop them from drinking. When my wino buddies were drunk, they often cried about their sorrows, just as I did. Sometimes we'd fight and argue over the dumbest things, and then find ourselves laughing or singing five minutes later. There was a comradary among us that I never found with heroin addicts.

I found out about the drug called methadone. I was told that it was used as a deterrent to using heroin, and that it possessed the same type of high. I hadn't used heroin in a long time, and lied my way into the program.

I didn't really know what to expect the day I received my first liquid dose of methadone, but was pleasantly surprised when I got that familiar warm feeling, that—all is right with my world feeling that I got from opiates. In fact, it was better than heroin. It lasted all day and it was free! I'd go get my dose in the morning, then return to the railroad tracks and drink with the winos.

Going into regular stores was not an option for us winos. We always stank of yesterday's booze and our clothes were dirty. We rarely ventured from skid row. We'd go to a little Mexican store, or the family owned Filipino stores in Chinatown, where they all knew us and never judged, but would sometimes scold, because they cared about us.

I walked around with a paper bag containing my toothbrush, comb, shampoo, and if I was lucky, a change of clothes. When I decided to take a bath, I would sneak into a boarding house a couple of blocks from the railroad tracks, and duck into their bathroom. I'd fill the tub with water and some shampoo and get in, clothes and all. When I was finished, I'd sneak out and walk back to the railroad tracks to drip dry.

The methadone really kept me going. It helped me feel like a human being. It allowed me to drink without getting too drunk. Then one day, after having been in the program for nine months, I went to the clinic and was informed by the nurse that I was being terminated. I hadn't used heroin while I'd been in the program, so I could only surmise that it was because I was always packing a pint of Thunderbird wine on my person, and was occasionally drunk when I went to get my dose. The nurse told me that I'd be placed on a two week detox and that my dose would be gradually reduced. I freaked out and got myself into the county alcohol detox unit in Salinas. Once there, I kicked pretty hard from the alcohol with the sweating, the shakes, and the nightmares that came whenever I began to drift off to sleep.

When I drank, I rarely ate, so I shouldn't have been surprised the first time I had delirium tremens, otherwise known as the DT's. That's when a person becomes delirious, and has terrible hallucinations from the lack of alcohol.

Usually, a person only experienced the DT's after many years of heavy drinking. Here I was, in my early 20's, seeing bugs crawling all over me, or feeling the flames of fire burning me up. It was terrifying.

About a week into my detox, I was sitting and eating my lunch, and that's the last thing I remember until I found myself lying on my bunk, having urinated on myself. A nurse was with me when I came to, and told me that I'd had a seizure. I had no memory of it happening, nor was there any warning. It left me feeling exhausted and weak. That was the first of many seizures I would have, as a result of alcohol withdrawal.

It was a short walk from the detox unit to the methadone clinic. For the two weeks that I was being cut down on my dose, I had withdrawals similar to coming off of heroin. My body ached and my bones hurt. Most of all, I missed the high. I didn't like being straight.

About my third week at detox, I was beginning to get that restless feeling, and knew all too well what that meant. I was clean and sober and ready to leave to do it all over again. Every single time I'd gotten cleaned up and was feeling healthy again, I conveniently forgot about the consequences of my drinking and drugging. The horrible experience of withdrawal would leave my mind completely. My thoughts were solely on that first drink and getting high.

I left on a Friday, because I knew I'd be able to get free booze from some weekend partying soldiers who were feeling generous. I left detox and headed for the clubs in Cannery Row in Monterey, because that's where I knew many of them would be.

After a month-long booze run, I went to see my friend, Father Larry, and told him I needed help, that I was coming off of alcohol. He arranged for me to stay with a family from the parish. That night, as I was lying on the living room couch, unable to sleep, I looked toward the front door. The top of the door had a clear glass inlay. Peering at it, I saw a sinister looking man's face, staring back at me! I freaked out and left the house, heading straight for the Catholic rectory.

I banged on the door to Father Larry's room. Then, I heard his voice. He was calling the cops. "No Father Larry, it's me, Sheila!" I shouted. He opened the door to see me standing there in a state of panic. "Would you please give me a bottle of altar wine?" I pleaded. "I think I just saw the devil." He said, "I know I shouldn't," but gave me the fifth of wine anyway. I thanked him and told him I was sorry, before scampering away, seeking a safe place to drink it. The altar wine sure did the job.

Father Larry tried to help me on several occasions when I was on the streets. Years later, I asked my friend, why he had continued to do so. He said that he never gave up hope that someday I'd make it.

Many a time I met the devil when I was out on the streets running amuck and other times, I had angels looking out for me. One such time was a morning when I woke up, fully clothed, in a twin bed. I looked around, and realized that I was in a young girl's bedroom. I got up, got dressed, and left the bedroom and found a nice young couple in their kitchen. They greeted me warmly and asked if I were hungry. I told them I wasn't, and thanked them for their generosity. I vaguely remembered being picked up by a man the night before as I was hitchhiking. I blacked out after that. There were other times when that sort of kindness came my way, after I'd passed out somewhere in public. Then there were the times when I woke up in jail, praying that I hadn't hurt someone while I was in a blackout.

I left the couple's house as quickly as I could. I was really embarrassed, and besides, I needed a drink. I found myself in a residential neighborhood and walked until I found a main road. I was picked up by another nice man. He seemed to like me. When you've lived as I did, you become quite perceptive at knowing who is who. And I was adept at getting what I wanted from a guy, if I sensed he was codependent and/or—a sucker.

I could tell that this guy was lonely and just wanted a woman to hang out with. I'd already been raped at least ten times by then and could tell, that was not his intention, nor did I feel he wanted to have sex with me, which was a relief.

As he drove, we talked, and since there seemed to be a good rapport between us, I ventured to ask him if he'd buy me a bottle of liquor. Strangely enough, he didn't have a problem with buying hard liquor in the early morning hours. He joined me in getting drunk as he drove us around Monterey. Then he asked me if I wanted some "bennies." "Hell yeah," I told him. So *that* was it—the guy was already high when he picked me up.

My mom and three younger brothers were living in Needles, CA, at that time. My mom was working with the Mojave tribe, and my brothers were in high school there. Once the speed took hold of me, I told my new friend that I wanted to go to Needles to visit my family. I had to have been pretty high to want to face my family in my condition. The man agreed to take me all the way there.

We drove for hours, drinking and popping bennies. When the man dropped me off in front of my mom's house, he handed me a baggie full of bennies and a few bucks.

After my mom opened her front door, she just stared at me. It took her a moment to realize it was really me. I hadn't let her know I was coming. She told me to come inside, despite the fact that I was drunk and had a six-pack with me. I was still her daughter and she never would have turned me away.

As we visited, she asked me what I was going to do with my life. I told her I'd been thinking of joining the Air Force. "Well, at least that's something," she told me. I had no idea why I told her that. Who was I kidding? I was a drug addict and alcoholic, and couldn't see myself living any other way.

My brothers were surprised to see me as well, and it took a while before they felt comfortable with me. I was nothing like the sister they remembered; I was drunk and high on speed. That evening, I told my mom I was going to the store to buy more beer. She told my younger brother, Kevin, to go with me. The next morning, I stayed in bed until my mom and the boys left. I knew I couldn't stay, not like that. I wrote my mom a letter before leaving the house, explaining why I had to go.

I continued hitchhiking east, through Arizona. I stayed drunk the whole time on cheap wine and beer. I finally ended up in New Mexico. By then, I was running as fast as I could—from myself. I went from skid row to skid row, until I got too sick to function, and turned myself into a hospital detox ward in Albuquerque. "I'm withdrawing from alcohol *and* heroin," I lied, because I wanted them to give me pain pills. I was administered Darvon N, as I'd hoped, and after three days, was transported to a residential program in downtown Albuquerque, called Odyssey House. That began my experience in "therapeutic community" drug programs.

Odyssey House had its base in New York. It began as a drug program for hard core heroin addicts. I wasn't that hard core, not yet. In other words, I hadn't been to prison as most of the residents in the program had been, but I was certainly not far from it if I continued my downward spiral through addiction. Sooner or later, most junkies become desperate enough and commit felonies.

The treatment program was heavy-duty, with lots of rules and regulations. We were all on some sort of work crew. The program would contract out with different companies that were in search of cheap labor. That's how programs like Odyssey House survived, because there was no federal funding available to them.

In the beginning, I was part of a crew that was digging trenches in the Sandia Mountains, just east of Albuquerque. We dug the trenches and filled them with rocks to prevent mud slides. It was during the heat of summer, but I enjoyed the physical labor and loved being out in nature.

When winter came, we loaded up a truck with camping gear, food, and other supplies, and headed for a cabin past Taos, N.M., where we'd been hired to cut trees. We cooked in the fireplace and slept on the huge cabin floor in sleeping bags. For bathing, we had our choice of heating water for a sponge bath, or going into the icy, cold creek. This crazy woman chose the latter. We washed our clothes in a big metal tub over a fire, stirring it with a huge tree branch. In the evenings, after dinner, we had our therapy groups and then sang songs. That's where I got in touch with the singer in me again.

After being in the mountains for a few weeks, I didn't want to return to Albuquerque. I felt alive out in the woods and I had no cravings for alcohol or drugs. But return we did. One day, I'd had enough of the program, and left. I wasn't ready for the level of honesty that was required. I wasn't ready to face myself or my guilt.

I caught a ride out of Albuquerque with some wannabe hippie- types, who took me as far as Gallup, N.M.

When we got there, I was invited to stay at their house and party. The young people had beer and peyote. I got pretty wasted. I decided to leave and go walking around Gallup, like an idiot. I was never satisfied staying in one place for very long when I was loaded. I always had the urge to see what I was missing at another party or another bar. But what I found instead...was always trouble.

I was picked up by a couple of Navajo guys who were returning from a rodeo. They fed me more beer as we drove around in their truck. The last thing I remembered was them raping me. I "came to," the next morning, to find myself lying on the ground. I had no idea where I was. An old Navajo man was out walking. He saw me in a jumbled heap in the dirt and came over to me. He could see that I was in trouble and walked me over to his small adobe house so I could get cleaned up. I'm sure he knew what had happened to me. After he fed me, I found my way to a main road and made it back to Monterey.

After burning my bridges in Monterey, I decided to try my luck living on the streets of San Jose, CA. While there, I was introduced to a drug called PCP, or Angel Dust. More like devil's dust if you ask me. San Jose was the PCP capital of the country. All I wanted to do after I smoked it was to hide in a corner. It was definitely not my kind of high.

One night, I was walking down a major boulevard, and this guy came out of nowhere, pulled me into an alley, and raped me. I was so pissed off at yet another rape that I slugged him in the face as I fought with him, which only made him madder. Afterwards, I went back out on the street and stuck my thumb out. I was picked up right away. I wanted a ride to another part of the city to try and hustle a drink, but asshole number two, had other plans. Soon, we were racing down the freeway, away from San Jose. I thought, *Son of a bitch—twice in one night.* "Stop this car or I'll jump out!" I demanded. I opened my door, just enough for him to see that I was serious. That's the last thing I remember.

When I came to, I was lying on the freeway pavement. There were flashing red lights all around me from police cars and an ambulance. I was moaning, "My leg, my leg." The EMTs told me that I'd been hit by a car. Apparently, I'd been knocked out when I landed on the ground and my head was bleeding. I also had a broken leg. I was rushed to the nearest hospital, but denied treatment, because I didn't have insurance. I was then transported to the county hospital, all the while, in tremendous pain.

Both bones below my knee were broken, but it was a clean break. As I lay in a cubicle, I screamed for pain medication but was told that because I was "under the influence," I'd have to wait. Sure, I'd had some alcohol several hours before, but just enough to stop the shakes. They stitched up my head and put me in a leg cast before giving me a shot of Demerol. After that shot, I wouldn't have cared if both legs were broken. I was in heaven.

I started thinking about what a miracle it was that I wasn't dead. It was definitely a wakeup call. I was only 25 years old, and had seen more of the shady side of life than any woman I knew. It was time to stop the madness. I contacted a Native American program I'd heard about called Four Winds Lodge. The Director of Four Winds Lodge came to the hospital to interview me, and I was accepted into the residential alcohol program.

Before I left the hospital, I was given a prescription for codeine, but I was determined not to get it filled, yet held onto the script anyway. I told myself I was through with drugs and alcohol—for real—I really mean it this time—that's it—no more—I'm going straight for good. Humm...How many times had I vowed and promised to quit? And how many more times would I go on breaking that promise?

I hobbled around on crutches for a while. It was a real lesson in humility, having to ask for help. Normally, I didn't ask anyone for help unless it was practically a life or death situation. I always had to be in control, and by asking for assistance, meant I'd have to depend on another human being, that I'd have to trust someone. On the rare occasion that I did ask for help and didn't receive it, I could tell myself, *See, no one really cares about you. No one will ever be there for you.* It became a self-fulfilling prophecy. I hated not being able to walk, but it kept me rooted to the program. There was no way I was going out on a binge on crutches.

We had fun in the program and went to lots of pow-wows. I met Dennis Banks, the co-founder of AIM (the American Indian Movement), at a pow-wow that we were taken to. One of his "women" was the secretary who was employed at our treatment program. I understood that he had women all over.

About three months into treatment, I went ahead and had my prescription filled for the codeine. I rationalized my need for it to myself, and didn't tell my counselor at the program.

On my next hospital visit, my cast was removed and replaced with a shorter one, and I was able to trade in my crutches for a cane. Before I left the doctor's office that day, I managed to acquire another prescription for codeine, even though I was no longer in pain. I could be quite persuasive when I wanted something bad enough.

When I ran out of codeine, I decided to try nutmeg. That's right, nutmeg, the spice. I'd heard that if you took enough, it was similar to a marijuana high. Hell, I didn't even care for marijuana. One night, I mixed a couple of tablespoons of nutmeg with chocolate milk and drank it. Ugh! To this day, I can't stomach anything made with nutmeg. But after I drank that concoction, I was high for two days! I thought I'd never come down.

Looking back, it was at the three month point that I began to get in touch with my deeper feelings of shame, grief, and anger. That's why I began to self-medicate at the Lodge. For me, it was the un-numbing process: the feelings that I'd held inside for years, were making their way to the surface. The shame I carried forced me to withdraw into myself, and I wouldn't talk to anyone about it; I feared what others would think of me. I became overwhelmed and panicky. So, instead of working through the feelings, I relapsed.

One night, I took a walk to the store, bought a six-pack, and brought it back to my room. That was pretty bold of me. After drinking all six beers, I passed out in my bed. The next morning, I woke up and found that I had wet the bed. I was so embarrassed that I packed my things and snuck away, before anyone knew I was gone.

Because I was physically disabled, I was able to get on welfare, and found a room to rent in a boarding house. Next, I located the Indian bar and became a daily customer. One night, I met a white guy there; he told me he had some codeine in his motel room. As soon as we got into the room, he threw me down on the bed and raped me. When he was finished, he grabbed some rope (this guy was definitely prepared) and bound my hands and my feet together, then he lay down on the bed next to me. I lay motionless, waiting for him to fall asleep.

When I was sure he was drifting off, I started the slow process of untying myself. It took hours, as I had to be very still and not wake him. I made my plan of escape, step by step, in my head. At the first sign of light, I made my move. Very quietly, I shifted my weight away from him, lifting myself from the bed. As I stood up, I looked over at him; his breathing was slow and even. I got dressed, then made my way to the door, and opened it. Once I was outside, I quietly closed the door behind me. The sun was coming up. The motel was facing a busy street, which was a relief.

Without looking back, I hobbled away, as fast as anyone could, in a leg cast. I hadn't gone but a few yards when I heard the door open. I swung around to see him start to barrel out the door and then stop, realizing he was half naked. He was pissed! I yelled back, "Fuck you, mother fucker," and kept on truckin.'

For the entire year of 1975, my wanderings lead me to skid rows in Phoenix and L.A. I was 26 years old and looked and felt like I was 40. I floundered around in Phoenix for several months, drinking and surviving on the streets and in the alleys with the Indians. There was an alcohol detox unit downtown called LARC (Local Alcohol Recovery Center). I ended up there on several occasions. When you first got there, you just looked for an empty mat on the floor and that's where you did your detoxing, along with about 30 other drunks, mostly Indians. It was cold turkey and depressing as hell. I always ended up leaving after a day or so.

I'd been in a leg cast for nine months already, and decided it was time to get rid of the damn thing. I cut the cast off with a knife. I was upset to see that my leg hadn't healed correctly, as it jutted out in the middle where the break had been. But mostly, I was just happy to be "mo-bile" again.

It was time to get out of Phoenix and head back up north to familiar territory. As was often the case, I'd be drinking while I was en route to my destination, and would end up stranded in places I didn't want to be in. So I started hitchhiking and landed in East L.A.

One day, I bummed enough money for a pint of bourbon. I was in the city of El Monte. That night, I went into a blackout, and when I came out of it, I found myself standing in the living room of someone's house. A woman was telling me she was going to call the cops. I was looking for the bedroom, and told her I was going to go to sleep. Evidently, I just wandered into some couple's house, as if I lived there. When I finally realized what was happening, I left right away. That wasn't the last time that I wandered into someone else's house, or on another's property, as if I lived there, because I was in a blackout.

It was around that time, that I decided to get the hell out of East L.A. and head back up north, before I got myself killed. I had a bottle of whiskey on me that night and was nursing it as I stood on a major boulevard, with my thumb out. A man picked me up who seemed friendly enough, but then again, I was a lousy judge of character when I was drunk. He asked me where I was headed. "Salinas," I told him. I passed out as he was driving, and came to, when the car stopped.

I sat up and looked around; it looked like we were in the mountains. It was pitch black out. The car was parked under a cluster of trees. I said to the driver, "Hey, what's going on?!" He didn't answer me. *Oh my God, here we go again*, I thought. He reached under his seat and pulled out some type of cord and tied my hands together. I felt my whole body going numb from sheer terror.

Every time I was raped, there was the fear of being killed. I'd had guns put to my head before, but this felt even more sinister. There were a couple of serial killers in California at that time who were still killing women. *My God*, I thought, *I finally met up with a serial killer.*

When my attacker covered my mouth with duct tape, I was stone-cold sober. I started praying in my head, harder than I ever had before. "Help me Jesus, don't let him kill me. I don't want to die like this!"

What's really a mind-blower, is that I was repeatedly putting myself in harm's way; playing Russian roulette with my life, every single day I was on the streets. My life had become one of a slow suicide, and for the most part, I didn't want to be alive. But when it actually came down to the threat of death, at the hands of another, the will to live became so strong, that I'd do anything within my power to prevent it. There were a couple of times when I was able to escape, by jumping out of cars and running like hell, when I felt I was in the presence of evil. Other times, I was able to talk my way out of being harmed; those times were few. But I could neither run, nor could I talk my way out of this horrific situation.

When the guy reached under the seat, and pulled out a butcher knife, I knew it was all over for me. *So this is how I'm going to die.* It was right up there with being burned to death, as far as I was concerned. I think at that point, I left my body, yet I was acutely aware of the movements of the man next to me.

Then, all of a sudden, my attacker spoke for the first time, saying, "Oh, I'm so sorry, did I hurt you?" as he carefully removed the duct tape from my mouth. A rush of relief flooded through me and I quickly responded, "Oh, no, I'm fine," as I watched him untie my hands.

I was afraid he might slip back into some evil place, so I began talking to him as if he were my best buddy. He was the perfect gentleman, as he then offered me a ride back down the mountain to a freeway ramp, where I could catch a ride going north. I don't know why that man did what he did, or what made him snap out of it. He had all that he needed to kill someone. I now attribute that to the Creator, for having spared my life, one more time.

Once I was back in Salinas, I headed for skid row, and after a couple of days of drinking cheap wine, I met Louie. I was on Main Street one night and had enough money for a fix of heroin. I went into the hamburger diner that was frequented by junkies. I saw him as I went inside.

Louie was Chicano, and a few years older than me. He was in typical Chicano attire: neatly creased khakis and a Pendleton shirt. I took a seat next to him at the counter and ordered a beer. I made small talk with the man and found out he'd just gotten out of the "joint." When I asked him where I could score some dope, he said, "You're looking at him." Bingo! We ended up back at his place, which was a room in a boarding house on the same street. After we had our fix, it was an instant relationship for both of us.

Louie knew that I'd prostituted myself in the past for heroin, and assured me that I wouldn't have to do that again, which was a relief. I was happy to be getting free heroin and beer.

Louie controlled the sale of heroin on the streets of Salinas. He belonged to the Nuestra Familia (New Family), a rival gang of the Mexican Mafia. A movie came out in the early 90's called *American Me*, which tells about the "NF" and how the group formed.

Gang members had distinguishing tattoos: teardrops, crosses on the webbing between the thumb and forefinger with four dots around it, symbolizing NF 14. I found it interesting that many of these guys had tattoos of the Blessed Mother covering the whole of their backs, yet did unspeakable things. Catholicism and family were sacred to them. Mothers were akin to saints.

I knew better than to listen in on conversations or to ask questions, while in the company of Louie and other gang members. When the two of us walked down Main Street to meet his supplier, I had to wait a half a block away and face the opposite direction, so as not to see the make of car, or who was in the car of the person he was meeting. I became addicted to danger, and there was always an element of danger while I was involved with Louie.

I had no problem fitting into the Chicano way of life. I wore creased Levis with small cuffs at the bottom, Pendleton shirts, and bandanas. I also wore a fedora hat and had the Chicano slang down pat. Since I grew up hearing my mother speak Spanish, and had a good grasp of the language, it wasn't difficult to learn the street/prison slang. I looked like a real "chola" (home girl). I went from being an LSD tripping hippie, to a skid row wino, to a junkie hooker, to a gang members woman. I was good at transforming myself to fit into whichever group I wanted to associate myself with. I sought to belong, to identify myself with a particular group. I had no identity of my own.

Louie only bought me beer to drink. I would have preferred hard liqueur, but he didn't want me getting drunk. If I was drunk, I was a liability because I might attract the cops.

Whenever we were on the street and he was "holding" (dealing heroin), we were constantly on watch for the vice cops. They knew him well. Sometimes they'd be walking toward him and Louie would take off running, but I'd stay behind until the coast was clear for us to meet up again.

We had to keep moving to different boarding houses when Louie felt that the cops were onto him, but still they found us, and sometimes they'd bust in on us while we were sleeping and do a search. They weren't concerned with me. They wanted to bust Louie with dope in his possession and send him back to prison.

We finally found a place that was more permanent. It was one huge room with a bed, a dresser, and a bathroom. It was on Market Street, hidden away in the back.

One time, Louie had to leave for a couple of days to go down south and pick up a large supply of heroin. He told his brother, Marcos, to stay there with me while he was gone, he didn't want me to be alone.

As soon as Louie left, I was free to hit the bars and get drunk. I came back to the pad one night and Marcos wasn't there. The next day, I found out that some guys from another gang had done a drive-by and had shot up the place. Marcos had been shot—in the ass. I thought it was pretty funny, unlike Louie, who was really angry with *me*. Instead of being relieved that I wasn't there to get shot, he was pissed off because I had gone to the bars to get drunk.

A couple of months into our relationship, Louie started getting violent with me, and it was nothing like I'd experienced with any man I'd been with before. A couple of times he strangled me to the point that I was passing out. Other times, he beat me so badly, that both of my eyes were swollen shut. Whenever we walked down the street, I had to look down, so that I wouldn't look at any men who passed us. If he even thought I was looking at another man, he'd beat me up right there on the street. Louie was insanely possessive. When he was dope sick, he was an animal. He said he'd killed before, and I believed him. There was a rage in him that was terrifying. He told me that if I ever left him he'd kill me; that threat kept me with him for several months.

It was 1978 and I was 27 years old. I was looking pretty rough and worn out. The initial glamour I'd found in the life of danger, had vanished, and left me feeling empty and lost. It just didn't fit anymore, and I wanted desperately to get clean and sober.

I found out about a treatment program in Watsonville called the Freedom House. Watsonville was just north of Monterey, on the coast. I contacted the program and was given an admit day. Strangely enough, Louie thought it a good idea and agreed to get clean himself because he wanted to get the cops off his back.

In order to be checked into treatment, I had to be at the administration office at 1:00pm. On the way to Watsonville, I caught rides with guys that were drinking, so I was buzzed by the time I got there. It was 5:00pm when I walked into the office for my intake. A therapist, named Barbara, was just locking up. I can't remember if I was persuasive or manipulative, or if she could tell that if I didn't get into treatment soon, it may be too late for me. Whatever the reason, she agreed to stay and get me checked in, and then transported me to the treatment facility.

The actual program site for the Freedom House was in the middle of strawberry fields. It was an old farm house with several unattached wooden buildings that served to house the men's dorm and the staff office. The men's dorm had about ten beds. The women's dorm was in the main house, just off of the living room. I'd be sharing a space of about 6x8 feet, with three other women.

The morning after I arrived, I started getting dope sick, but wasn't allowed to stay in bed. After breakfast, we had to assemble in the living room for "morning meeting," which was a combination of announcements, residents singing songs, and silly games. *I am just too cool for this shit*, I remember thinking.

When morning meeting was over, we were directed by a senior resident to go outside and stand in a circle. *Now what*, I'm thinking. As the leader walked around the circle, he whispered the name of an animal in everyone's ear. Then, at the count of three, we all had to yell out the sound of our animal. I was a donkey. Well, you can imagine what happened next. At the count of three, I sounded out with a "hee-haw," while the others stood silent. Then, they all busted out laughing. I was pissed! I didn't appreciate being made a fool of. That was the initiation of a newcomer.

Next, was exercising. I asked to be excused from doing jumping jacks and other standing exercises because, after all, I was sick. Request denied. *What kind of a cruel place is this?* I wondered. Then we all had to return to our bedrooms and make sure that our areas were "tight" and clean. Even our shoes had to be perfectly lined up. *What the hell is this, boot camp!* I thought.

I was assigned to a work crew, housekeeping. The person in charge of each work crew was a resident, which I really had a hard time with. It was bad enough that I had a problem with authority, but to have another junkie giving me orders, really pissed me off. I kept my anger to myself, though, yet my facial expressions and my body language, surely must've given me away.

The next few days were rough. I was kicking pretty hard. But even as my body began to get well, my emotional state worsened. I was easily triggered by residents and staff, especially when anyone told me what to do; I became paranoid, feeling as though I were being watched; and my moods were up and down. Yet, I did my best to appear aloof, and if I tried hard enough, I could slip back into a state of numbness.

Most of the residents there were heroin addicts and Chicano. I fit right in. In the beginning, I noticed that without my drugs and alcohol, as well as my "image" as a tough, street chick, I didn't know how to act. I felt lost. At the very least, I had to hold on to an outward appearance of being "hip, slick, and cool," or I felt vulnerable, naked. It was a process that took several months, but as I became more honest and comfortable with being me, the outward images that I had used to define myself by, no longer served a purpose.

Several of the programs for addicts back then in California, were based on a method developed by a man named Chuck Dederick, who in 1958, began a therapeutic community program called Synanon. Synanon was highly controversial, due to its confrontational counseling style called "attack therapy," yet it proved to be more successful in treating seriously hard core drug addicts, than traditional mental health therapies, because it was able to break down the addict's thick wall of denial. Freedom House utilized many of the methods of Synanon.

Because the Freedom House operated as a therapeutic community model, versus a medical model; there was no medical staff on board and we weren't referred to as patients; that implied that we were sick, and needed something from outside ourselves to "fix" us. The therapeutic community was more of a social model, whereby, residents worked together to help themselves and each other, in changing behaviors that were counter-productive to a drug-free lifestyle. The program stressed client, as well as social, responsibility. It was all about owning one's mistakes and bad choices, instead of blaming the family, the legal system, and society.

"I am my brother's keeper" was often quoted by staff. This meant that if I witnessed a resident behaving in a way that was harmful, I was bound to help. The help came in the way of confrontation. If I had a beef with another resident, or had witnessed someone behaving in a way that was less than honest, I wrote the incident down on a little piece of paper called a "slip," then dropped it into the wooden slip box. When we had our group session, we confronted the person we had an issue with. This method of having to wait until group, before taking issue with someone, was very therapeutic. As addicts, we were used to reacting in anger, on the spot, instead of allowing time to pass; to be able to cool off and gain perspective. The confrontation group also enabled us to become aware of how our behavior affected others. We were each other's mirrors.

I was scared to death of those encounter groups; I didn't want to be confronted, and worked hard at making sure I didn't ruffle anyone's feathers. I personalized any type of negative feedback I received. I had no defense against being confronted because I had no sense of who I really was. I defined myself according to my past roles as hooker, drunk, and addict. I was afraid that if I looked any deeper, I'd encounter a beast. Other times, I felt like a walking shadow; like I was nothing, a nobody.

I'd been at the Freedom House for two weeks and was in a confrontation group, sitting on my hands, so no one could see they were shaking. I did my best to appear invisible, but it didn't work because all of a sudden, Dan, one of the counselors, turned to me and said, "So Sheila, do you talk?" "No," I said flatly, as my face turned red. Thank God he didn't push it. I was so fragile then. One day, one of the male residents said to me, "When I look at you, I see so much pain in your eyes that *I* feel like crying." I hadn't realized how visible my sadness was to others.

    A major part of treatment was about getting in touch with our feelings. One day, Dan had us all go outside and stand in a circle. *Oh no, what crazy, scary thing is he going to make us do now,* I thought. Man, how I dreaded those exercises. "At the count of three," he commanded, "I want you all to growl as loud as you can. One—two—" A barely audible "meow," left my lips. I was sure that Dan hadn't noticed. How could he have, over the ferocious roars of lions and tigers from the others? "It's interesting," Dan began..., *Oh, hell no, here he goes,* "that the two people who have the most rage," he continued, "Juan and Sheila...hardly let out a sound. Hmm, now how did he know that about me? I didn't realize it then, but I was afraid of my anger and of losing control.

    I'd been at Freedom House for three months. As I said before, there was something about hitting three months of sobriety that was like a switch going off in my brain—to go no further. It was as if I kept hitting this huge steel door of pain, and I was too afraid to see what lie behind it. At that point, I still didn't trust myself. My feelings terrified me. I hadn't experienced what it would be like to go into what seemed like, a bottomless well of grief. What if I didn't make it back to sanity and was completely shattered? So, I did what I'd always done, and distracted myself by thinking about a man, and that man was Louie. Men and heroin had been my painkillers.

    Even though I had acclimated to the program fairly easily, and had gotten close to several of the residents, especially a young woman named Vicky; it wasn't enough to keep me there. I was afraid that Louie had found someone else.

I had a major issue with rejection and abandonment that went back to my childhood. I didn't realize the impact that my childhood had on my behavior and choices, until much later. I just knew that I would panic at the mere thought of being abandoned.

So one day, I went to the staff office and told them I was splitting. Dan told me angrily, "Be honest, you just want to get loaded." That wasn't it at all. As I began walking up the dirt road that led away from Freedom House, my friend Vicky was crying. I felt guilty about leaving her, but I had to go.

I went to where Louie and I had lived, and knocked on the door. He opened it and let me in, but he wasn't alone. There was a young woman there that I knew from the streets. She was a heroin addict and very attractive. Louie was high and didn't seem all that glad to see me. I went to my dresser, opened one of the drawers, and saw the women's clothes inside. That's when I lost it. Neither one of them said a word as I ranted and raved. Louie had agreed to get clean himself while I was in treatment; we were going to start over. I felt betrayed and hurt. The fact that I even wanted to continue a relationship with a man who had repeatedly tried to kill me, was insane. I took off and got drunk.

The next morning, I returned to see Louie and found him alone. I don't know why I went back. I must've wanted an explanation. He said he was sorry and wanted me back. I told him I wouldn't, not after what he'd done. That's when *he* lost it. He picked up a knife and forced me to undress.

After he raped me, I got up from the bed and tried to get away from him, but he picked up a piece of linked chain, and whipped me with it. I ran toward the door, but he beat me to it and bolted it shut, then grabbed me and threw me down on the bed. I watched in slow motion, as he retrieved the knife, and brought it toward my gut. I held his wrist with both hands and one thought: *He is not going to kill me!* I pushed his hand away with a force I didn't know I had.

He finally let go of the knife, got up, and walked away from the bed. He was crazed! I had no idea what he was thinking or planning next, but I wasn't going to wait around to find out. I lay there on that bed and gauged the distance between me and the bolted door. Louie was about 20 feet from me.

As soon as his back was turned, I leapt from the bed, ran to the door, unlocked it and ran outside stark naked, practically into the two police officers who were standing there. Evidently, someone had reported hearing my screams.

The cops told Louie to come outside and told me to go put my clothes on. They could see that I'd been beaten and asked me if I wanted to press charges. Louie made eye contact with me, a look that said he would have me killed if I did. With an evil grin he said calmly, "Go ahead, tell them." I told the cops that I just wanted to get out of there. I refused to press charges.

I left Salinas, realizing that I'd blown it by leaving the program, and hitchhiked back to Watsonville. On the way there, I managed to get drunk again. I stayed that way for several days before contacting the Freedom House about being re-admitted.

Back at the farmhouse in the middle of the strawberry fields, I knew the drill. When I entered the living room, I was directed to sit in the "chair," in the corner of the room and face the wall. The purpose of the chair was to sit and think about what I'd done. I was not to talk to, nor have any contact with the other residents, because I was not considered to be a part of the community yet.

I was wearing white bell bottomed pants, and blood had seeped through them from the beating. I smelled like piss; I'd passed out the night before from drinking and had wet my pants. I sat there while other residents sat not far from me, talking, or participating in group sessions. I ate facing that wall. I felt humiliated and wished I could disappear into the woodwork.

After three days, the program director, Rafael, instructed Lorencia, a senior resident, to take me to the bathroom and stay with me while I bathed. When she saw the welts on my lower body from the chain beating, she looked at me sympathetically, and I felt ashamed.

I was given clean clothes to wear and led back into the living room, where Rafael was seated in his chair at the front of the room. The residents were sitting in a horseshoe around him. I was instructed to sit among them. Group was on. They were to decide whether or not they wanted me back in the program. I was scared, but relieved to be cleaned up and no longer sitting on that chair.

Rafael was a hard-core, ex-addict. He was an East coast Puerto Rican and had an authoritative presence. Rafael *expected* respect. And for God's sake, you'd better not mispronounce his name. "My name is Ra—fa—*yell*," he'd yell. He was a piece of work. But most of us didn't take him seriously.

Rafael, as was his style, began by shaming me about how bad I smelled before I'd been allowed to bathe, and for leaving the program. After he'd had his say, the residents gave me their feedback, which wasn't too hard to take. I think they felt as if I'd suffered enough. Then it was my turn. I had to convince them all how badly I wanted to stay. It wasn't difficult. I was very open and genuine as I expressed to them how I knew I couldn't make it on my own anymore, that I needed their help. I was unanimously accepted back into the program.

I was given what was termed a "learning experience." I was to work in the kitchen for 12 hours a day and couldn't eat meals with the others. I was put on a "monad" which meant that I couldn't talk to anyone, unless it was during group sessions. Then there was a writing exercise I had to complete. I was willing to do whatever I had to. I wasn't going back to the streets. It had become much too dangerous.

After a month, I was allowed back into the community and felt like a human being again. My relationship with my friend Vicky would never be the same. She'd been too hurt by my leaving the program and was afraid to trust me again. But a couple of months after I'd been back, a young woman entered treatment, and we liked each other from the start. Olga was quiet, like me. We eventually bonded like sisters. Today, we're a couple of old gals and are still close.

There was no time limit as to how long we were in treatment. It was very individual, but a year was the average stay. What I learned in that program, was more valuable to me than all the years of trainings and college courses I would ever take. The Freedom House experience helped make me an intuitive and empathetic counselor, much later in my life.

The staff was aware of my three month relapse point. I'd been back for about that amount of time when one day, in a group session, the three counselors who were facilitating, decided it was time to help Sheila get in touch with her anger. I knew I had a lot of anger from all that had happened to me, but managed to keep a tight lid on it because, like I said, it scared the hell out of me. The counselors knew this. It was uncanny, the way staff seemed to see right through us residents, as if they were psychic. But it was because they were all ex-heroin addicts themselves, who'd also been through treatment.

The female counselors started out by saying things to try to piss me off like, "Hey, prune face," and "You must be constipated from all that anger you're holding on to." Then a male resident said, "Call her a bitch, she hates that." I knew what they were trying to do, but I just sat there, staring them down, with a "Fuck all of you" look on my scowling face. Then Stan, the male counselor said, "All you're good for is hustling on the street corner." I exploded with an energy that blew everyone away, including myself. I screamed at him, calling him every name I could think of. I was raging at that poor man who suddenly became all the men who had ever humiliated me.

I was applauded to have finally gotten in touch with my anger. As soon as group was over, I had a bowel movement that was long overdue. I *had* been holding on to my shit! What I learned about myself from that experience, was that even though my expression of anger came in the form of verbal rage, I was able to physically control myself by staying seated in my chair, without destroying furniture or throwing things around, as I had initially feared.

Some time after that group had ended, I found out that the counselor, Stan, had really been affected by my having unloaded on him the way I did; he'd taken it personally. Years later, I found out that Stan started using again, and died from a heroin overdose.

After I'd been back in the program for a while, one of the counselors, Ricardo, told me that Louie had contacted the Freedom House soon after I'd returned, demanding to know if I was there. Ricardo said that when he informed Louie of the confidentiality policy, that Louie threatened to put a "hit" on him and the rest of the staff. Ricardo didn't seem to be phased by Louie's threats and nothing ever came of it.

Every three months the staff would provide us with a "Dissipation." This was primarily a Gestalt therapy group intensive, and would last for 24 hours. Gestalt therapy focuses on unresolved issues from the past, by bringing them into the present; whereby, the client is assisted in getting in touch with their feelings of anger and grief through role play. In my personal experience, it was extremely healing.

Not everyone was allowed to participate in the dissipation. The staff would choose about ten of us; those whom they felt were emotionally ready to face their guilt, as well as traumatic events from the past.

We'd spend the entire time in the living room, which had been stripped of everything. White sheets covered the windows. It was like we were in our own little cocoon. During the group, staff would play songs on the record player; songs that would trigger past traumas and grief. We sat on bean bags and one by one, did our work. Some of the men were Vietnam vets, who were able to get in touch with their personal horror from that war, and grieve.

In my first dissipation group, I got in touch my dad's death. In my second dissipation, we were about 12 hours into the group and I was full of emotion, but I was stuck, and staff knew this. They decided they would help me along by playing a song about a woman who was a drunk. All of a sudden, a powerful energy from within became unleashed, and I began beating relentlessly on the throw pillows, roaring and screaming with rage. The anger I got in touch with was for myself and my mom.

What I learned from those group intensives, as well as the regular process groups, was that the more I expressed my anger, the more ability I had in controlling it. I learned that to gain control of my emotions, I first had to lose control, in a safe environment; the more un-numb I became, the more alive I felt. I eventually got the connection between unexpressed emotions and my need to use substances. I began to trust my ability to express anger toward another person. I also began to entrust the group with the guilt I'd been carrying around with me, which up until then, seemed unforgivable. As I shared my secrets, one by one, they didn't seem as huge to me once they were out in the open, and it enabled others to share their secrets too. It helps when you know you're not alone. I went from being completely dishonest, manipulative, and shut down; to being open, truthful, and in touch with my feelings.

Back then in treatment programs, the term "Higher Power," hadn't been coined, and we didn't talk about God; yet, spiritual principles were the basis of the program: love, faith, hope, honesty, forgiveness, and acceptance. In essence, we were taught to trust our intuition, our conscience, and to do the right thing and to say what needed to be said. I was able to trust the staff and to honor my own therapeutic process.

Now, in case you may be thinking, *Wow, it seems like Sheila finally got it together and will live happily ever after, drug and alcohol free...*I hate to disappoint you; unfortunately, it would take many years for me to heal from all I'd experienced; not to mention, the trauma I managed to accumulate during subsequent relapses. It would be years before I was able to forgive myself—which would allow me to love myself—to feel that I deserved to be happy. I was extremely hard on myself. But I did make huge strides toward that goal, and would never lose the awareness, the wisdom, or the growth that I received from the Freedom House experience, and the programs that followed.

Back then, I was still rarely in my body, except when I was in touch with my feelings in group. Feelings are energy. As I cried and yelled, and screamed, I was releasing that energy from my body; yet, it would take much longer for me to feel comfortable in my own skin, because of all the stored trauma memories that had accumulated in my legs, back, shoulders, chest, abdomen, and hands.

Weeks turned into months at the Freedom House, and I took to it like a duck in water. I felt valued there and safe. I felt like I belonged. But I never did get comfortable with being confronted in group. I did my best to ensure that I didn't do anything to upset anyone, but I had an attitude problem, and sometimes it showed. I did; however, get more comfortable with confronting my peers. In the beginning I had a really tough time with that one. I had been raised to feel as if I had no right to be angry; I had to appear cheerful and grateful all the time.

The concept of "inner child" was difficult for me to grasp at first. The staff would say things like, "Give your child within a voice," and "Let her scream," or "Be your four-year-old and tell your dad how it felt when he took you to the foster home." That type of therapy is called psychodrama, and was difficult for me to do. First of all, it felt like I was pretending; it seemed silly and embarrassing. Secondly, it was hard to understand how the exercises were supposed to help me in the present. What I learned, though, was when I allowed myself to give in to the exercise, it became all too real, and it didn't matter if the person being addressed were present or not, or if they were even alive.

It wasn't all work and no play at the Freedom House. We had a lot of fun too. At one point, I was in charge of week-end activities. Sometimes we went to the beach. We played volleyball and other outdoor games, as well as indoor parlor type games, like charades. Sometimes we dressed up like rockers from the 50's, and danced to oldies records on the stereo. Other times, we put on skits, like the ones from Saturday Night Live, and we laughed until we cried. It was important to know that we could have fun being straight.

Passes were given to residents who were in phase 2, but I wasn't interested in going anywhere, since I had no family to visit. Besides, I was afraid to leave my safety net within the program. The staff finally had to force me to go on passes.

When an addict quits the drugs and alcohol, they often become attracted to the opposite sex. I still didn't feel whole within myself, and was easily attracted to some of the men in the program. Once I knew that I was becoming distracted by my crush on a guy, I did what was expected, and would "cop to it" in group. Usually, the poor guy would be sitting there, red-faced, not having a clue, because I never acted on my feelings. I seemed to be the only one getting these crushes and it was embarrassing. Sometimes the staff would jokingly ask me in passing, "So, Sheila, who do you have feelings for this week?"

The counselor, Dan, didn't miss a beat. He was always right on the money with his observations regarding us residents. One evening, he was facilitating our group. I'd already been in treatment for over a year. He addressed the men in the group by asking, "How come you guys never confront Sheila?" Some of them said that they respected me too much, or that they knew how sensitive I was. Then Dan turned to me and asked, "What if you're in a relationship, and the guy calls you a bitch?" "I'd probably get drunk," I responded. Dan knew how I gave my power away to men, and expressed his concern for me, because I was close to graduating from treatment.

When you're interacting on such deep levels with peers whom you live with for months at a time, there's a natural bonding that occurs, which can be stronger than the ones you have with your own family, not in terms of love, but because of the depth of the internal landscape you have traversed together. To this day, I remember all my peers. Many of them have since died from drug overdoses or suicide. It's a miracle I'm not among them.

I graduated after having been in the program for a year and a half, and transferred to the re-entry facility downtown, that housed about six of us. I found employment at a women's crisis program in Santa Cruz, then signed up for a couple of college courses.

Several of the residents were smoking pot. I finally allowed them to convince me that it was okay to smoke it. I rationalized it by telling myself that, after all, it wasn't heroin; besides, I'd never had a problem with marijuana. What's really weird is that staff knew about it, and although they didn't condone it, there were no consequences given to those of us who smoked dope.

I look back at all the times I sabotaged myself; all the times I completed a treatment program with flying colors, was deemed "most likely to succeed," only to completely trash all my hard earned progress. I understand the why of it now, and feel sad for the woman who had a subconscious death wish; yet, she was willing to try one more time…and one more time again.

I bought an older model, maroon-colored, Mercury Marquis. It had skirts over the back tires, which I thought was sharp looking. I put a few old tires in the trunk to make it drop down in the back, making it look like a low-rider car.

On the week-ends, I started driving to Monterey to the night clubs. I'd smoke a joint before I went into the bar and would sit there, nursing a soda, hoping to meet a guy. One night, I met a Chicano soldier who was stationed at Fort Ord. After that first night, Jacob and I began seeing each other on a weekly basis.

Jacob smoked pot and liked his beer. I'd go pick him up on Fridays and we'd spend the week-end together in a motel. One night, we were in the motel room and had an argument. Without giving it a second thought, I grabbed one of his beers and drank it. And I didn't stop with just one. I proceeded to get drunk. I hadn't had alcohol for almost two years, and found myself picking up right where I'd left off. Jacob knew I was an alcoholic because I'd told him; yet, he didn't know the extent of it until he witnessed my Jekyll and Hyde behavior that night. The next morning, I had a horrible hangover, and vowed not to repeat that behavior again.

I moved from the re-entry facility and rented a room in the back of a woman's house that had been added on. It was quite small and had a wood burning stove. I was still involved with Jacob and lived for the times we were together. That wasn't good. It was like I just existed during the weekdays. We still smoked our pot and he even quit drinking around me so I wouldn't get tempted.

Around that time, I was drinking this Mexican espresso coffee every morning. I was smoking pot almost daily and eating lots of sweats. I began feeling crazy, and my moods were all over the place. I'd either feel really intense and angry, or depressed and exhausted. I went to see a psychiatrist, who promptly diagnosed me as manic-depressive. I disagreed with her diagnosis and went to see a therapist in Santa Cruz, who questioned me about my diet. I told him what I'd been consuming and the symptoms I was having. He said he wasn't surprised I was feeling as I did, with all the pot, sugar, and espresso coffee I was using. His diagnosis was a medical one. He told me to cut out the pot smoking, all sugar products, and the coffee. He suggested a diet for me to follow that involved smaller meals, several times a day, and more protein. He also suggested that I be tested for hypoglycemia, which I later did, and was told that I was a borderline hypoglycemic. For about four days, I felt like I was detoxing from drugs, which I was, but I stuck with it and began to feel more balanced emotionally.

Those who consume large amounts of alcohol over a long period of time, are at risk for developing hypoglycemia, because they either don't eat, or they don't eat healthy foods. Thank God I went for a second opinion, and found out that my problem wasn't a mental illness, but rather, an issue of diet. But what created my craving for espresso coffee, sugar, and pot, *was* the problem. I wasn't living according to my values. I was in a relationship with a man who was good to me, but not good *for* me, because he drank and smoked pot. We were never together and not stoned. I was losing myself and losing self-esteem.

One night, Jacob wanted to go to a nightclub. After we got there, he ordered himself some drinks, which pissed me off, so I decided to have some hard liquor myself. By the time we got back to my place, I was pretty drunk.

When I woke up the next morning, I was sick and hung-over. I asked Jacob what had happened, because I knew I'd blacked out. I was horrified when he told me that I'd picked up the axe next to the wood stove, gone over to him as he lay in bed, and with both hands, started to bring it over my head toward him. Then, he said, I stopped and put it down. I was dangerous in a black-out. Well, needless to say,

Jacob ended our relationship. I fell to pieces and went on a binge that lasted a couple of months.

I contacted my friend Olga, who had graduated from the Freedom House by then. She arranged for me to go to the re-entry house and detox there. After a few days, I was well enough to go back to Freedom House. The new director, Tom, had been one of the counselors when I was there before. He confronted me by saying that I was, "flirting with death." It sounded cold, but I knew he was right. I was really pushing it to the limit.

I felt like such a failure going back to treatment for the third time. I felt defective. I thought there must be something really wrong with me, and began to doubt that I'd ever really make it. How many times did I have to hit rock bottom before I was ready to choose life? Well, I got with the program and began working on myself. When I drank and used drugs, I didn't do it half-way. The same held true for all the times I was in treatment. It wasn't long before I was feeling good about myself again. I remember being in group once and saying that I felt like I was in love, but with myself, and what a revelation that was!

I moved into phase 2 fairly quickly, and got a job working at Planned Parenthood in Santa Cruz. I didn't feel fulfilled there, though. The last time I'd been at Freedom House I'd realized how much I wanted to be a drug counselor, and still felt that way. I did great in the process groups as far as assisting my peers in working through their issues. My perceptions and my feedback were always right on target.

Then...Alex arrived for treatment. He was tall, dark, and handsome. I knew enough to stay away from him and it worked, that is, until the day that he told me of his attraction for *me*. Oh, shit! Why did he have to go and do that?

It was as if the strong, wise Sheila was swept off to another planet, leaving the little girl, codependent me, feeling totally out of control. That empty hole I had inside me, which I'd finally filled with myself, was replaced with an addiction that was more powerful that any drug. I was addicted to the *feeling* of being in love, just as much as I was addicted to the need to be needed. The faces changed, but it was always the same guy. And Alex was a "bad boy" and a user of women. Yep, just the man I needed for a good ole' fashioned sabotage.

I admitted in the group, that Alex and I had an attraction for one another. We were put on a monad. We could only speak to one another in group sessions. That only served to deepen my attraction to him. Here I was, light years away from the guy in terms of personal growth, but felt unable to stop the powerful draw I felt toward him.

One day, Alex wrote me a note asking me to leave treatment with him. I felt I had no choice, even though I clearly did. We had to wait until I got my paycheck, which was to his advantage, as was the fact that I had a car. He had it made with gullible me. We agreed to meet in Santa Cruz.

I cashed my check and Alex and I spent the next several days drunk, in a motel room. After my money was gone, so was Alex. As I was driving back to Watsonville, my car broke down on the freeway and I just left it there. I was really angry with myself. So what did I do? I went back to Salinas and my wino lifestyle.

It was all downhill from there. I started buddying around with a couple of Indian guys who were from Arizona. We spent our days drinking wine on the railroad tracks. Some of the old gang were getting cirrhosis of the liver and dying off.

I was beginning to experience problems with my memory and my speech. I'd have to drink half a fifth of wine, just to stop the horrible trembling and paranoia. I was having black-outs on a regular basis. I was a pathetic mess. Even in my sickly condition, I managed to turn tricks for booze money, but half the time I got raped.

Sometimes, when I was drinking with my Indian buddies, these kids would come around and throw rocks at us. We'd be too weak to defend ourselves. I didn't even have a change of clothes anymore and my Levis became shiny and greasy, just like the other bums. I'd hit yet another rock bottom.

Turning 30 years old was not something I was looking forward to, in fact, like most women, I thought *Oh God, I'm getting old.* Looking back now, I think of how emotionally immature I still was at that age. Anyway, on June the 9th, the day before my 30th birthday, I found a place to crash in an abandoned house, with several other winos that I knew. That night, I went to sleep with $10.00 in my pocket and a pint of wine for a "wake up." The next morning, I found that everyone had gone, and so was my wine and my money. What bastards...Of all days!

A few days later, I decided to check myself into a women's halfway house that I'd heard about. It was a good two miles from the railroad tracks. I was so sick and weak that I doubted whether or not I could make it that far, but I was desperate.

I looked up at this big, beautiful, two-story house with a sign on it that read, Door to Hope. I prayed that they would take me in my condition. I barely made it up the steps and into the staff office. I was in bad shape and the staff on duty could see that. I was immediately taken to a lovely room downstairs and put to bed. The staff was wonderful as they helped me through a very tough withdrawal, complete with hallucinations.

When I finished detoxing, I was put in a room with another woman and began my recovery. I soon gained a wardrobe of very nice clothing, from the donations we received from the community. We were provided with make-up and toiletries as well. During the day, we had household chores and classes, and at night, we were transported to AA meetings. I began to feel pretty again and enjoyed dressing nicely. I gained some dignity, in that I was no longer living a tramp's life.

For many years, I'd wanted to learn how to play the guitar. I bought a used one, and since I couldn't afford lessons, taught myself. I started out with songs by Janis Joplin and Neil Young. I'm sure that I drove my roommates crazy as I struggled with chords and strumming, but they were very gracious about it. Only after I became better at my playing, did the women tease me about how it had been rough on their ears. Playing guitar became my new obsession.

Joan was a social worker at Door to Hope. She assisted the women with employment and in transitioning back out into the community. After several months of working a recovery program, I felt I was ready to move to the next level, which meant getting a job. Joan was aware of a program called CETA, which paid for on-the-job training. She knew about my interest in becoming a counselor and was eager to support me in my goals toward attaining that. There was an outpatient substance abuse program in Salinas called, Sunrise House, that served individuals as well as families. Joan contacted the director, Elgie, and scheduled an interview for me. If hired, Elgie would have to agree to pay for half of my salary and CETA would pay the rest.

I arrived for what would be the first of many interviews I'd have with behavioral health and substance abuse agencies. I sat, somewhat nervously, in front of Elgie and the rest of the staff of counselors and therapists. I wasn't familiar with the whole interviewing process and didn't know what to expect.

The staff began asking me questions about myself and my experience in working with substance abusers. I informed them of the excellent training I received while at the Freedom House. As I began to answer their questions, I sensed their approval as they nodded their heads and smiled at me.

Afterwards, I went back home, to Door to Hope, and awaited Elgie's phone call. When it finally came, it was terrific news! I was on cloud nine and couldn't wait to start. During my first week there, one of the counselors said that I blew them away during the interview, because I was so real. She said I was a natural in terms of being a counselor. I had found my calling.

I left Door to Hope after I collected a couple paychecks, and rented a studio in a very nice older home, just down the street. I'd never lived alone before, sober, and didn't want to be too far away from my support system.

The studio had a bed that swung out from the closet and it was furnished. I bought myself a little black and white TV and Door to Hope helped me out with dishes and other household necessities. I rode a bicycle to and from work. I was living as an independent, responsible woman and I loved the way that felt.

I decided to return to college and registered for a full load. My major was undecided at that point, but I was especially interested in psychology. I completed the first semester with a B+ average. That's when I realized I was more intelligent than I'd thought.

When I went to register for the second semester, I saw that a previous instructor, Brad, was teaching a sociology class I'd signed up for. I enjoyed Brad's style and the passion he displayed in what he taught. He and I became good friends and we remain so to this day.

In the evenings, I'd watch TV and then hit the books. I was experiencing many "firsts" in my new lifestyle, and it felt so good to be clean and sober and productive. I bought myself a nicer guitar and continued to play. I remembered how I used to make up songs when I was a kid and thought, *Why not write my own songs?* Just the thought of doing such a thing gave me the biggest rush. I sat down on the carpet with my guitar that night and wrote my first song, *Yesterdays Pages*. It was a Bob Dylan-type ballad about my journey from addiction to recovery. I found that I could only write songs about something I'd experienced firsthand.

Elgie really took me under his wing. He helped me realize my giftedness and told me that my experience as an addict was valuable to my work. Elgie gave me my first experience as a public speaker. He began taking me to high schools, where I would speak to gymnasiums full of students about my drug use and recovery.

I remained closely connected to the AA community. I found out about an AA dance at Sun Street Center, the men's alcohol and drug rehab. I wanted to go, not so much to dance, but to listen to the music and eat the food. I was a sucker for free food. Part way through the dance, a slow song was being played. I saw this good looking Chicano man walking toward me. I wasn't very comfortable with slow dancing, but accepted his invitation, nonetheless. He said his name was Richard, and that he lived there at the center. We spent the rest of the evening talking and enjoying each other's company. When I was ready to leave, he asked for my phone number, saying he'd call the next day.

After that night, Richard and I were in daily contact with each other. Sometimes he'd get a 24-hour pass and stay at my apartment. Oh, I was in love! That feeling should have been a red flag in itself, but I chose to ignore it. Instead, I let Richard move in with me before he even completed his treatment at the rehab.

We had a lot of fun together and were both working a recovery program, although I really had a jump on Richard in that department; yet, I was determined to help him catch up...

Richard had been in the Army and wanted to use his GI bill to go to school. He'd learned how to cut hair when he was in prison and decided to go to beauty school. I loved that idea because it meant free perms and haircuts for me.

I wanted to live in a rural area. I've always been more of a country girl anyway. Besides, Richard hadn't been sober that long and I wanted to get him away from easy access to alcohol. I was a classic codependent, thinking that I actually had the power to save him from temptation.

I found a rental about fifteen minutes outside of Salinas, in a town called Prunedale. Richard and I went to check it out and were pleased with it. It was a quonset hut with a big yard and very few neighbors. It was also right off the freeway, which made it convenient. We moved in right away and acquired some furniture. It was summer, my favorite season. We had barbeques and went to the gorge for swimming and picnics on the week-ends.

It was 1983 and I was 32 years old. One of my cousins in L.A. was getting married, so I saw it as an opportunity to go visit my relatives and to introduce them to

Richard. My mom had been living in South Dakota, working on one of the reservations at that time. She flew out to L.A. as well. I was excited to see her. I hadn't seen her since my strange visit to Needles, when I was still drinking. My mom and I had been in touch through letters and phone calls, but since she'd moved out of state, I couldn't afford to fly out and see her.

During our visit, Richard and I informed my family of our decision to get married. They all liked Richard because he was helpful and friendly. They were happy that I'd found someone who treated me well, and that I was finally getting my life together.

As you recall, I'd always sabotaged myself when things were going too well. But I didn't do that this time. I'd reconnected with my family and I didn't want to mess that up. I also valued my position as a counselor, because I had a responsibility to my clients. I'd been clean and sober for about two years and felt strongly about maintaining what I'd worked so hard for. I had my own home and I had my music. I was reasonably happy and emotionally stable. I also valued my relationship with Richard and was looking forward to marrying him.

Then, it all began to unravel. One evening after work, when I went to pick Richard up from school, I was told that he'd come in, but that he'd picked up his check and left. I had no idea where he was. I drove home and waited, anxiously. He didn't come home all night and didn't call. I knew what that meant. He'd relapsed.

I was too upset to go into work the next day, I called in sick. The pain was horrendous. Of course, I wouldn't have been in pain at all, had I remained single, or chose to be involved with a man who was not a newly recovering alcoholic, or one who didn't trigger my childhood pain of abandonment. But I wasn't ready to stop my pattern of having to save men who were addicts, because as long as I was with men who needed me, I felt I was in control. So you see, I *did* sabotage myself when I decided to hook up with Richard in the first place.

I eventually found Richard in skid row, drunk. I was an emotional wreck, but so relieved to get him home. I couldn't believe how attached I was to Richard, and a part of me hated him for that.

Richard began to relapse about every three months after that. I was on an emotional roller-coaster. I walked on egg shells, watching his moods and forgetting about myself and my own needs. The relationship became strained. I had a hard time focusing at work because I was so obsessed with Richard.

I was pacing the house anxiously one evening, wondering where he was, when I heard a car drive up. I peered out the window and saw him getting out of the passenger side, and then the car left.

As he came staggering up the porch, I quickly bolted the door. I figured I'd teach him a lesson. When he couldn't open the door, he began banging on it shouting, "Open the fucking door!" When he realized I wasn't about to let him in, he busted it down, leaving it barely hanging from its hinges. I was terrified. He was out of his mind with rage because I'd had the nerve to lock him out. Well excuse the hell outa me! I was the one paying the rent *and* the bills, not Richard.

To get me back for locking him out, Richard picked up my guitar and smashed it to pieces. He knew what that guitar meant to me. I'd never seen him like that before and I feared for my safety. I ran out of the house and down the dirt road that was adjacent to the freeway, screaming for help.

He caught up to me and grabbed me by the hair, dragging me back to the house. He told me to get my purse and to drive him to Salinas. Once we were there, he ordered me to drive to an ATM machine and withdraw $40.00. After I got the money, he took it from me and had me drive to a heroin dealer's house. If he was going to shoot dope with *my* money, then by God, he was going to get enough for me too, especially since he'd just shattered my world.

The next morning, I called my boss and told him I was quitting because I'd relapsed. At least I had enough integrity to know I couldn't help others after what I'd done, and I certainly couldn't face the staff.

My relationship with Richard didn't end there, but it would never be the same. We became two sick people, shooting dope and getting drunk together, because we didn't know how to say it was over. We pretended that what he did to me never happened. When my money ran out I started turning tricks for heroin and only went home to shower. I couldn't stand to be in that house because it was no longer a home.

Richard and I woke up one morning and knew we had to leave because there was no money to pay the rent. There was a real heaviness that day. We'd been together for two years and neither one of us had a thing to say to each other. It was over. I drove him to a halfway house and returned to pack my things.

I had an AA lady friend who lived nearby, who offered to store my belongings at her home in her storage shed. Once that was accomplished, I packed a suitcase and drove to Salinas. I went to the human services department and got a voucher to stay in a rooming house for a month. I deserted the car in a parking lot, knowing it would be repossessed anyway, since I still owed payments.

I was turning tricks and it wasn't long before I was strung out on heroin and booze again. I stayed as wasted as I possibly could because of the grief I felt over the loss of the relationship, the loss of my live-li-hood, of my home, and most of all, the loss of myself, as a sober and productive woman. I felt guilty, because once again, I'd let my family down.

Richard ended up back on the streets, which came as no surprise to me. We'd run into each other from time to time. It would hurt seeing him and I'd lash out at him if I was drunk. But after a few months, he was just one more asshole who had used me and then fucked up my life. At least…that's the way I chose to see it.

One night, I was out doing my thing on Market Street, when along comes this Latin looking guy in a long coat, sporting a fedora hat. Now that was a sharply dressed man. I'd never seen him before and figured he could only be in that part of town for one reason; he was looking to cop, or he was one. I went up to him and started making small talk. He was definitely no cop. He said his name was Angelo and that he'd just arrived from New Jersey. Well, it was my lucky day, because this Puerto Rican flashed a hundred dollar bill at me, and offered to buy me some heroin if I could score for him. The man was loaded with cash.

I did not leave Angelo's sight, as I helped him spend his money on heroin and nightclubbing. Angelo and I became an item. We lived in a room that was above a Mexican bar. Then his money ran out and I started turning tricks again. Angelo didn't like it, but what could he say? After all, I was buying him dope.

I took possession of a street corner in Chinatown and hustled from it. I went out every night, sometimes Angelo came with me so he could get the license plate number of the car I got into.

When I scored my heroin, I'd get my needle and cooker from wherever I'd stashed it, and walk the short distance to the Filipino pool hall to fix my dope. I was "skin popping," which meant I wasn't mainlining, but would stick the heroin filled syringe in my buttocks. That way, when the narcs stopped me on the street and had me roll up my sleeves, I didn't have any marks or ugly tracks on my arms.

The men in the pool hall would be busy gambling and drinking. I'm sure they knew what I was up to, but no one ever bothered me. Filipinos always treated me decent, in fact, I had a Filipino friend, Jimmy, who was deaf, and he knew martial arts. He was always in Chinatown, hanging around outside of the Filipino market. He was very protective of me and once, when I was being hassled by a drunk, Jimmy threw the guy a kick that landed him on his ass.

Maureen and Stan were on a mission. They were a married couple who had recently arrived from New York City. They were ex-heroin addicts who became a fixture in Chinatown and skid row. They were trying to save souls for Jesus. We ran into each other on occasion, and they were determined to rescue me from the devil's web.

Once, I was in the pool hall bathroom, just getting ready to shoot up, and someone started banging on the door, scaring the hell out of me shouting, "Sheila, we know you're in there. We want to help you." It was them. *Oh shit*, I thought, *these Jesus freaks are going to get me busted, making all that racket*. "Get the fuck away from me," I hissed. I was not in the mood to be helped or saved.

It was a cold January night in 1984. I was hanging out in front of the Mexican bar on Market Street, doing nothing in particular, when a woman I knew approached me. She had a six-pack and invited me up to her room to have a beer with her and her boyfriend. When we walked in, her man was there, and so was this guy that they'd just met on the street. I didn't like his vibes, and the blunt person that I am, I told him so. I finished my beer and left.

The next day, I saw the couple sitting across the street from the bar, in the park. I went over to hang out with them. The woman told me that it was a good thing I left when I did, because their visitor told them he had planned to rape me.

While we were still sitting in the park, a couple of men in suits approached us. They said they were detectives and proceeded to question us about the guy from the night before; when was the last time we saw him, and so on. They wouldn't say why they were looking for him, but later that day, the news had hit the streets. That man had gone to the Korean market a couple of blocks away, the night before, to rob the place. The owner, a Korean woman, refused to give him the money, so he stabbed her 22 times. Wow, another close call for me!

All the hookers in Chinatown had black pimps. Pimps and I didn't get along because I didn't play that game. I was a solo act. One night, I was standing on the corner in Chinatown and a big fancy car pulled up next to me. There were three pimps in the car. "I hear you don't like us," one of them said. "As a matter of fact, I don't," I replied. They didn't say another word, but the powered window went up, ever so slowly, and they slowly drove away. I knew I'd just signed my death warrant.

Just a week before, a black hooker had grabbed me, and put a knife to my throat to try to scare me. It worked. The next day, I bought a knife and when I saw her, I pulled it out on her. She got scared and took off. I'd only recently begun to make enemies on the streets, and that wasn't good. I later heard that those pimps planned to kill me.

I usually hung around the family-owned Filipino store during the day. They knew what I did, but they liked me anyway. The cops would slowly cruise Chinatown on a regular basis. When I saw them coming I'd duck inside, grab the broom, and start sweeping the sidewalk so they would think I was helping out at the store.

One evening, I was standing in front of their store, drinking a beer. A few feet away was an attractive woman working the streets. There seemed to be something different about her, or something I recognized in myself. We started a conversation. I told her that I'd been a counselor. She said she'd been a court reporter. Then we looked at each other, as if to say, "How the hell did we end up here, doing this!"

I woke up around 4:00pm, to begin my nightly ritual of getting ready to hit the streets. I drank my usual pint of wine to stop my hands from shaking, so I could cook up my dope without spilling it. Then I showered, dressed, brushed my hair, and put on my makeup. I could never look at myself in the mirror unless I was high. When I was high, I thought I was lookin' good.

After I got into recovery, a woman in AA, who'd seen me walking down the street one day, told me, "You looked like you died and forgot to lie down." Heroin had a way of distorting what I saw in the mirror.

On one of those nights, after I finished getting ready, I left Angelo in the motel room and walked the few blocks to my street corner.

A car pulled up next to me. I looked inside and saw four guys in it. I knew better than to get in a car with more than one man in it, but I was getting careless and taking more dangerous risks than usual. I was getting real tired of it all, so maybe I was setting myself up to be killed.

After getting in the back seat, I directed them to my motel room, which was where I took care of business. Angelo would hide behind the shower curtain in case there was trouble. But instead of them driving to the motel, they headed out of town to some isolated area that I'd never been to before.

When they stopped, three of them got out while the one inside raped me. When he finished, the next one climbed in, and the next, and then the last one had his turn. While number four was raping me, the other guys stood outside the car and were rummaging through my purse. I didn't have money or anything of value in my purse, except for my pictures.

I looked over and saw them pulling out those photos and talking about them. They were pictures of my kids, the only ones that I had of them. Knowing that those pigs had their hands on those pictures, felt more violating, than the vile acts I was being forced to perform.

Then, to my horror, I heard one of the men say to the others, "She's seen our faces. We're gonna have to kill her." As the last man was raping me, I sensed that he wasn't as cold-blooded as the others, so I pleaded with him, "Please don't let them kill me." Then I said, "Do you have a sister?" He immediately told me to shut up, but I could see that I'd hit a nerve, and continued to talk about the possibility of that happening to his sister, as he continued telling me to shut up. But that's all I had to fight back with. Once again, I prayed to myself, for my life.

Then—it was over. They all piled into the car, gave me back my purse, and drove back to town. I couldn't believe it. I was spared once more from an ugly death. Before they dropped me off, they told me to keep my mouth shut about what happened, or else. Yeah, like I was going to call the cops, me, a prostitute. That's the reason why so many hookers end up getting raped. Their attackers know it won't be reported.

When I walked into the motel room, Angelo's eyes got real wide as he stared at me, asking me what happened. I was a mess, with blood running down my legs, but all I said was, "Nothing." I wasn't about to sit there and process my feelings. I was in survival mode. All I wanted to do was clean myself up and get back out on the street and make some money, so I could feed my addiction.

I stayed out all night, hustling, fixing dope, and drinking. The sun was coming up and I found myself in some guy's car, and didn't remember how I got there. But I was in need of another fix and for some reason, the guy just gave me some money. We were parked on Main Street, and he said he'd wait for me in his car, while I went inside the Mexican restaurant to score my heroin. I figured it would be okay to leave my purse in his car.

I got my dope and went into the bathroom to fix it. This time, I decided, I was going to mainline it. As soon as I stuck the needle in my vein, it broke off. I watched in despair as the brown liquid spilled down my arm. I went back out to where the man was waiting for me, and he was gone!

I was distraught at losing the pictures of my kids. I began walking toward the railroad tracks. Thank God, I at least had a pint of wine on me. I took it out of my pocket to take a drink, and the damn thing slipped out of my grasp, busting into pieces on the gravel below. I stared down at the broken glass and dropped down to the dirt. I began wailing as I hadn't done in a long time. Just then, I heard a voice next to me saying, "Sheila, are you ready now?" *What the...?!* The

Jesus freaks seemed to have materialized from nowhere. "Yes—I'm ready—I'm done." It was March 23rd, 1984, and I was 32 years old.

Part Four

Recovering My Spirit:
A Fierce and Sudden Hunger

After driving me to their home, the couple from New York City led me inside and showed me where I was going to do my detox. They were giving me the use of their bedroom, which had its own bathroom. These were the people I'd made fun of for the past year and avoided like the plague. Maureen and Jack were the real thing; they never called themselves Christians—they lived it. They knew exactly what I would be going through, they'd kicked heroin themselves. It would be the first time I'd be withdrawing from both heroin and alcohol without any medication: no Darvon, no methadone, and no Librium. It was gonna be cold turkey and I was scared to death; yet, I also knew that my body and mind couldn't take what I'd been putting it through any longer. The combination of alcohol and heroin had taken a toll on me, and I was beyond exhausted from that lifestyle. I also knew that cold turkey was the only way for me; I didn't ever want to forget how bad it was. I wanted to quit, and stay quit.

Maureen had me change into one of her nightgowns before putting me to bed, and then left the room. When she returned, she had a pitcher of water and a glass of fresh orange juice. I wasn't allowed to get up, unless I had to use the bathroom. There were two other rules: I couldn't smoke or cuss. Well fuck...I was too sick to do either!

As the hours went by, my withdrawals steadily worsened. It started with sweating, then the chills, then nausea, and then diarrhea. I tried to keep the liquids down, but wasn't able to. That night I couldn't sleep. I just lay in that bed and tried to stop the steady stream of traumatic events and guilt that flooded my consciousness. I missed Angelo and felt terribly alone. I tossed-turned-moaned and thrashed amidst the covers.

The next day was worse. I tried to get up to go to the bathroom and found myself unable to walk because I was so weak, and had to crawl on my hands and knees to the toilet. Maureen and Jack heard me and came to my rescue. By then I was on the bathroom floor, and losing it from both ends. They cleaned me up and put me back to bed.

Later that night, I was having horrible nightmares of being suffocated and choked. I sensed an evil presence in the room. Alcoholic nightmares occur when you are in a half-awake state and the body feels paralyzed and trapped. I must have cried out for help. All of a sudden, I found myself sitting up in bed, dizzy from the room spinning, as Maureen and Jack hovered over me, praying loudly, "Help her Jesus, help her Jesus!" I felt like I was in an exorcism, and the force of their praying was scaring me more than the nightmares.

On the morning of the fourth day, I woke up and felt like I'd been through hell, but I was done with the worst of it. I showered and put on the clothes that Maureen had kindly washed for me. I went into the living room, where I found then both sitting. I asked for my cigarettes and thanked them for all their help, and for being there when I was finally ready to quit. The Creator really had his hand on me that time.

It was a beautiful spring day as I started walking toward town. I lit up a smoke and felt so grateful to be on the other side of that experience. I had no intention of getting loaded. I wondered where Angelo could be. I really wanted to see him, but I couldn't chance walking around skid row; I didn't want to run into someone who wanted me dead. So I went straight to the halfway house that I'd taken Richard to when we'd split up. I'd burned my bridges at Door to Hope. When I got there, I was interviewed by the Director,

Charles, who readily accepted me into the program. Charles was a recovering addict/alcoholic himself.

The big older home had room for about fifteen residents. We had weekly house meetings and AA meetings. I got along with everyone, some of whom I knew from the streets. I had to get on food stamps and welfare to pay for my stay.

I started feeling depressed after I'd been clean for a month or so. I went to see a psychiatrist, who put me on an anti-depressant medication, Elavil. The medication didn't seem to be helping me though, because my depression was not clinical, but due to feelings that I had yet to process, from all that had happened during my last relapse.

I'd gotten in touch with Angelo and he would visit me often. We even went to AA meetings together. He was staying clean himself and got a job as a taxi driver.

Not long after I'd entered the rehab, I was reading the daily newspaper. On the front page there was an article about a prostitute who'd been murdered. When I looked at the woman's picture I was stunned! It was that nice woman I'd talked to in front of the Filipino store, the court reporter. The article stated that she'd been picked up by a "John," a Marine, and that she had taken him back to the home she shared with her parents. Reportedly, her parents had been away on vacation at the time of the murder. I read on, in horror, as it described what that animal did to her. It stated that she fought hard for her life as he tortured and then degutted her. *My God*, I thought again, *that could have been me! And why wasn't it me?*

I contacted my social sciences teacher, Brad. I needed to be in touch with friends who'd been supportive to me and my recovery in the past. Mike, one of the residents living in the halfway house, told me he was taking one of Brad's sociology classes. I mentioned it to Brad, and told him that Mike had been in prison; which we both saw as a positive thing, as the man was trying to better himself, by getting an education. Unfortunately for me though, the next time Brad saw Mike, he shared what I'd told him about Mike having been in prison. When Mike returned from school that day, he was really angry with me.

The director, Charles, was off that evening, so we were on our own. During our in-house AA meeting that night, Mike began talking strangely, and told the group that I was a "snitch." Then, he pulled out a knife and held us all hostage in the living room, while he focused his verbal attacks on me. Sometimes he'd let us go to the bathroom, one at a time, but kept a close watch in case someone tried to call the police. It was unreal! Mike obviously had some severe mental problems. He was most likely schizophrenic. Around midnight, he finally let us go. The cops were called and he was apprehended. I was so traumatized by that incident that I ended up leaving the next day.

For the next couple of months, I stayed with different women in the AA program. Angelo would visit me at which ever house I was staying. I don't think I was ever in love with Angelo, not like I'd been with Richard, but I was addicted to him just the same. Angelo was charming in his own way, and I loved his Puerto Rican, East coast accent. He was never abusive and we rarely had arguments. He was basically a good person and I felt safe with him.

Sylvia was a kind woman that I had bonded with during one of my stays at Door to Hope. I went to a women's AA meeting one night, and saw her there. I told her about my circumstances, about not having a stable place to live. She offered to let me live at her home with her fiancé. I felt very comfortable with Sylvia and Greg. They were both in AA, and took me with them to meetings on a regular basis.

I was still seeing Angelo, but was keeping it a secret. I felt dishonest about the relationship, yet feared letting him go. He was my pain killer. I wasn't ready to feel the full extent of my pain yet. But the Creator knew differently and gave me a push in that direction.

One afternoon, I found myself sneaking off to town. I was feeling needy and wanted to see Angelo. I had to know that he was still in my life and that he hadn't relapsed. When I got to his boarding house, I took the stairs up to his room and knocked on the door. There was no answer, but I heard movement inside. I peeked through a crack in the door to see what he was doing. What I saw instead, was a black woman, putting on her clothes. There was no Angelo. I was furious and demanded she open the door. When she didn't, I kicked it in. I must have looked like a mad woman because she was really scared. I yelled at her, "What the hell are you doing in here?" She said she hadn't had a place to stay, and that Angelo had let her sleep there. "Bullshit," I yelled. I looked at the little table next to the bed, and saw a spoon with cotton in it, and a syringe. Then I turned to grab the woman, but she ran out of the room and practically flew down the stairs, with me on her heels. But I let her go and decided to wait upstairs for Angelo. I was fuming! I couldn't wait to see that son of a bitch. Here I was, busting my ass, going to my meetings, working on myself, and he's fucking other women and shooting dope. I felt very self-righteous all of a sudden. God, I couldn't wait to see his face when *he* knew that *I* knew. I didn't have to wait long.

When he came in the room he looked guilty as hell. He lied about sleeping with the woman, and of course, I didn't buy it. I felt insane as I picked up a screw driver and put it to his neck shouting, "I'll kill you!" I really just wanted to scare him, but realized how crazy my behavior was and I dropped it. "We're done," I yelled, and walked out the door.

Angelo knew the street I lived on, but not the house. For about two weeks after that incident, I noticed him roaming my street, but he didn't see me.

One day, Angelo became desperate as I heard him calling out to me from down the street, so I had to go out there and tell him to stop. He was pleading with me as he said, "I need a strong woman like you to help me." Normally, that would have hooked me, but not this time.

Then one night, Sylvia and Greg heard Angelo yelling outside and said, "Who the hell is that?" As they opened the front door, they were just in time to hear Angelo's loud pleading voice, "Sheila, I love you. I have to talk to you. I'm sorry, blah blah blah." I was mortified. *This idiot is going to ruin it for me*, I thought. So I was forced to come clean with them about the relationship. How could I not? I was the Sheila he was yelling for. I let them know I had ended it with him. They asked me if I wanted them to call the police. I told them, "No."

That began the letting go process. But it wasn't just about letting go of a man. It was a whole pattern that I'd set up, whereby, I first became attracted to, and then addicted to, men who were abusive, men who were alcoholics and/or addicts, emotionally unavailable men, emotionally unavailable abusive alcoholic addict men, men with a history of prison, Vietnam vets, Vietnam vets who'd been to prison and were abusive alcoholics and emotionally unavailable, men who weren't nurtured by their mothers and/or were abused by their fathers and went to Vietnam, only to return more screwed up then they would have been had they not gone at all, and who also used alcohol and/or drugs as a coping mechanism, or any variation thereof. There was one type of male I was never attracted to: responsible, employed, educated, and straight. Why? They didn't need fixing...they didn't need me and were therefore, BORING. Besides, if a "normal" man were attracted to me, I figured there must be something terribly wrong with him. Talk about being relationship challenged...

So Angelo was no longer in the picture, and I was hurting. But the hurt went much, much, deeper than any pain associated with the man himself. Angelo was merely the catalyst that opened up an already infected wound that had formed a thick, protective scar.

At a very young age, I incorporated a set of core beliefs, according to the way I perceived myself in the world. Here are just a few: As long as I take care of you, you will need me and never leave. I am responsible for your actions and your feelings. Your needs are more important than mine.

I didn't know if I was capable of letting go of a pattern—a pattern I'd worked years to perfect and maintain, just so I could feel emotionally safe. But it just wasn't working anymore; this pattern that kept me from looking at my own unmet needs as a child and as an adult. But was I strong enough? Was I ready? Creator knew it was time for me to finally walk through this one.

When I began to let go of my addiction to Angelo, the combination of old grief and new grief was so overwhelming that I shut down and tried to control it. As a result, my anxiety level skyrocketed; I was scared to death of feeling that pain.

One day, I was in my bedroom at Sylvia's house, and I was so overwhelmed with panic that I was afraid I'd relapse. I was having a hard time breathing, my throat was closing up. I just wanted to run out of the house and keep on running. But that's what I'd always done, wasn't it? Here I was, up against that steel door again, and I just knew I had to do something different. And I had to do it quick, or I was sure something terrible was going to happen. I took a huge risk. I ran to the living room where Sylvia was and cried out to her, "Help me Sylvia, I need help." I didn't know what her reaction would be and I feared the worst. Instead, Sylvia very lovingly held me and let me sob. She *heard* me. I wasn't this shameful, pathetic, messed up creature, just because I was falling to pieces. I'd acted on instinct and had gone beyond myself, beyond the dreadful anxiety that threatened to swallow me up and kill me. What a major lesson I learned that day—I cried out for help and I got it.

For the next couple of weeks when I went to my AA meetings, I just allowed myself to sob. I cried for missing Angelo—I cried for all the loneliness of a lifetime—I cried for what I'd done to myself and to my kids—I cried for a little girl who didn't get her needs met, and who wasn't allowed to cry—I cried for the young woman who wanted to disappear and not exist. I cried without shame.

I began to trust myself and allowed others to care about me again. But wait…hadn't I done a lot of this work when I was at the Freedom House? Yes, I had. But this was the first time that *I* had made the decision to end a relationship. *I* had ended a relationship with a man who *needed* me. That alone empowered me. And yes, I had done some of this work before, but there's a saying: "One step back and two steps forward." Each time I was in recovery, I progressed and grew a little bit more than I had the time before.

Angelo gave up on coming around. I was no longer addicted to him, and in my heart, I wished him well. I was stable enough to look for a job, and found one in a small grocery store. I bought myself a used bike to ride to work. It felt good to be productive and to be receiving a paycheck. I started saving my money to get my own place. I bought myself another guitar and continued writing music.

During this time, I was in touch with my mom, just as I'd been all the other times I'd gotten clean. She was always relieved when I got back into my recovery, but it had to have taken its toll on her. I knew how she worried about me. I rarely called her when I was on the run because I felt so ashamed, but later I realized that she would have preferred just knowing I was alive. We addicts can be so self-centered while we're in our dis-ease. We think we're only hurting ourselves, but that's far from true.

Another lady friend I had in the AA program told me that she was vacating her studio apartment. She asked me if I wanted to take over her lease. First, I had to find a job that was closer to where I'd be living. Luckily, I found a job as a cashier at a Chevron gas station, and moved into my little studio with a Murphy bed. I loved it. The studios were all set apart, like little bungalows, and had attached garages. I knew a guy from AA who had a truck. We went to Prunedale and picked up the belongings I had in storage.

I hadn't lived alone for about three years or so. It was difficult for a while, but I had to get used to being comfortable with myself. Over the years, I've heard many women say that they'd always lived with a man or a roommate, that they were afraid of living alone. I think everyone should have the experience of living by themselves, until they can feel comfortable being in their own company. It was a great growth experience for me.

I found myself an AA sponsor and I had a good support group of women who were in the program. I noticed that it didn't take me long to bounce back from my lengthy and traumatic relapse. I was pretty resilient when it came to getting back on track. I continued to work through my issues with my sponsor and in meetings. And I had no desire to be in a relationship.

There's another saying: "When the student is ready, the teacher will appear." Evidently, I was ready for something new in the way of a spiritual growth experience. One day, I went to visit my friend Brad and his wife. A former student of Brad's was also at their house. Eric was a composer and played the flute. We hit it off right away and soon became close buddies. Eric liked the songs I'd written. Sometimes I'd play my guitar and sing, while he accompanied me with his flute. He had psychic abilities as well, and that intrigued me. He practiced meditation and talked about how it helped him.

One night, Eric invited me to an older couple's home for a group meditation with the four of us. Before the meditation started, the couple explained to me how we would sit in silence for fifteen minutes with our eyes closed. I felt a little intimidated by that. It meant letting go and that was scary. I felt safe enough though, in the company of the couple and with Eric, to at least give meditation a chance. They made it sound so simple, "Just follow your breath and empty your mind," they instructed. *Easy for you to say*, I'm thinking. My thoughts were all over the place that first night.

Eric and I went back to their home a couple more times, and I knew that meditation was a discipline I was ready to take on. I began meditating on a daily basis.

One day, I was sitting on the carpet in my usual position for meditation, when all of a sudden I felt this incredible surge of energy rushing through me. I just allowed it to happen. My whole body was vibrating and shaking with this wonderful energy. Later, I described it to someone as a spiritual tune-up.

Meditation began changing me in subtle, positive ways. I began to feel this connection that I'd never experienced before; to myself, to the human race, and to the spirit world. My mind was clearer and I was able to understand and see my life in a whole new way. It was the beginning of my spiritual wakening.

A phenomenon called synchronicity began to occur. I found myself drawing the people and situations into my life that supported my new way of being; the same way I had attracted people and situations into my life when I was living on the dark side.

One day, I had the TV turned on to some talk show. I was cleaning house, not really paying attention to the program, until I heard something that caused me to stop and take notice. The topic was on reincarnation. Now, I'd never really given it much thought, but at that moment, it was as if I'd always believed in reincarnation. It made sense that we experience different lifetimes in order to grow spiritually.

I began reading about Buddhism, and found that it resonated with my soul. One night, I was at work in my little cage at the gas station, when an Anglo man walked up to me, asking if I were interested in Buddhism. *No way*, I thought. *This is too weird.* I'd just been thinking about how I might like to become a Buddhist. That's what I mean by synchronicity. Needless to say, I told this young man, who was to be a sort of sponsor to me, that yes, I was definitely interested, and agreed to attend a chanting session with him.

I had my initiation into the Japanese school of Buddhism known as Nichiren. I arrived at the Temple and stood before the Buddhist Priest. He tapped my head with a rolled up scroll and said some words in Japanese. Then I was presented with the Buddhist string of beads to use while I chanted. There were many Japanese Buddhists present and it seemed that they were recruiting people of all nationalities into their order. The next thing that happened was that my Buddhist "sponsor" came to my apartment to set up my alter. It included water, incense, and my prayer beads. I was given the words to chant in Japanese: Nam Myoho Renge Kyo, which is translated as meaning: "I take refuge in the sublime Dharma of the Lotus Sutra." The Lotus Sutra is one of the major Buddhists texts, which explains that the Buddha is an eternal being, that he willingly submits himself to the cycle of rebirth, in order to save humanity. This seemed plausible to me. I feel that Christ was one of those incarnations, that he was a prophet, a healer, and a teacher for that time period, who also said that everyone had the abilities that He did; that enlightenment was possible for us all, as it was for Him.

So I chanted every day, in the way I was taught. I also attended the group chanting in the evening. I continued with my daily meditations because I saw more benefit in that, than chanting in another language. I'd been involved in the Buddhist way for about a month. I hadn't altogether bought into it, but was soon to become disillusioned with that particular group and its spiritual benefit to me personally.

I was given a ride to attend a Nichiren Buddhist convention in San Jose, CA. One by one, people went up to the podium and gave testimonials about what the chanting had done for them. I was surprised when I heard most of them sharing about how the chanting was helping them in attaining material wealth. This was not, as I understood it, the principles and teachings of what I understood as Buddhism. During a break, I went outside to smoke, and I questioned a couple of the participants about what I'd heard so far. I must've hit a nerve because one of them said loudly, "This way is the only way to enlightenment." "That's bullshit," I said. Whenever I heard any group preach that their way was the only way, it was a definite turn off for me. I told them that I believe there are many paths to enlightenment. Now all eyes were on me like I was the enemy. At that point, I was just hoping I still had a ride back home to Salinas.

The next day, I discontinued the chanting and dismantled my altar, replacing it with the items that are sacred to me. I have a lot of respect for the principles and beliefs of the Nichiren form of Buddhism; they're pretty universal, it just wasn't my way.

I decided to start seeing a psychologist. I wanted to work on my anxiety. I chose one that I'd previously met at behavioral health trainings, when I was employed as a counselor at the Sunrise House. Martin was a gentle soul and very personable. At our first session, he said he was surprised that I was seeking help for an emotional problem; that he'd previously experienced me as a confident and very together woman. That was me, all right. I always had to look like I had my shit together when I worked professionally, even when I was coming apart on the inside.

In one of our sessions, Martin asked me what my greatest fear was. I told him I was afraid of dying. He said, "I don't think that's your biggest fear. I think you're more afraid of living." Suddenly, I was gasping for air as my throat was closing up. That old feeling of imminent doom hit me. I jumped up and ran out of the office and out of the building to the sidewalk. Martin came after me. He was able to get me through the panic attack by allowing me to cry and to shake. My body trembled and vibrated as the energy of fear was being released. So many times in my life when I'd been terrified, I held on to that fear and didn't allow myself to just shake, I couldn't. I was living in survival mode most of the time. When a person doesn't feel their fear, it often shows up as anxiety and panic attacks.

I was glad that Martin was there for me that day. It was because I trusted him, that I was able to completely lose it. I knew he wouldn't leave me hanging. My panic attacks were never that bad again, because I had faced a major fear. Martin reminded me that when I felt overwhelmed with anxiety, all I had to do was call someone and cry, instead of literally running from my feelings. I also realized that I *was* afraid of living and of being successful. I'd been able to experience success in the past, but only for short periods of time, before I found ways to trash it.

It was 1985, and I had this great idea about putting on a little benefit concert. I contacted three other singer/songwriters, local to the area, who were willing to participate in the concert. My friend Brad said that we could hold it at his church in their auditorium. I told Brad that I'd donate the ticket sales from the concert to his church. Then I contacted Father Larry, who was able to get me grant monies to cover advertising and refreshments. I'd found a guitar player who was willing to accompany me while I sang. The day of the concert came, and even though it was a small crowd of about fifty people, it turned out well. After it was over, I was so elated that it took a while for me to come down from my high. I had faced yet another huge fear of mine, singing my own music in public.

Around that time, I got back in touch with Olga, my friend from the Freedom House in Watsonville. She told me that the Freedom House had shut down due to lack of funding. There was an adult therapeutic community program in Santa Cruz called Sunflower House, and they had taken over the site that had once been the Freedom House, making it a sister program for adolescents. It was called Sunflower Youth House. Olga said that she'd been working at the youth program as a counselor for the past few years. I let her know that I'd been in recovery for a year and asked her about possible job openings there. She put me in touch with the program director, Patricia, who told me that they needed a night manager.

It had been about eight years since I'd last been to the facility, the farm, that held so many memories for me, and I was excited. My shift began at 11:00pm and all the residents were asleep at that time. I did hourly rounds, checking the boys and girls dorms to make sure there was no hanky panky going on, and that they were all accounted for. Then I'd walk around the spacious grounds that I knew so well, with a flash light and a baseball bat. I took my job seriously, in that I was responsible for the protection of those kids. When I was on the streets, I did a lousy job of protecting myself, but when it came to protecting others, I was Mighty Mouse and Underdog all rolled into one. "Here I come to save the daaayyy…"

I was still in the spiritual seeking stage and I went to see my first psychic. His name was Patrick and he lived in Pacific Grove. As I sat across from him, he began drawing with different colored pencils. I was a little scared about what he might see, or that he'd give me some bad news; yet, I was also very curious.

Patrick finished his drawing and showed it me. He called it a rose drawing. What I saw, was a rose with a stem. He explained that the length of the stem indicated how many lifetimes I've had. The stem went to the bottom of the paper; therefore, I'm a "very old soul," Patrick told me. The rose itself, he said, symbolized how enlightened I was. The bud had opened about one fourth of the way. He said that meditation played a major role in being able to fully awaken.

He'd also drawn two leaves that were near the stem, but not connected to it. The leaves, he said, symbolized children. He saw that I had given birth to two children, but that we'd been separated. I was amazed by that. I asked him about the whereabouts of my kids and he said they were near Canada, but couldn't be more specific than that. He went on, with eyes closed, telling me which lifetimes were trying to get my attention at that stage of my life. The purpose was to learn from the previous lifetimes and move on.

One that was being highlighted was a life I had in Spain as a spinster woman, and how I had to take care of my elderly and sick father who was also cruel. It was a sad and lonely life. The teaching from that, Patrick said, was that I had to let go of my need to take care of sick men. *No kidding!*

The other lifetime was one in which I was a wandering vagabond sort of guy, somewhere in the UK, and that I survived because I had a great sense of humor. I'd travel on foot going here and there and making people laugh. The lesson from that lifetime was that I'm too serious in this one and that I need to laugh things off more and lighten up.

Patrick shared some other things about me that he was aware of. He could see that I'd had a hard life and a poor self-image. Patrick told me I'd better start telling myself, "I'm the best thing since popcorn." I had a lot to think about as I drove home from that reading.

Being raised by a Native American mother, I knew about bad spirits and witchings. So, I was no stranger to weird occurrences in my life. As I progressed in my spiritual development, through my meditations and spiritual practices, I knew that not only would I attract good spirits, but also bad spirits in the human form. This was a risk I was willing to take. I just had to make sure I was protecting myself at all times, and not with guns and knives.

I attended a class on energy work in Santa Cruz one night. After the class was over, I got in my car and entered the freeway entrance on Highway 1, to return home to Salinas. As soon as I got on the freeway, I noticed that my speedometer was going crazy; the needle was moving rapidly from right to left. I just figured it was broken and moved over to get in the slow lane. Then, to my left, a dark colored pickup truck came rushing up and cut in front of me, then slowed down a bit, causing me to also slow down. So I moved a lane to my left, and this guy promptly got in front of me again and slowed down. I'm thinking, *Who is this idiot?"* This went on for five miles or so. My speedometer was still going nuts. Finally, when he'd forced me down to about 20 miles an hour I thought, *That's it…I've had it!* I always did have guts, but sometimes I was more of a fool than a warrior, as I often acted on impulse, instead of instinct. So when this guy finally slowed down to a stop, I stopped right behind him. I kept my lights on and turned on the interior light. I wanted to get his license plate number and I wanted this asshole to see exactly what I was doing. I was ready to get out of my car, to go up to him, and ask him what the hell his problem was. I mean, I was really gonna let him have it. But then, all of my gung ho left me as my intuition told me that I'd better get away from this man like…five minutes ago. What was really weird was that for the past few miles, he and I were the only cars on the freeway going southbound. It was as if this were happening in another dimension altogether.

I put my car in drive and sped down the freeway. He didn't get in front of me after that, but stayed behind me. Maybe my act of boldness diffused some of his power.

It wasn't that far to the next town, Watsonville, and I had a plan. We both approached the red light, just after entering Watsonville, at the same time. I was in the left lane and he was in the right. As soon as I stopped for the light, I rolled my passenger window down. I looked over to my right and into the face of a white male with the most chilling, evil, grin. I grinned right back at him, unafraid, my eyes gleaming with "fuck you" darts. When the light turned green I motioned for him to follow me. I proceeded to lead evil man straight to the police station a couple of blocks away. As I was turning left to enter the police station parking lot, I looked in my rearview mirror and didn't see him. He had vanished! I quickly turned around to get back on the main street, and I didn't see him anywhere, so I continued on to Salinas.

By the time I reached my driveway, the speedometer was back to normal. That man, or witch, was literally trying to take me off of my spiritual path. I was sure of it. But by me keeping my power, I was able to block *his* power from hurting me. He didn't get my spirit.

I'd been employed with the Sunflower Youth House for about four months, when one morning, the director, Patricia, said she wanted to speak with me. My first thought was, *I'm getting fired.* I still lacked confidence in myself, and thought the worst in situations where I felt like I was being summoned to the principal's office. When I sat down with her, she informed me that a position was opening up for a counselor, and wanted to know if I'd be interested in it. "Are you kidding me?" I told her. I assured her that I was definitely interested, so she set up an interview with herself and the rest of the daytime staff. During the interview, the staff had concerns about my level of stability, as they were aware of my track record when it came to sustained recovery.

In the end, they were satisfied with my answers and I was hired.

I decided to move to Watsonville to be closer to work. I'd been driving an old Chevy that was barely able to make the long drive from Salinas. I rented a cute little loft that was above an antique store in Watsonville. The rent was minimal because the owners basically wanted someone there for security reasons.

In 1986, I'd been working at the Youth House for over a year, and decided to go to the Healing Arts School in Santa Cruz, to learn massage and Chinese medicine. I wanted to supplement my income and for some reason, had been drawn to massage. There was a wide curriculum to choose from. I registered for a certification in Swedish massage and Jin Shin Do acupressure.

I liked the atmosphere of the school. We began each class with a group meditation. We weren't taught physiology. Instead, we were instructed in the techniques of massage, polarity, and energy work. I don't know what I was expecting when I started the classes. I certainly wasn't prepared for such a relaxed attitude about nudity.

The first night, after we were taught how to massage the back, we had to pair up. I glanced around, and was embarrassed, as I saw students stripping in front of everyone, like they were flower children. *Holy crap*, I'm thinking. *Now, what have I gotten myself into?* You may be thinking, *Hell this woman was a hooker, so what was the big deal?* Well, despite my past lifestyle, the real me was always very modest when it came to my body and the way that I dressed.

I began to feel less self-conscious about my body as the classes progressed, and it became a most positive and healing experience for me, as I'd rarely allowed myself the practice of safe touch.

We were taught how to pick up on the energy of the person being massaged, as well as knowing where there were energy blocks in the body. Although we were learning the techniques of deep tissue massage, what was more important was the ability to use our intuition in guiding us through the session.

The instructor said that we shouldn't use our minds to guide our hands, but the other way around. "The hands know what to do," she'd say. After completing a massage we were told that we should feel as good as the client if we were channeling energy from the Source.

Sometimes, the students I worked on told me that my hands felt really hot, and I felt it too. I also noticed that there were times when my upper body, especially my arms and hands, would vibrate with a lot of energy when I was working on someone.

After completing my course in massage, I went on to learn acupressure and the basics of Chinese medicine, which interested me even more. Acupressure was based on the same system as acupuncture, except that the fingers are the conduits of energy, versus the needles.

Before I completed my training, I began looking for a one-bedroom house. I needed a bedroom to do my treatments in. I found a little house to rent that was owned by an older Portuguese couple. They lived in the front house and mine was in the back. I bought myself a fold-out futon couch and slept in the living room.

I began advertising for body work as soon as I completed school. A lot of people at that time hadn't heard of acupressure, so most of my clients came for massage. I was averaging about $200.00 a month with my practice.

One night, I was working on a male client. I was halfway through the massage and it was time for him to roll over onto his back. I held the sheet toward myself so that I didn't see his nakedness. When he rolled over, I laid the sheet back over him, but he pulled it down saying, "Massage this," as he pointed to his erection. "Get your ass up and get the hell out of my house!" I demanded.

I went into the kitchen as he was dressing, got a butcher knife, and stood by the open front door. As he was walking toward me, he had a stupid smirk on his face as he held out a $20.00 bill. I snatched it and quickly locked the door behind him. That situation affected me so badly, that I decided against bringing any more men into my home, and eventually had a steady clientele of women.

The teenagers at the youth house were the same ages as my own kids would have been. I'd wonder what Lisa and Travis were like. Sometimes I'd form an attachment to a resident that I sensed might resemble my child in looks or personality. I felt guilty at times because I was helping these youngsters heal from trauma, when I had caused my own kids so much pain.

When I had three years of sobriety, I decided to start looking for my kids. I felt that I was emotionally ready to do so. I tried several agencies, but to no avail.

I went back to see Patrick, the psychic, to see if he was able to pick up more information on their location. He wasn't. He assured me though, that we would be reunited, but not through an agency, and not until they were older and on their own. He said that they would be the ones to find *me*. That was encouraging. I'd been told that adopted children usually become interested in finding their birth parents when they were in their early 20s, or when they began having their own children. I just kept hoping and praying that mine would seek me out.

Sometimes Olga, myself, and a couple of the other female counselors would go to Santa Cruz for the afternoon. Espresso coffee shops were becoming popular. We'd head for the coffee house and get ourselves a latte, then go to an Oriental bath house. We'd reserve a huge hot tub and sauna room for ourselves. The attendants would bring us a pot of tea and we'd drink our tea and soak. That was a new experience for me and I found it to be very relaxing. I could handle going out with a group of woman to the hot tubs, but other than that, I wasn't comfortable socializing outside of work.

Most people experienced me as being too serious and intense. I was constantly being told by staff to "lighten up." But I would lighten up in my own time. I had such a fear of relapsing that I was very controlled and rigid. I had a difficult time relaxing, unless I was meditating. So I'd find ways to bow out when it came to going to dinners or events where I knew there would be joking and small talk. And the idea of going on a date was out of the question. I was in no way ready for that; besides, I was determined to continue working on myself and my spirituality. Except for Olga, who accepted me for who I was, several of the women at work would hassle me about not dating, as if there was something wrong with being single. Yet, I noticed that *their* relationships didn't appear to be all that healthy.

Even though my co-workers called me an "isolator," I felt perfectly comfortable in my home alone. Take the word *alone* and divide it in two. It becomes al-one, or all one. There is a strength in being all-one with self.

On the weekends, weather permitting, I'd drive to Monterey and walk the beach or swim. I enjoyed being out in nature and preferred it to the company of people. I was and still am, an introvert, and there's nothing wrong with that.

Sometimes I'd take my guitar and write songs as I relaxed on the beach or at the river. When I was out in nature, alone, I felt the most connected to myself and the Creator. I had my best meditations when it was just me, the water, and the trees. We all have a symbiotic relationship with Grandmother Earth, but we often get so caught up in the demands of everyday life, we forget how a simple trip to the water—to the woods—to the forest, can bring us back to a peaceful state. Animals can have that effect on us too.

My landlady, the Portuguese woman, asked me one day, if I wanted to have her cat. It was a beautiful Siamese cat with no tail. I'd never had a cat before, I'd always preferred dogs, but I told her I'd take the cat. Its name was, "Miss Piggy." That name had to go, for one thing, *she*, was a *he*. I called him Karma, because I figured he was going to teach me something of value.

One morning, I had a client coming over for an acupressure treatment. I heard her car pull up, so I opened the front door to greet her, and gasped, as I looked down at the dead rat on my doorstep. Karma was watching me from afar. When the woman came up to the door, she said simply, "Oh, the cat brought you a gift." After that, I learned to accept his little "gifts" and then dispose of them when he wasn't aware of my doing so.

Everyone I knew had at least one credit card, so I thought that I'd apply for one myself. When I received my American Express card in the mail, I was elated. I was making good money and was able to pay my charges off quickly. Then I got another credit card. So I decided to see if I could qualify for a new car. I'd never owned a new car before and was excited at the prospect. I went to a Chevy dealership, and a few hours later, I drove away in my brand new silver Chevy.

It was summer, and I had some vacation time coming. I called my mom, who was still living in South Dakota, and told her I was driving out for a visit.

I made it to Lower Brule, South Dakota, in three days. I had a great time with my mom and ate a lot of corn soup and fry bread at her friends' houses. I loved watching wild horses running. I saw herds of buffalo for the first time. My mom remarked to me that my energy felt real good. I attributed that to my meditating every day and feeling generally good about myself and satisfaction with my life.

One evening, we were in her kitchen, talking. She was making me some fry bread. Out of the blue, she turned the conversation into a serious matter. She told me how wrong it was of her, to have never allowed my dad to talk to Matthew and me about our birth mother when we were growing up. Then she surprised me again with, "Did you think I didn't love you when you were younger?" "Sometimes," I said. She lowered her head, and when she looked up, I saw sadness in her eyes. Then she asked me, "Is there anything you want to tell me about how I raised you? I know what I did to you was abusive, and I am so sorry for that," she said sincerely. "No," I answered, "I dealt with all that in treatment."

The fact that my mom acknowledged what she had done, made a huge difference to me. I didn't realize how much I'd longed to hear her say those few words.

Then she said, "But you really got back at me when you'd be off drinking, and I wouldn't hear from you for months at a time. I'd be worried sick about you." *Wow*, I thought, as I continued to listen. "Sometimes, I'd be driving with your brothers in the car when they were younger, with tears running down my face, and they'd ask me what was wrong. 'I don't know where Sheila is,' I'd say." I'd never thought about how *my* actions had affected *her*.

The morning I was leaving to return to California, I was looking out the back door, gazing out at the rolling hills of the plains, when my mom came up to me from behind and wrapped her arms around my waist. "I'm really glad that our paths came together," she said. It was a tearful moment for me, as I realized how deeply I loved her. That was a very healing visit.

When I pulled into my driveway, I was tired from the road and looking forward to seeing my cat, Karma. I knew he'd be okay, because I'd left him with enough food and water to last him for the ten days I was gone.

When I opened the front door, he stood there, meowing like crazy, as if to say, "Where the hell have you been and why did you leave me?" I was to learn what cats did when they were angry for being left behind. I carried my bags into the bedroom, and opened my closet, to put some things away, when my attention was drawn to my shoes. That darn cat had crapped in all of them! Well, initially I'd hoped that he would be a teacher in a spiritual sense. That was not what I had in mind when I named him Karma.

The "new age" movement became popular in the 80's. I'd go to some of the little shops in downtown Santa Cruz, and they'd be filled with crystals, wands, incense, Tibetan bells, singing bowls, and books galore on chakras, spirituality, and Buddhism. There was new age music, and tie-dyed t-shirts. It was like a re-birth of the hippy movement. Santa Cruz was like a little San Francisco. The sidewalks were filled with jugglers, sidewalk acoustic guitar players and other free-spirited types.

Talking about auras was the topic of conversation, with many of the young people. I knew them to be the energy field around humans and all living things. Some people are gifted in their ability to see auras. I'm not able to see the colors emanating from a person; I just feel their energy as light or dark. Many people have this ability.

I went to psychic fairs whenever I could. I loved being around such high vibrations of energy. I continued to get psychic readings when I could afford them. I met with real ones and ran into a few fakes. Once, I went to get a reading from a psychic who advertised with a sign in front of her house—a crystal ball lady—you know the type. From the moment she started talking, I knew she was full of shit. At the end of the reading, she said I had evil spirits around me, and for $20.00 more, she could get rid of them. "No thanks," I told her. "I can do that myself..."

I also began to focus on my own abilities, which I didn't see so much as psychic, but as spiritual gifts from the Creator. What had the most meaning for me was Native Ways. My mom didn't share a lot with me about such things as I was growing up, because her tribe, the Quechan Indians, had been catholicized and most of their traditional ways had been lost. I knew nothing about my Cherokee people, because I wasn't in touch with any of them. So I went with what felt right to me, which was smudging with sage and cedar. I also paid attention to what my dreams were showing me. Eagles and eagle feathers appeared several times to me in my dreams.

Although I practiced my spirituality in my own way, in the privacy of my own home, I was always open to consciousness-raising techniques that would further my healing and increase my awareness. Once, the Sunflower

House executive director, Paul, provided the staff with an amazing training, it really opened my eyes on many levels.

It was a beautiful, sunny morning in Santa Cruz, as I arrived at the home of the couple who were conducting the training. As each staff member arrived, a feeling of excitement and expectancy was in the air. We all assembled in the large living room and listened, as the facilitators told us all about holotropic breathwork.

This type of breathwork, they said, was developed by Dr. Stanislov Groff and his wife. It involved a particular way of breathing, similar to the way a baby breathes: very rapid abdominal breathing. I learned that as we get older, most of us breathe incorrectly. We don't take the breath all the way down to the abdomen. Instead, we breathe shallowly and only fill the chest with air.

When we experience a traumatic event, we often stop breathing, which causes tension and energy blocks. If you've ever witnessed a dog when it's frightened, you probably noticed that it allows the flow of energy to be released, by shaking. That's because they live in the now. Dogs don't hold on to what happened yesterday. We humans hold on to so much energy, that it blocks us from living fully in the present moment.

After the breathing technique was explained to us, we all paired up and spread out on the large living room carpet. Olga and I agreed to be partners. She lay down, as did the others who were doing the exercise first. Music began to play that sounded very tribal, with drumming and other rhythmic and ancient sounds. That type of music helps the person journey to other dimensions.

Olga began her rapid breathing. My job was to observe and support her. After several minutes, it started sounding real strange in that room. Some were crying like newborn infants, while others were talking weird and making sounds that I couldn't even describe. I thought, *Man, these folks are really on some kind of trip.* I doubted that this breathing thing would work for me though, because of my fear of the unknown. I always had to know what I was walking into, what the outcome would be, which is why I wanted Olga to go first.

After about thirty minutes, everyone started to come back to the earth plane on their own. When Olga opened her eyes, she said that she felt like she was giving birth. Maybe she was giving birth to herself. After a break, the rest of us were ready to begin.

I lay down and began the rapid breathing. It wasn't easy breathing like that, but I forced myself to go on. After what may have been fifteen minutes, I felt my hands curl inward and my feet and legs curl up, as I spontaneously went into a fetal position. After that, I wasn't doing the breath work. It was doing me. I remember being in the womb and that I didn't want to come into this lifetime, I knew it would be a hard one. Then I heard myself, as I was outside of myself, crying like a newborn. After that ordeal, I saw the most beautiful Siberian tiger in full technicolor. This went way beyond anything I'd experienced in my meditations. It was like I was right in front of that tiger. It was a beautiful still picture that came and went several times.

Next, I observed myself going through a hole in the floor to the earth. I mean, this was nothing like a dream, it was real. I found myself holding onto the edge of a very long tunnel. The tunnel was grayish and cylindrical. At the very end of the tunnel was one huge green eye. I later realized that the eye was me, my spirit. I was afraid to go through that tunnel, afraid to let go, but when I couldn't hold on any longer, I was sucked downward, as if by a vacuum.

I flew down that tunnel at an amazing speed. As I got closer to the eye, I decided that I wanted to stop. I wish now that I wouldn't have. I don't know if I spoke in my head or out loud, when I said, "That's it. I don't want to see anymore," and opened my eyes. Afterwards, I could barely walk. I felt exhausted and at the same time felt like I'd taken a hit of acid. Everything seemed fluid and I was totally in the moment. *Wow*, I thought, *this breathwork really works*. I must have released a lot of energy that was holding me back.

It was explained to us by our facilitators, that we all had the experience we were meant to have. For me, the tiger meant quiet strength. Maybe the tiger was me. Or maybe it meant that at that time in my life, I was being gifted with tiger medicine, I don't know. I do know that it was one of the most profound spiritual experiences of my life. What I realized was that there are more dimensions than the one we live in. I began to see babies much differently, knowing that they are still connected to where we all come from, just because of how they breathe. It's a shame, that as we get older, we forget.

During the 70's and 80's, the only real requirement for being a drug and alcohol counselor, at least in California, was to have a history of substance abuse, with at least two years of clean time. Around 1987, the state required its counselors to become credentialed. This would afford us a level of professionalism that until that time, we didn't have. It also meant a pay increase. It included case work and an oral exam.

Once I completed all of the requirements, I was granted my Therapeutic Communities of America Certification, or, TCA. This particular certification would allow me to work in any substance abuse therapeutic community in the U.S. I went from making $7.50 an hour to $8.00, which was good pay in 1987.

In 1988, my mother left South Dakota and moved to Flagstaff, Arizona, because she was offered a position with the university in their Native Studies Program. Soon after she moved to Flagstaff, my brother, Frankie, who'd been living in Thailand and working as an underwater welder, decided to relocate to Phoenix, and got a job working in construction.

I loved living near the ocean, but I was ready to live near family, so the fact that my mom and brother were in Arizona, was the deciding factor in my decision to move to Phoenix. Besides, I wanted to be around more Natives.

I located several substance abuse programs in the Phoenix area and found a youth program that was interviewing for a counselor position. I did a phone interview and got the job. I gave Sunflower House my two-week resignation.

I sent my brother Frankie some money, asking him to secure me a nice furnished apartment. He put a deposit down on a place not far from where he lived.

I realized that my Chevy sedan wouldn't be practical. I'd need a pickup truck for loading all my belongings. I was moving to the hottest state in the country, so what did I get?...a black pickup with a sun roof. What was I thinking?!

The realization that I was leaving California began to sink in. California had always been my home. Sure, I'd been to Phoenix before, when I was living a drunkard's life, and wasn't even in reality. This would be different, and I had some real fears about leaving my support system and my home.

I'd been employed with the Sunflower Youth House for three years. My clients were having an especially difficult time with me leaving. I'd been their counselor for several months, and attachments had formed.

    One evening, I was at work and it was time to start group. What happened instead was a real treat. The other counselor on duty, David, told me where to sit, as I watched the clients perform a skit that they'd put together for me. They depicted me in situations as they had experienced me during my employment there. One client began the skit with, "You never knew what Sheila was going to look like when she came to work. One day she looked like this..."and one of the girls came in the room wearing a pair of very flared bell-bottom Levis, a hippie looking top, and a big scarf around her head. "Then, another day, she would look like..."and a different girl came in with straight leg Levis and a Pendleton shirt, and yet another in a professional looking outfit. I laughed so hard I cried. Sure enough, that was me. But at that stage in my recovery, I wasn't a chameleon. I dressed according to my mood. Next, other clients read poems that they'd written about me. Before the group ended, David said he wanted to play a song that reminded him of me. It was, *Rhiannon*, by Stevie Nicks. I loved her music. Her words, "woman taken by the wind," rang so true for me.

    Whenever a staff member was resigning, we would give them a good send-off by taking them to dinner, and would all chip in on a nice present, so I knew it was coming. Ever since I was a child, I had a difficult time with birthdays, or any occasion where I was being honored, and this was no different. But I wasn't taken to dinner. I had my send-off at Pat, the director's house. When I got there, I saw that it was a Mexican pot luck. They knew that Mexican food was my favorite. After we ate, we went to the living room and sat around in a circle. One of the counselors brought out a royal blue piece of leather, and attached it to a round loom. It was to be a shield. As the empty shield made its way around the circle, each staff member took a small leather pouch and filled it with an item they had brought, and attached it to the shield. There was a crystal, a bit of dirt from the grounds at the youth house, M&M's, a guitar pick, stones, feathers, and other items that they knew had meaning for me. I was very touched, and never would have expected such a sacred gift as that.

Olga came by on the morning of my departure to help me pack the rest of my things into the truck and to see me off. The last thing to go into the truck was Karma. I'd purchased some kitty downers and had just given him one. I didn't want him to be stressed out and meowing during the long drive. Olga and I said our tearful goodbyes, and I was on my way.

When I got to Phoenix, Frankie helped me unpack the truck and move me in. It was nice to be living near my brother for a change. Karma wouldn't come out from under the bed for a week. I should have taken that as a sign. I realized that I was in an area of high crime. Much later, I realized that the whole city was a crime zone.

My job at the youth program was nothing like I'd expected. It was a far cry from Sunflower Youth House in California. It lacked integrity and common sense.

One day, I came on duty to see a boy doing pushups, while a male counselor stood over him. When I asked the counselor why the kid was doing pushups, he said that he broke a rule. "What rule is that?" I asked. He said the boy had cursed. *Well fuck*, I thought, *give the kid a break. This ain't boot camp*.

The kids were treated as if they were criminals. After a month, I couldn't hang anymore. The groups were ineffective, there were no writing assignments, and the consequences being dished out had no therapeutic value, whatsoever. In other words, those people didn't know shit about helping drug-addicted youth! So I quit, because I refused to be part of a system I didn't buy into.

The intelligent, responsible thing to do, would have been to make sure I had another job to go to, before I quit the first one. But as you know, I was often impulsive in my decision making. But I soon found another position working in another youth program. That one was worse. When I found out that I'd be expected to perform "take-downs," techniques that involved physically restraining a kid, I thought, *you've got to be kidding me*. I only lasted there for a week.

I went into a depression. I don't know what I expected when I moved to Phoenix. The youth house I'd worked for in California, combined with my experience at the Freedom House, raised the bar on treatment programs, and no program I ever worked for in the future, would measure up to their high level of standards.

I began to search vigorously for a counseling position. There seemed to be nothing available in the employment section of the paper. A couple of weeks went by. I was almost broke and had maxed out my credit cards.

One day, I was feeling desperate, so I took a drive to the outskirts of Phoenix, into the desert. I got out of my truck and looked up at a red rock mountain, and cried out, "What is it you want me to do? Lead me to where you want me to work. If Phoenix is where I'm supposed to be, then show me where to look for a job, where I'll be happy and can do the most good." I drove home, got out the phone book, went to the yellow pages, and started looking under alcohol programs. A program practically jumped out at me, it was called Indian Rehabilitation.

I called the number and spoke with Carol, the director. I asked her if she had a position available for a counselor. She said that she'd just filled a position. My heart sank. I told her a little about myself and she said she'd like to meet me.

Indian Rehab was a residential program for adult male Natives. There were two houses. One was the administrative house and the one next door to it was where the men lived and where the counselors had their offices. Both of the houses were two-story and at least 50 years old.

When I walked into the administrative house, I was met by Carol, who ushered me into her office. She was a little bit of a thing, with long brown hair and was very personable. She was Irish, but had married a Dine' (Navajo) man. She told me that the young woman she'd just hired had no experience as a counselor and was thinking of using her for another position. Carol seemed impressed with me. Then I showed her my counselor certification. She said that since her program was not a therapeutic community, I'd be required to get the Arizona certification. But because of my experience, Carol offered me the position, with the understanding that I'd work toward getting my state certification. I went home happy.

By the end of my first week I had a full caseload of clients. There was no new employee orientation. I hit the ground running, learning as I went along. The days were filled with classes and groups and I was thrown in the mix as co-facilitator for a short time, before I was expected to teach classes and facilitate groups on my own.

One morning, one of the counselors was conducting a "Talking Circle." He invited me to join them. After everyone was assembled in the room, he smudged us all with cedar. Then he explained the purpose of the ceremony. "It's not so you can talk about others," he told the residents. "You have to talk about yourself. When you're holding that eagle feather, you have to speak from your heart." As the eagle feather began making its way around the circle of residents, I began to feel a profound sadness and didn't know why. When the feather was handed to me, I held the stem in my hand, and began to sob. They were tears of gratitude.

I took the Arizona alcohol and drug abuse counselor exam. I passed it on my third try. That was the most difficult exam I've ever taken. It felt good though, to receive the certificate in the mail with my new title as a CADAC.

I refused to be in the company of anyone who was using alcohol, and I had zero tolerance for drunks that came around Indian Rehab, which was often, since our program was right down town. I didn't want the residents being tempted to relapse. Once, I was facilitating a group session in the front room, and noticed a drunken Indian guy on the front lawn. I went out there and really let him have it. The residents were lined up at the window, watching me. Later, one of them told me, "Wow, Sheila, I've never seen you like that before!" They didn't know that I was Mighty Mouse…

Part of the reason I didn't want to be around anyone who was drinking, or drunk, was that I didn't want to be reminded of my past lifestyle. I didn't even want to smell it. It wasn't until much later that I realized why I had such stringent boundaries when it came to booze. I still hadn't made peace with the drunk that *I* had been.

When it came to my place of residence, that was sacred space, and I was adamant about keeping it free of the bad spirit of alcohol. My brother, Frankie, came to my apartment one day to visit. He had a can of beer with him. Brother or not, I immediately and self-righteously told him,

"You can't bring that in here!" He seemed surprised by that, but dumped it out in the sink.

I knew Frankie had an alcohol problem. But I didn't want to alienate him by preaching. He wasn't a 24-7 alcoholic like I'd been, he was able to maintain a job, but when he drank, he usually got drunk.

One week-end, I went to Flagstaff to stay with my mom. We'd both been asleep when the phone rang. It was Frankie. My mom sounded really upset. When she got off the phone, I asked her what was wrong. She was on the verge of tears. She said my brother had been arrested for DWI and that he'd rolled his truck. "Is he okay," I stammered. "Yes, he's not hurt," she said. We both got dressed and drove to the police station to get Frankie.

My brother was devastated by what had happened. That's what it took for him to realize that he needed help. Frankie and I had been close before, but that incident brought us closer.

All my brothers and I dealt with the loss of our dad and our childhood abuse in different ways. For Frankie and me, it was to self-medicate. My mom arranged for Frankie to go into treatment. The program was just outside of Phoenix. Since I was employed at Indian Rehab, he couldn't go there.

I went to pick my brother up the day he completed treatment. That night, we went to an AA meeting together. That felt very special to me. The next day, I took him to our mom's house in Flagstaff. Frankie eventually left for Hawaii, where he got a job as an underwater welder. I was sorry to see my brother go, but grateful for the opportunity to be there for him, and to share in his recovery experience.

Not long after Frankie left, my mom was off to South Dakota again. She'd been offered a position as director of the Indian Health Clinic on another reservation. I really felt lonely after my brother and my mom left, but work kept me busy, and I still had my cat, Karma.

I knew I had to get out and start meeting people that were like-minded. I heard about a picnic that was taking place one weekend. It was being held at South Mountain. What interested me about the picnic was that it was for psychics. I decided to check it out. While I was there, I met a guy named John. John had blond hair and blue eyes, and I found him to be very engaging and upbeat. We talked for a while and exchanged phone numbers.

John and I shared a common interest in meditation and anything relating to spiritual growth and healing. Because John was psychic, he often knew what I was thinking. One time, he asked me if I'd been thinking of a woman named Olga. I had, in fact, been missing my friend Olga. It's a bit unnerving, being with someone who can read your thoughts.

Eventually, our relationship turned physical. I'd been celibate for five years, so it was a big deal for me. I felt emotionally safe with John, yet I didn't feel a strong attraction to him.

My birthday was coming up. John wanted to take me on a boat ride to Ensenada, Mexico. Wow! That was a first. I'd never been with a man that was willing to do something that special for me. We drove from Phoenix to San Diego, and spent the night there with a friend of his. Since the boat ride wasn't scheduled until later the next day, I asked John if he could drive me to the Naval Base. I wanted to find my birth mother's gravesite.

As we were approaching the cemetery, I began feeling anxious. It was Sunday, and there was no one available to tell me what section her grave was in. The cemetery was huge. John and I searched through rows and rows of tombstones, looking for my birth mother. I tried to picture myself there as a child, but I couldn't remember where it was. I *felt* like a little kid, as I frantically searched each head stone for my mother's name. After an hour or so, I gave up. John was very supportive and sensitive to my feelings of sadness and disappointment.

John and I had a nice time in Mexico; yet, it lacked romance. I liked the man, but was beginning to feel more like a sister to him than a lover. As we were driving back to Phoenix, I knew I had to let him know my true feelings. "John," I said. "I like you, I like spending time with you, but I'm just not attracted to men with blond hair and blue eyes. I tried, but it's not working." "I'm glad you told me that," John replied, "because I'm more attracted to blondes, myself." What a relief that was. We agreed to stay friends.

The counselors where I worked were all full-blooded Indian. One was Papago, one was Navajo, and another was Mojave. I was the only counselor that was "watered down," as we call it. When clients or staff asked me what tribe I was I'd say, "I'm Irish, but I was raised by a Quechan mother who's from Fort Yuma." I didn't acknowledge being Cherokee. My mom told me not to, because a lot of lighter-skinned people, who weren't even Indian, said they were Cherokee. "Tell them you're Lakota," she said. "When you used to visit me in South Dakota," she went on, "my friends would tell me that you could pass for being Lakota any day." But of course I never did.

There was a sweat lodge in the back yard of the residents' house. I began going to sweat on a regular basis. The Mojave counselor who ran the sweat would allow outsiders to attend as well. We'd start by introducing ourselves by name and by tribe. Once when we were going around the circle, identifying ourselves, it came to a young, blond, white woman who said her name, and then said she was the granddaughter of a Cherokee princess. *Holy shit*, I thought. I couldn't believe my ears. I'd heard Indians joking about white women saying that very thing. I'm sure some of the guys had a good laugh about that.

One of the staff members would volunteer to take residents to peyote, or tee-pee meetings, on the Pima reservation. I had my first introduction to the Native American church when I was about five years clean and sober. I continued to go to several more after that, but I had to stop going, once I realized that I liked the "medicine" too much. I was afraid of taking some peyote tea home and abusing it.

I wanted a relationship before I got much older, so I decided to advertise in the singles section of the paper. The heading went something like this: "39-year-old—single—professional—woman seeking Vietnam vet." I couldn't relate to men who hadn't experienced horrific life events, and I was still drawn to men who'd led a soldier's life. I had quite a few responses.

Hector was Chicano, and in his early forties. When I walked into the lobby of the restaurant where we'd agreed to meet, I didn't feel an immediate attraction. He was somewhat overweight and no taller than I was. We introduced ourselves and went to our table. The first thing he asked me was why I wanted to be involved with a Vietnam vet. "We're all crazy you know." Hector said he'd done three tours in Nam and called himself "dinky dau," which is Vietnamese for crazy. That's what the Vietnamese called our soldiers. Hector had an intensity about him, just like I did. I liked Hector. He was a man's man. We would become the best of friends.

One day, I went to Hectors' apartment and he showed me his gun collection. My dad had been a cop, and I'd only *seen* his gun, but I'd never held one before. Hector had every weapon there was, from a 38 special to an AK47. He asked me if I'd like to go target shooting. "Hell yeah, I would!" Hector taught me how to hold a weapon, how to breathe, and how to pull the trigger.

I was hooked! Sometimes we went out with Hector's M16, but my favorite was the M14. I would've made a good sniper; I was good at long range firing. I loved rifles, so I went and bought myself a Marlin semi-automatic. I met other vet friends of Hector's, and sometimes we'd all go target shooting outside the city limits. Hector began calling me, "Warrior Woman." He thought it was great that a woman took to shooting the way I had.

As Hector shared his personal experiences with me, I shared traumatic events from my own life. I felt emotionally safe with Hector. Once, he told me that what I'd been through, was worse than any Vietnam vet he knew.

Hector had been a corporal in the Marine Corp. He had a black bag that he'd brought back from Nam. The bag was in storage and he hadn't seen its contents for over 20 years. After we'd been friends for a while, Hector said he was ready to open the bag, and that he wanted me there when he did. I went to his apartment that day. He brought the black bag out and we sat on the floor. He carefully unzipped it and took the items out, one by one. Since he'd been a corporal, he had medical paraphernalia; he had some type of speed pills, which soldiers often used in Nam to keep them awake and alert. There were propaganda leaflets that the Viet Cong dropped from their aircraft, there were pictures of Hector and his buddies, and other artifacts and souvenirs. Hector had some comical stories to tell about those items. He often used humor to hide behind his grief, and that's what he did then. It was a profound experience for me. I felt privileged to share it with my friend.

Part Five
Losing My Grip: P.T.S.D.

I was in no way prepared for what was about to occur when I was in my sixth year of recovery. It began, seemingly out of nowhere, with shame attacks and paranoia. They were unlike the panic attacks I'd experienced before. They usually hit me when I was at work. I'd have to do deep breathing exercises in my office before I was able to facilitate a class, or a group. Classes were the worst. I'd be standing at the chalkboard, facing all these men, so sure that they could see right through me, that they could see my past, and all the awful things I'd done, as well as the rapes.

At times, I isolated in my office and had horrible crying spells. I didn't understand what was happening to me. The not knowing, terrified me. I'd heard about Post Traumatic Stress Disorder, but associated it with veterans. I didn't connect it to myself. I just feared I was losing my mind.

I wasn't comfortable living in the apartment anymore. I became easily startled by any type of noise coming through the walls from other tenants. I was lucky to find a one-bedroom house, which had been built in the thirties. That house had personality and I loved it. I had a real porch and a front yard.

All the while, I was still having a hard time controlling my emotions, and for the first time, I began experiencing insomnia. Then, something else began to occur when I least expected it. I'd be driving somewhere, when all of a sudden, I wouldn't know where I was. I'd become disoriented and would panic. I'd have to park the car while I broke down in tears.

I was afraid to talk to any of the staff at work about what I was going through. I was a counselor, after all, a professional woman. I was responsible for the well-being of my clients. I had to hold it together. I didn't want to get fired. What in God's name would I do then? I'd lose everything! At that point, I should've high-tailed it back to California; to my support system, where I could've gotten help. I don't know why I didn't; except for pride and feeling like a failure.

The pressure continued to build. I did my best to hide it, but when a person is under a great amount of emotional upheaval, it comes out one way or another. I was a pressure cooker, ready to explode. I knew enough to realize it had to do with past sexual trauma. But why now?

Anger became my protective outer layer against feeling out of control and afraid. Staff was becoming aware of my inappropriate displays of sarcasm and rudeness, but it wasn't addressed, until one day, when I finally exploded. Something that a staff member said or did "tripped my trigger," and I started yelling and threw some papers on the floor.

Carol, the director, called me into her office. She knew that I was having problems. I was placed on six months' probation and had to get into therapy. Man, I was really slipping. I went to my therapy sessions, but it wasn't helping much. I'd stopped meditating not long after I moved to Phoenix. That was a discipline that I *never* should have let go of.

Someone who was a great help to me during that time, was my buddy Hector. He'd been diagnosed with PTSD, and knew exactly what I was going through. When I went into the "twilight zone," I'd call Hector. He was "Johnny on the spot." If he said he'd be at my place in fifteen minutes, by God, he was there in fifteen minutes. He'd take me for a long drive, and make me talk until I was able to come down from my episode. What a lifeline he was for me.

Guiding Star Lodge was an affiliate of Indian Rehabilitation and was just a few blocks down the street. It served Native women and their children. I'd been working at the men's facility for close to three years, when Carol decided that she wanted me to transfer over to the women's program. I think she felt it would be a good move for me, because of my past trauma with men, but it had the opposite effect.

Within a week or so of my transfer to the woman's program, I began my downward spiral. Every single client I had on my caseload, admitted to having been sexually abused as a child. I was getting triggered right and left. It didn't take long before I came completely undone. I was no longer effective as a therapist. A couple of my female coworkers were aware of what was going on with me. They were very supportive, and spent a great deal of time with me in my office, as I sat crying, overwhelmed by the force of my pain.

One night, I drove home from work. As I got out of my truck, Karma leapt down from his tree branch to greet me, as he always did when I got home. I opened my front door and just stood there, frozen. My things were all thrown about. My TV and stereo were gone. In slow motion, I walked to the bedroom. All my jewelry was gone, and all of the clothes in my dresser were gone, even my underwear. I looked in the open closet and saw that all my Levis, most of my blouses, my coats, and my shoes…all gone. *Oh—my—God!*

I went into a state of numbness for about a day, then I started to feel rage for having been violated, which in turn, woke up all the other times I'd been violated. I was in a full-blown Post Traumatic Stress episode. I became hyper-vigilant at home. Whenever I heard the slightest noise outside my house, I'd go out with my rifle and case the area.

I heard about a gun show that was taking place in Phoenix. I went, with the intention of purchasing a hand gun. I ended up buying a 22 revolver. I had no conscious thought of shooting myself when I bought the gun, but later that day, I found myself sitting on my bed, pointing the nozzle at different parts of my head. I didn't want to end up a vegetable or in a wheelchair, so I had to do it right. I just wanted to end the pain. I'd been living with my symptoms for over a year already. I couldn't see a way out. I didn't think there *was* a way out. No one had told me that after being clean and sober for so many years, I'd be lost in a nightmare. I couldn't understand, how after having worked so hard on myself, I would be feeling so much worse. Anyway, the fact that I might miss a fatal shot made me change my mind about that method altogether. I didn't have any pills to take either. What the hell was I going to do?

I called Hector and told him how I almost shot myself. He came right over and confiscated my guns. He said he'd give them back when I was more stable. I didn't know when that would be. I knew I couldn't go on in the state I was in, I needed help real bad.

I contacted my boss and told her I was suicidal and needed to get myself to a hospital. Her response surprised me. Instead of telling me she was glad I was getting some help, she was upset that I was "abandoning my clients." What the hell, I had very nearly abandoned myself—and for keeps! I'd given Carol's program three years of my life. I arranged for Karma to be taken care of and checked myself into Good Samaritan Hospital.

When I was admitted to the behavioral health unit of the hospital, I assumed that I'd be there for a while, like a month; at least that's what I'd hoped. They didn't tell me in the beginning that I'd only be there for ten days.

While I was in the psych unit, it became clear to me that I couldn't return to work. I called Carol and informed her of my decision. Once I was admitted to the hospital though, I think she realized the seriousness of my condition, and told me to go ahead and file for unemployment.

The psychiatrist diagnosed me with major depression and bi-polar disorder, and started me on an anti-depressant. At that time, the only ones receiving a diagnosis of PTSD, were Vietnam combat veterans. Whereas, those of us who experienced the same symptoms as a result of severe and prolonged trauma, were often misdiagnosed as having bi-polar disorder, because the symptoms were similar, but the causes were not.

A person has a diagnosis of PTSD, if they've been exposed to a traumatic event or events, either by experiencing it themselves or by witnessing it in another, such as combat vets seeing their buddies blown up in front of them. The same thing can happen for children who grow up in dysfunctional families, where any of the following are present: physical and/or sexual abuse, addiction, abandonment, and neglect. Symptoms of PTSD include: the traumatic event being perpetually re-experienced through nightmares, flashbacks, psychological numbing, and memory blocks of the event, inability to feel love or joy, sleep problems, irritability, angry outbursts, trouble concentrating, hyper-vigilance, and being easily startled. A person with PTSD can be easily triggered by an event that reminds them of the past trauma, as if it were happening in the present. Depression, suicidal ideation and attempts, are also common.

On the other hand, bi-polar is a brain disorder, characterized by episodes of mania and depression. There are several forms of this disorder. A manic episode may be experienced by feelings of intense excitability, euphoria, or as irritability. A person having a manic episode can go for prolonged periods without sleep and may have an exaggerated sense of self. Then comes the crash, which is the depressive part of bi-polar, and the person often becomes suicidal. Episodes of mania or depression may come on without any apparent reason, unlike PTSD. Any lay-person with half a brain, can figure out the differences between the two disorders. Yet, I would continue to be misdiagnosed by psychiatrists for years to come.

Even though I knew I had to be in the hospital, because I couldn't trust myself to be alone, I had a deep sense of failure, as I could no longer function in my profession. The therapy groups helped me, in that I was able to process a lot of my feelings, and because I didn't have to pretend that I had it all together.

After a week of being in the hospital, the psychiatrist informed me that I was being discharged in three days. "But I'm still feeling suicidal," I admitted. "Our policy," he stated, "is to keep patients only until they are out of crisis." *How much more in crisis did I have to be!?*

When I got home, I called the friend who had Karma, and told him not to bring him back; I wasn't ready to take care of him. Then I contacted the mental health clinic that I'd been referred to by the hospital staff.

On the day of my first appointment at Comcare mental health clinic, I was seen by a social worker who explained the outpatient program to me. She said she'd be providing me with case management and that a psychiatrist would see me on a monthly basis to monitor my medication. I was put on a second medication, Trazadone, for insomnia. I didn't like that I had to take medication. I saw it as another failure in my ability to take care of myself. But I took the meds and stayed home, feeling hopeless and helpless.

One day, I knew I was in trouble again. I called 911. When the paramedics entered my living room, I had the strangest sensation. I told them that I felt like I was in a movie; like I was observing everything, but wasn't connected to it. I couldn't feel my body. Whatever I was experiencing was so traumatic that I left my body. This experience is termed "depersonalization," and is a symptom of one having a dissociative disorder.

I was led into the ambulance and taken to the county hospital. The attendants ushered me into a waiting room and just left me there. As I stood there, wondering what I should do, an old prune-faced woman said, "Next." I'm thinking, *I'm not a* next. I didn't understand why the EMTs hadn't taken me back to see someone right away. I was already on the edge and feeling completely out of control. I went up to the plexiglas window with the little hole in it, and "prune face" addressed me as if she were bored, with a look that said, "Well, hurry up, I don't have all day." Something in me just snapped. I yelled, "Fuck all of you!" and rushed out of there, slamming the plate-glass door behind me. This wouldn't have happened had they taken me to a regular hospital. I had hospital insurance, after all.

I ran to a bench on the hospital grounds, shaking. I'd been brought by ambulance so I couldn't just drive away. I'd just sat down when the cop car came to where I was sitting. The officers got out of their car and come over to me. "Stand up," they ordered, and proceeded to put me in handcuffs. Then an officer began putting his hands in my pockets, probably checking for weapons. "Don't touch me!" I yelled. I felt violated. I told the cops that I couldn't feel my legs. I was in such distress that it felt like my limbs were detaching from me.

I was put in the police car and driven back down the road to the county hospital. At that point, I had no idea what was going to happen. I felt nothing but terror. The cops took me to a room, took the cuffs off me, then left.

The room was enclosed in glass and I was locked in. I felt like a sitting duck, like I was on display. Just as I thought it couldn't get any worse, it did! Old prune face came in and handed me a set of hospital pajamas, ordering me to undress. I lost it. I went from helplessness to rage in no time flat. "You perverted fucking bitch!" I screamed, and then I was five years old, and prune face was my foster father, staring at my nakedness.

The adult in me realized that I had to play this thing off, so I could get the hell out of there and go home; instead, I was taken to the psychiatric floor and let loose with about fifty other mental patients. The movie, *One Flew over the Cuckoo's Nest,* came to mind, and all the nurses looked like Nurse Ratchet.

The next morning I saw the psychiatrist. He told me that I was there under a court order and would not be released until he felt I was ready. So now I knew what I had to do. I went straight into survival mode. I'd have to do my best acting and convince the good doctor that I wasn't nuts.

We were allowed to smoke, but only four times a day. When the nurses woke us up in the morning, we had just enough time to get up, brush our teeth, and be in the huge day room for breakfast. We couldn't return to our rooms until it was time to go to sleep at night. I was so freaked out that I spent the entire day in a chair with my back against the wall, where I could watch the other patients. They were a scary bunch, as were the male and female nurses, as I watched them putting strait jackets on patients who were out of control. It took a week, but I was finally able to convince the psychiatrist that I was no longer a danger to myself. He too, diagnosed me with bi-polar disorder and prescribed the drug Lithium, along with another anti-depressant and Benadryl for sleep.

Hector came to pick me up. We went to get my new prescriptions filled and he took me home. I was relieved to be out of that horrible place, but I'd been re-traumatized by the whole experience. Absolutely nothing of any therapeutic value happened for me there. In fact, I felt worse off than before.

I continued with my appointments at the mental health clinic, but I refused to take the Lithium. I also began attending a 12-step meeting called Codependency Anonymous, or CODA. CODA was started by a married couple in Phoenix. The 12-step program then spread throughout the states.

Codependency is an underlying disorder in all addictions: substance abuse, gambling, sexual addiction, overspending, eating disorders, and so on. The purpose of the 12-step program is to learn how to have healthy relationships. Those who attended Codependency Anonymous meetings were people who came from shame-based, dysfunctional families, where their emotional needs weren't met as children, and where there were boundary violations.

What I found in those meetings, were people who had also experienced some sort of trauma in their lives. It was a good fit for me. I'd put the needs of others above myself for most of my life and found it difficult to say "no." I was able to set limits and boundaries when it came to my clients and friends, but not when it came to my relationships with men. That's where I became enmeshed and was not able to tell where I ended and they began.

Codependency Anonymous was often called the graduate school of AA. Because of the help I was getting through Comcare, as well as the CODA meetings and the medication, I was beginning to feel that I was on my way back from the abyss. But that stage of my journey was just beginning.

I was a firm believer in physical exercise, and had been going to a gym several times a week while I'd been employed at Indian Rehab. Exercise not only helped my depression and anxiety, it also helped me to feel in control and in my body. Since I was no longer able to afford the gym, I decided to start walking along the canal.

One day, while walking there, I turned around and noticed a man a good distance behind, walking at a fast pace. Not thinking much of it, I continued my walk. Then, I felt him gaining on me. Just as I was about to turn around, he grabbed me from behind with one arm, and with his free hand, grabbed my crotch. People with PTSD often have a delayed response to things of a shocking nature. I froze momentarily, unable to move, and then he faced me with that sick smirk that I hate. That's when I came unglued.

As he was running away, laughing, I started running after him screaming, "You mother fuckerrrrr!" He took off down a side street and disappeared. I ran to my truck and rushed home. I was on a mission. I went in the house and retrieved my rifle, got back in my truck, and returned to the scene of the crime. By now it was dark. I parked my truck and walked over to the canal. I lay down near some bushes, with my rifle, waiting. I was going to take him by surprise and shoot him in the crotch.

Why I assumed that my attacker was just gonna come diddy boppin' by again, is beyond me. I was out of touch with reality. That asshole became every man who had ever raped me. At some point, I stood up and noticed there were people not far from me, watching, with looks of fear. And that brought me back to reality. I returned to my truck and drove back home.

For the next few days, I didn't leave my house. I was in a lot of emotional turmoil from what that man triggered in me. I wanted to die. That's how bad I was hurting. I'd met a woman in the CODA meetings who I felt safe talking to. I called her and told her I needed help. She suggested I contact the battered women's shelter. Well, I wasn't a battered woman currently, but I called them anyway, and reported what was going on with me. The woman on the other end of the phone, said to come right in, that I qualified. I packed a suitcase, locked up the house, and left for the shelter.

I must have felt tremendously safe there emotionally, to have allowed my inner wounded child to go so deeply into the original pain and terror of being in the foster home. That's what was coming up for me. There was a small, nicely furnished therapy room, directly off of the staff office. When I felt very young and small, I'd go there, get on my hands and knees, hide in the corner, and cry. Staff was aware of my childhood regressions, and allowed me all the space and time I needed, to work through the pain. Several of the women staff were Masters level therapists. Many of them were survivors of childhood sexual abuse themselves.

One day, I was in a session with my therapist. I was sitting in a rocking chair, rocking back and forth, soothing myself. I was sharing about my birth mother. The therapist was saying how frightening it must have been for me at thirteen months of age, my mother going to the hospital one day, and never coming back. Just then, something switched in my brain. I spontaneously slid down to the floor from the rocking chair, and began crawling around. I was looking for my mother and crying like a toddler. At the end of that session, my therapist got on the floor and held me while I sobbed, which allowed me the healing I needed. What I went through with the therapist was much different than what I imagined happening when I was a baby; my father coming home from the hospital after my mother died, so full of his own grief, that he wasn't able to comfort me.

I'd already spent many years in therapy healing old wounds, but nothing compared to that session. Through my years of healing, I'd finish a piece of powerful work and feel really good for a period of time, and then I'd get triggered by another past trauma and get frustrated, wondering, *When does this shit ever end?!* What I came to understand was that for every traumatic event I experienced, there were layers upon layers of healing that needed to be done.

Many people are under the impression that trauma experienced as a baby doesn't affect them, because they don't remember it. That's not true. Those memories don't go away, and if not healed, will influence adult behaviors and future relationships. Those children will often grow up and subconsciously gravitate toward someone who is similar emotionally to a parental figure. If the parent was an alcoholic, they may continue to be attracted to alcoholics, because it's familiar. Or they may do the opposite and choose a career and independence over being married and having children, because it's safer. I've experienced being both ways.

At the end of the session that day, when my therapist was able to bring me back into the present, I felt something I had rarely experienced. It was joy. That's the benefit of healing old wounds with someone who is nurturing and affirming. For the rest of the day, I was a happy five year old that trusted the adults who were in charge of me. I asked for paper and crayons and drew pictures. The adult in me was aware of my child-state and wondered when I would catch up to being 40. By the next day, I was completely back.

Chicanos Por La Causa (Chicanos for the cause) was a residential/outpatient program for Hispanic males, and they were accepting applications for a counselor position. After 90 days at the women's shelter and a lot of hard work on myself, I was ready to leave. I'd missed Karma and was glad to get him back home with me. I felt strong and solid and was ready to get back into the work force. I dropped off my application at CPLC. The position was for their substance abuse outpatient program. I went for an interview and got the job. The pay was $9.50 an hour, about $1.50 an hour more than I'd made at my last position.

My new boss, James, was the program director. He was also very active in Narcotics Anonymous and had been clean for several years himself. At that time, I had close to eight years of recovery.

I was given a small office and a computer. It was 1992, and I'd never used a computer before, but I had to learn in order to do my documentation. I completed client intakes, made assessments, and facilitated an evening group. Since my program was a one-woman show, I was able to develop my own program, and a series of classes that I felt were pertinent to substance abusing clients.

My time off was fairly structured. I was exercising three times a week at the gym, attending my CODA meetings, taking my medications, and making my appointments at Comcare.

In the winter months I'd go mountain climbing or take walks in the desert. During the summer, I'd float on a raft at the lake or go down the Salt River in an inter-tube. I loved being in the water. I also spent a lot of time playing my guitar and writing music.

I decided that I had enough songs to record an album, or rather, a cassette. CD's hadn't come out yet. I located a young man who had a studio in the basement of his house. He also played guitar. I brought him my music, and he liked it. He charged $20.00 an hour, which wasn't bad. I asked him if he could play my guitar parts for me because my guitar playing was limited; besides, I wanted to concentrate on the singing only. We set an appointment to record my first song, and man, I was hooked. I fell in love with that microphone. That's where my deep alto voice really came alive.

I titled my cassette *Baptism by Fire*, because that was really what my music was all about. My songs were about my journey. I enjoyed singing in every style, but I did my best singing if it was rock. It took about four months to finish the cassette. Then I went to a printer and had the jacket made; with my picture on the cover, and the titles of the songs on the back. That whole process was a blast. I don't have the words to tell you how I felt when I had my cassettes in hand. It was a dream come true.

Once I saw the power in my ability to create such a great work of art, I realized an important key to continued sobriety, for myself and other addicts. I had discovered something that was invaluable. I had to make this a part of my teachings to clients. "Creativity," I'd say, "is the flip side of destruction. Find your creative side, and you will connect with your spiritual side and the Creator. When you are in the creative flow," I would say, "there is no compulsion to medicate with substances." I incorporated creative classes into my work as a counselor. I even used my own music when I did group work, because it was therapeutic; it allowed them to get in touch with their feelings.

What's interesting about alcoholics and addicts, is that most of us are very intelligent, sensitive, creative people. Look at prison art. For me, it was sad to see a Native American man selling his drawings, kachinas, or other handmade crafts for booze. I had pawned my guitar for the same reason. I'd sold my beadwork for a drink. It reminds me of the movie, *The Man with the Golden Arm*. Frank Sinatra, who played a junkie, took his most treasured possession; his horn, and pawned it for heroin. It was like he was selling his soul.

I loved my Karma, but noticed that he'd been spending more and more time at a neighbor man's house. I knew they both liked each other, so one day, I asked the neighbor if he would like to keep my cat. This may be hard for you to understand, but I wanted to give my cat away because I was too attached to him. Lots of cats were being hit by cars on our street. I knew that if my cat was killed, it would be much harder for me to handle, than if he was not with me, but alive and well. My neighbor agreed to take Karma.

Since I was still having PTSD episodes, I began attending a weekly trauma support group. It consisted of Nam vets and women who'd been abused. It was a place for me to continue to heal. If I had been raped just a handful of times, or had only experienced the threat of death at the hands of another say, one time, I might have been done working on myself. With all the years of therapy and treatment I'd experienced thus far, I surely would have been as close to healed as one could be. Even though I was light years away from where I'd been when I first started my healing journey, I didn't know then, that I had a few more years to go, before I would be able to say, " The worst of it is over."

James had been program director of Chicanos Por La Causa for several years. He was a white boy, but everyone liked James, staff and clients alike. I looked up to him because he wasn't just a junkie who'd gotten clean. He wanted to better himself by getting an education as well. James earned his Master's degree soon after I came on board with the agency. One day, James announced that he'd been offered a position with another treatment program in Arizona, and he resigned. James had been gone for about a year when we found out that he'd committed suicide with a fatal gunshot wound to his head. We were all shocked. No one knew why he chose to end his life. It just goes to show you that working in substance abuse is a tough field, especially if one is in recovery oneself, because the counselor is constantly being reminded of their own past. Not only that, because there is such a low success rate for substance abusers, a therapist can often feel like a failure.

I can only guess at what happened to James. But knowing him as I did, I suspected it may have had something to do with a relationship gone bad, and that he subsequently relapsed on heroin. I'd seen it happen before.

Something else occured around that time that had a profound effect on me. I had a lady friend named Miriam. I met her while I was at the battered women's shelter. She was a volunteer therapist who would provide therapy to those of us who wished it. Miriam was an incest survivor and had undergone the most severe abuse as a child, as anyone I had ever personally known. She was an inspiration to me. We became close after I'd left the shelter. She was the only woman friend I had who I knew I could call when I was in the throes of my PTSD, who knew exactly how I was feeling, and how to help me through it. The friendship was pretty one-sided though, because I was always the one who needed *her* help.

Miriam had a daughter, Janus, who was about the same age as my daughter, Lisa, would have been. Janus had a daughter, Shelby, who was three years old. One day, I was at work and I had the urge to call Miriam. When she answered the phone, I could tell something was wrong. She sounded far away and spoke in a monotone, so unlike the bubbly Miriam I'd come to know. "Did you hear what happened?" she asked. "No. What happened?" Sounding eerily matter-of-fact she said, "Last night, my daughter shot my granddaughter in the head and then shot herself." "Oh my God, Miriam!"

I was dumbstruck. It took a minute to process what she'd just said. She told me that her daughter, Janus, was dead, but that Shelby was still alive and in intensive care. All I could think of saying was, "How can I help?" She knew I did massage and asked me if I would go to the hospital and massage her back. "Of course, I'll be right over." *What an honor*, I thought, *that I can be of some help to this grieving woman*. I couldn't come close to imagining what she was going through.

On the drive over, I thought of my own daughter and prayed that wherever she and her brother were, that they were all right. Up until then, I thought I'd been through more than any woman I'd known. Until then, I thought I had the corner on mother grief.

When I arrived at the hospital, I found Miriam surrounded by her friends and family. As I worked on nurturing and supporting my friend, she explained more of what had made her daughter do such a thing. She said that Janus had left a suicide note, blaming social services for their lack of support and assistance. Evidently, Janus felt that she and her three-year-old child would be better off dead. The young woman had to have been severely depressed and desperate, to have come to *that* conclusion.

Miraculously, Shelby survived with a bullet in her head. What was truly amazing was what took place when the paramedics arrived on the scene, just after it had happened. One of the paramedics rushed over to Shelby, and upon seeing her condition, he started crying. He told Miriam that Shelby started to pat him on the leg. She was comforting *him!* That little girl was called, "The Miracle Child," because she was a survivor.

During the days that followed, I was able to see Miriam's strength, and her will to go on. Once you've known someone who's gone through something like that, you begin to see the pettiness of your own problems.

Due to unforeseen events, I was to lose touch with Miriam until about three years later. It just so happened that the day I went to visit her, her granddaughter, Shelby, was there as well. She was an amazing and loving six-year-old girl. I visited Miriam several times after that, and the little girl and I bonded in our love for music and singing. She was wise beyond her years, and had an affinity with the dolphin. She knew what her mother had done, and because of all the love and support she received from her family, was able to adjust fairly well emotionally, and with minor neurological damage, with the bullet still lodged in her head.

Raul was a social worker who came to work at Chicanos Por La Causa. The new Director, Alfredo, wanted him to facilitate groups with me, since I had more experience in the field. He and I seemed to hit it off pretty well, probably because he was a Vietnam vet. Raul knew just what to say to hook me. He told me how beautiful I was and began to flirt with me. Raul and I began an affair. Staff members were discouraged from getting involved, but I justified it by telling myself that after all, there was a married couple working at our agency.

We decided to live together, and between our two salaries, we could afford to rent a decent house. We found a large two-bedroom with a garage, in suburbia. I loved that house. It was the first real house I'd ever lived in as an adult. Raul bought me a washer and dryer because I said I wanted one. The rest of the furniture was mine. Not surprisingly, it wasn't long before there were problems in the relationship.

One day we were at home, and I was going through a tough period again. I was reliving pain associated with my sexual abuse. Another layer was surfacing. Raul was with me. I thought he would help me through it. I was sobbing with my head down. All of a sudden, I felt something on my face. It was his *penis!* He wanted to put it in my mouth! I freaked out and jumped up. It felt like I was being re-traumatized. I wanted to know why the hell he would do something so sick, and his response was, "I thought it would make you feel better." *Are you for real?!* I'd already told him about what had happened to me in the foster home, and here he was…a social worker for God's sake. I left him standing there, probably with his dick in his hand, and took off in my truck.

As I was returning home, I was livid. He'd really triggered me. *That man will pay for what he did,* I told myself. When I got home, he was gone. I sat down to think. He was a Vietnam vet, and I was going to trigger *his* PTSD. It wasn't long before I heard his car drive up. He came in and greeted me before going into the bathroom. When he came out, he started walking into the living room, then stopped in mid-step. With my rifle aimed at him I said, "Turn around and get on your knees. I'm going to put a bullet through your head, you sick son of a bitch!" I just wanted to fuck with his head, to get him back. I wasn't planning on actually shooting him. He started walking toward the kitchen, acting as if he were ignoring me. So I got up and opened the front door, aimed the rifle at his car, and fired off a shot. "Oops," I said. "I didn't know the safety was off. There goes your front tire." He just stood there, but the wheels were turning in his head. He was thinking, *This woman is in a PTSD episode, so I have to be the therapist and bring her back to her senses.* He proceeded to try and get me out of my right brain, my emotions, to my left brain, the thinking part of the brain, by asking me questions aimed at bringing me into the present. I was already hip to the drill; I'd used it with my own clients.

I was through having my revenge, so I just told him how much he disgusted me. I told him he'd better leave before someone got hurt, and that it wasn't going to be me. He moved out the next day.

I was a far cry from the Sheila that was walking a spiritual path. The scary part was that I didn't even see it. I'd felt justified in pulling a weapon on someone. How could I have made that okay? So yeah…Raul was a bonified creep. I could have done the right thing, the honest thing, like ordering him to leave. By doing that I would have been honoring myself, but I chose revenge. That incident set something in motion and there was no turning back.

Raul was a social worker. I had entrusted him with my story of childhood abuse. And he completely broadsided me when he pulled out his penis. It was the closest I ever came to reliving my molestation in the foster home. Perhaps if I hadn't been so traumatized by Raul's actions, I could have seen it as an opportunity to heal. But the feelings were so powerful that I went straight into survival mode, and it wasn't long before I was running on empty.

The next couple of days at work were difficult. I started losing it. I made a scene in the parking lot, calling Raul a child molester. Other staff witnessed it and reported me to the director. A week later, my new supervisor summoned me to his office. He said that I was in relapse mode and that I had an anger problem. I told him, "Fuck you!" as I stormed out of his office. The next day I was asked to resign.

After that, the only job I could find was working at a methadone maintenance program. I hated it, but tried to do the best job I could. The hours didn't agree with me. I had to be there by 4:00am to open up. Once I was late opening up because I slept through my alarm. From then on, my boss didn't seem to trust me.

There was a young college student who lived directly in back of my house. My back wall connected to his living room. He was a very nice young man who loved to play his piano. One night, it was about 7:30pm, and I was trying to get to sleep. He was playing that damn piano, and I snapped. I got my rifle, went to the back of my house, and started banging his front door with the butt of the gun. My next door neighbor opened his side door to see what all the yelling was about. When he saw the rifle, he quickly went back inside and shut his door. The piano player saw me through his window, but wouldn't open his door. I wouldn't have opened my door either, if there was a mad-woman yelling at me with a rifle. I threatened him with shooting up his piano, then went back inside and tried to calm down so I could get some sleep. I went to work the next day like nothing had happened, and did my work.

A few days later, the electricity went out on my block. It was summer, and that meant no air conditioning. I kept calling the electric company, trying to find out what was going on, but wasn't getting any answers. Finally, I got in the truck and went barreling into their main office, as if they had done me a grave injustice, just to fuck with Sheila. I was being verbally abusive and loud, telling them that I was going to spend the night there if I had to, in their nice air-conditioned office, until they fixed the electrical problem. I was completely out of control. When it clicked that they might call the cops, I left.

Around that time, when neighbors would be partying and getting loud, I'd walk outside with my rifle. I'd stand in my front yard until they saw me. Then I started taking the rifle and walking around the block in the daytime, whenever I heard too much noise. The sound of people outside my house was a major trigger for me. It would take me hours and sometimes days to come down from those episodes.

I was completely taken by surprise by this new wave of PTSD, and I was pissed off that it was back! I was still going to CODA meetings and seeing my psychiatrist, who had prescribed a tranquilizer for me to take, but at that point, none of it seemed to help. I felt powerless and helpless beyond measure. I was heading for a fall of massive proportions and didn't even see it coming.

I continued to dislike where I worked, and the type of work I was doing, because I felt purposeless. I was sick of watching the clients stroll in like the walking dead to get their dose of "feel good." The clients knew my stance on the whole methadone thing. Most of them saw me as a threat and avoided me like the plague. I felt like a complete failure to be working in that clinic, which I saw as the armpit of all treatment programs. I was a mess, but was sure that I was holding it together and that no one noticed. One day, a coworker asked me why the boss was always watching me. That triggered me even more because it felt invasive. I went to the main office to file a grievance against my boss. A meeting was scheduled to address the issue.

It was a Friday afternoon, on that November day of 1993. All the staff had just left for the day. I was on my way out the door, when my boss approached me. He kindly let me know that he'd been notified about the meeting that was scheduled to take place the following Monday. I told him I'd see him there and we said good night.

Part Six
A Warrior Gains Strength From Every Death

I walked to the parking lot and got in my truck, leaving my boss to lock up the office. I definitely planned on being present for my grievance meeting in three days; just as I had every intention of going straight home, as I did every Friday after work. I was four blocks away from my house, when I found myself turning into the store parking lot, without having made a conscious decision to do so, as if I were in a trance. I felt a strange calmness as I stood in the liquor store. My objective was exceedingly clear when I pointed to a fifth of Black Velvet, high on the shelf. If I was gonna check out of this life, I may as well do it with the good stuff, right? I paid for my purchase and drove the short distance home.

As I stood in my kitchen, there was no negotiating with myself, no second thoughts. I opened the cupboard, and took out a glass. I filled it half way with the whiskey, then added soda. There was no turning back now.

I'd been sober for nine years and eight months. I'd heard of people relapsing after nearing seven years and ten years. As I understood it, those were people who were just beginning to get in touch with the pain that had caused them to drink or drug in the first place. Unlike those folks, I had visited and revisited my past trauma, but was stuck somewhere in my process. I also knew that relapse began long before one took the first drink or drug. I was in such deep denial I couldn't see that I'd been in relapse mode for a very long time. That's how powerful denial can be.

I sat on my couch, staring at the glass in my hand. I took the first drink. The tranquilizers…I'd take them later…to finish the job. For the time being, I just wanted to sit—and drink—and think. I could allow myself to think now. It was safe to do so. I didn't want to call anyone to talk about how bad I felt. I needed no one to talk me down from a PTSD episode. I just wanted to sit there, alone with myself. Thinking made me feel, but now I could feel and it wouldn't kill me.

As I drank the poisoned liquid, I thought about how hard I'd worked on myself, over so many years of recovery, starting with the Freedom House when I was 27. I was now 42 years old. I thought about all the clients I had helped. *I think I've helped enough people*, I thought. Part of my codependency was that I felt I had to save everyone. I reflected on how I'd never experienced a healthy relationship with a man, about how I'd never be well enough to have one, and how sad that was. I was so tired—tired of working through issues—tired of feeling better, only to experience another layer of shame and panic, much worse than the one before it. I was tired of feeling as if I were losing my mind.

I don't know when it happened—when I decided to set myself up—so that my only recourse would be to end my life. If there was one thing I couldn't live with, it was the guilt of purposely harming another human being and causing them fear. So that's what I'd done. I'd threatened people with my weapon. I didn't realize any of this until much later. I only knew that the nightmare had to end.

I'd been feeling out of control, but this last act was in my hands, within my power, and at least I had *that*. I thought about how far I'd come and what guts I had for facing my demons. But it had become a never ending parade of demons that just wouldn't stop coming. I thought about the afterlife and didn't fear it; I'd already lived in hell on earth. I thought about my children, who would be young adults now, and how I'd missed them all those years. I thought about my mom. Thinking about her tore at my heart. I felt guilty leaving her. She'd been my rock, even though I was never able to confide in her about how horrible I'd been feeling.

Over the past few years, we'd had several visits. She'd pay for plane fare and fly me out to South Dakota. She'd spoil me by cooking for me and she'd buy me clothes, or whatever I needed. We'd laugh a lot and just enjoy being in each other's company. She finally became the mother I always wanted. I hadn't seen any of my brothers for a few years. They all had their careers and their families, but we always stayed in touch by phone and letters. My mom was the one I was most concerned about, yet I came to the sick conclusion that my death would be better for her. She wouldn't ever have to worry about me again. I wasn't aware of feeling sorry for myself. I wasn't aware of feeling anything at all, and it was nice for a change. I was comfortably numb.

I went through my things and put a pile together of mementos and important papers for my mom. Next, I got out paper and pen and wrote a letter for whoever found me, with instructions and contact numbers for my mom and the landlord. Then I wrote a letter to be given to my mom. Included in her letter, I placed one for my children. My mom and I had initiated several searches for them over the years, and I asked that she continue the search. When I felt that I'd covered all my bases, I sat and finished most of the bottle. I wasn't drinking for one last hurrah. I knew there would be no chance of my plan failing as long as I combined the pills with the alcohol. I don't remember feeling drunk. I do remember feeling like what I was doing was justifiable. I felt done with my life.

It was about midnight when I was ready to get the pills. I went to the kitchen and uncapped the bottles of Benadryl and the tranquilizers. I poured them all out. There were more than enough to do the job. I swallowed them and went to lie down in bed. I was ready to go "home."

I opened my eyes! I looked over at the alarm clock. It was sometime before noon. I sat straight up in bed. What the fuck! I'm not supposed to be here. I couldn't believe it. *Oh shit,* I thought. *Why am I still here?!* Oh, God, this is not funny. Now I have to call it a relapse.

I got up and went to sit in the living room. I didn't get it. 20 years before I'd been clinically dead from taking *fewer* pills and *no* alcohol, and I would've died had I not made it to the emergency. And now?—all I had was a bad hangover. I was really upset at still being alive. I picked up the whiskey bottle and saw that I had a drink left. I poured the contents into a glass. I had to think. Shit...! I knew I was out of pills, so I couldn't try another attempt; besides, damnit, God wouldn't let me die. I'd just have to keep drinking. It's actually funny now, thinking about it, but at the time, it was tragic.

For the next several days, I continued to drink. Once an alcoholic begins drinking, there is a compulsion to continue. It's like a switch that goes off in the brain. Whenever I relapsed, as you know, I drank to the brink of disaster. This was no different. I didn't call work and obviously didn't go in. I had screwed that up. I drank—passed out—came to—drank some more—blacked-out—and I drove drunk.

One night, I went to where my friend Hector worked and told him what had happened. Well, he could see that for himself. He was disappointed in me and concerned. He took my truck and parked it, not telling me where it was, and kept the keys. One morning, Hector came by to check up on me. He brought me a six-pack of beer, and left with my guns.

My boss called me several times, as well as my mom, but I didn't answer the phone. I felt too guilty.

I decided that I needed to be around other drunks. I remembered passing by Indian School Road when I'd been sober, and seeing a lot of Indians drinking there. So that's where I went. I'd walk the few blocks to my new skid row and drink with people who drank like me.

One late afternoon, I was drinking my vodka in an alley, and an Indian guy came by with a quart of beer in his hand. "Joe," I exclaimed, "are you drinking again too?" Joe was Tohono Odham (Papago). We knew each other from when I was working at Indian Rehab. He used to come by for AA meetings. He said he'd just fallen off the wagon himself. We stood there chatting for a while, and decided to take the party back to my house.

Joe was shocked that I was drinking, but was glad to be in my company. A drowning person doesn't like to drown alone. He told me that he'd always had a crush on me. I was flattered. Then I brought out my music cassette and played it for him. "That's really you?" he exclaimed. He loved my songs. Then he went into this whole Elvis Presley bit and tried singing like him, but failed miserably.

I didn't want Joe to leave. After my failed suicide attempt and relapse, I didn't want to be alone, and I didn't feel as depressed with Joe there. He didn't want to leave me either, and so he stayed.

Joe wasn't working, and we were spending what little money I had on alcohol. My rage began to resurface and things got a little crazy between us. I'd kick Joe out and then beg him to come back. I was angry with him for not getting a job, and at myself for the whole damn situation.

After being on a two-week drunk, my body couldn't take it anymore. Joe quit too, but wasn't as sick as I was. I spent two days in bed detoxing, while Joe cleaned up the terrible mess in the house. There were booze bottles everywhere and clothes and trash thrown all about. It was one of those messes where you don't know *where* to begin. It was mostly my mess, but Joe did a good job cleaning up. Well, after all, that was the least he could do.

My case manager came by to check on me while I was detoxing. He wanted to make sure I was okay because I'd missed my appointment. I went back to the clinic and resumed my mental health treatment. Needless to say, my psychiatrist discontinued my tranquilizer after hearing about my failed suicide attempt.

One day, a Vietnam vet friend of mine came by to make sure I was all right. He asked me if I remembered calling him, and I said I didn't. He proceeded to tell me about a call I'd made to him, when I was in a blackout. He said that he talked me out of shooting myself. According to my friend, I had my rifle under my chin and my new 22 automatic hand gun to my head. I was spared yet again.

Hector let me have my truck back when he knew that I'd quit drinking. He still checked up on me, as did a couple of other Nam vets that were friends of mine.

I called my mom and told her what I'd done. She was just glad to finally hear from me, and to know that I was all right. She knew something was up when I wouldn't answer her calls.

Joe got a job as a telemarketer. His first check gave us enough money to move into a duplex, where the rent was more affordable. We settled into our new place, and Joe continued to work. But every few months, he'd go on a drinking binge. I'd be beside myself, worrying about him. I'd drive around skid row, searching the alleys and looking behind dumpsters. When he'd return home a couple of days later, I'd be furious, but relieved.

One day, I was feeling depressed, but didn't want to drink. I asked Joe if he knew where we could get some pot. He did. We agreed to only smoke in the evening, after he came home from work. This went on for about a month, and then I found myself smoking it during the day. What was I thinking? I'd attempted suicide, gone on a drunken binge, was living with a mind-altering man, and smoking pot. I was spared from my suicide attempt, only to live a sham of a life, without direction or meaning. I was still running. Sure, Joe was intelligent, funny, creative, and loving, but he was a binge-drinking alcoholic. I was going to save him, though. Deja vu? Hadn't I been there, done that? Why was it so difficult for me to learn from experience? All I knew was that I loved Joe. I didn't love myself, but was sure I loved *him*.

Joe had spent eight years in the Army. He'd been an Airborne Ranger and had fought in a war that, according to military records, had never happened: the war in Central America. That really fucked with Joe a lot. What attracted me to him, aside from his being a veteran, was that we had a lot in common. For one thing, we both had PTSD, and for another, we were "wound mates." We had similar childhoods. I'd healed from a few layers of mine, but he had never done any healing around his issues. He was a toddler, when his mother left him with a Mexican woman in Tucson. Joe's mom didn't return for him until he was seven years old, after she'd remarried a Sicilian man. I met Joe's parents and we got along well. When Joe was at work, I often went to visit them.

I had a new psychiatrist who agreed with the many doctors I'd had before him, that I was bi-polar. He was determined to put me on Lithium. After a while, I started thinking that maybe he was right. I was still experiencing bouts of depression and alternating episodes of rage. So I started taking Lithium. It was horrible! It gave me diarrhea, and my hands shook, causing me to drop things. I felt "blah" all the time and had no motivation. Lithium wasn't for me, so I was prescribed another bi-polar medication.

My case manager encouraged me to apply for social security disability because of my mental illness. She helped me complete the paperwork. I had a paper trail going back 23 years, so I didn't think I'd have a problem. And I didn't. Nine months after I mailed in my application, I was awarded my benefits. I received close to $5,000 from back pay.

It was such a relief to have a monthly check coming in. Joe and I had stopped smoking pot and I resumed my membership at the gym. Joe had gotten a job at a sports club where he could work out for free. He was managing to stay sober. I decided to practice my guitar playing until I was good enough to sing my own songs at the local coffeehouses. That was a new and validating experience for me.

On September 8th, 1994, it was my son's birthday. I'd talked to Joe on numerous occasions about my kids. He knew how badly I wanted to find them and was very supportive of my search for them. I'd hoped that they would try and find me when they turned 18, but they hadn't. I was losing hope of ever seeing them again. I was sitting on the couch with Joe that day, and crying as I told him, "My son is 23 today. Do you think I'll ever see my kids again?" "Sure you will," he assured me. I said to Joe, "I bet my son is drunk right now. Something tells me he's an alcoholic."

Two weeks later, Joe and I were kicking back in the living room, reading and enjoying some quiet time, when the mail arrived. I flipped through it and saw a letter addressed to me from the social security office. I opened it. Inside was another envelope, but it wasn't from social security. I opened the envelope and pulled out a two-paged, written letter. Confused, I looked to the end of the letter for a name. I almost collapsed. "Oh my God, Joe, it's from my daughter!" My hands shook as I read her words. She said that social security told her they would forward her letter to both of her birth parents, if we could be located. The purpose of her writing, Lisa said, was to get our medical history, as she and Travis both had children. "Joe, I'm a grandma!" I was crying for joy as I looked at him, saying, "Joe, is this really happening?" He was thrilled himself. He knew what that letter meant to me.

Lisa said that she and her brother lived in Michigan. Her words were those of a woman who was being guarded, and of course, she should be. She probably didn't want to be too open and end up getting hurt, but at the same time, the letter was very direct, and I didn't care that it was formal, with little emotion. I knew where they were. I knew they were okay and I had an address.

It was finally over: the worrying, the wondering if they were alive, and the anguish from missing them. The psychic, Patrick, had been right when he said they were near the Canadian border.

There was; however, some disturbing news in her letter. Lisa wrote that social security had informed her that her father, Earnie, was deceased. He had died on New Year's Day of the previous year, 1993. That was very sad, but for the time being, my focus was on my wonderful news.

The first thing I did was to write a letter to Lisa. I let her know I'd dreamed about that day for 22 years. I gave her my address and phone number, asking her to please call me.

Joe had gone to work and I was watching TV, when the phone rang. When I answered it, a woman said "Hello," with a strong Midwestern accent, but she sounded like me with her deep voice. It was Lisa. She got right to the point, saying, "So, what happened?" She didn't sound upset, just very curious. We talked for a long time. She said that she had a boy and a girl, with another baby on the way, and that Travis had one son. I was a grandmother of three. I loved it! I told her that I wanted to fly out and see them all as soon as possible. Lisa was anxious to see me too.

It was around 9:00pm when my son, Travis, called me. It was a couple days after his sister had called. His voice sounded so much like his dad, that it was eerie. Travis was really talkative and sounded excited to be speaking with me. He wanted to know things like, what was my favorite type of music. When I told him I liked classic rock, he said he liked country music, and that his favorite singer was Hank Williams Jr. What a trip! My son was a cowboy. I didn't know it then, but he'd been drinking that night.

For the next few days, I was walking on air. It was a miracle! The first person I called about the news was my mom. She'd been helping me carry that awful burden for so many years and was really happy for me.

Right before I left for Michigan, I decided to do a little investigating around my husband's death. Earnie had been living in the Sacramento area before he died. Evidently, his mom and brothers had moved there from our home town of Red Bluff, several years before.

I requested a copy of the coroner's report, and it stated that Earnie had died of a heroin overdose. There had been an unusually high dose of heroin in his system. That seemed odd to me. I was able to locate Michael, one of Earnie's brothers, in Sacramento. When he answered the phone, I said, "Is this Michael?" and he replied, "Hello, Sheila." I asked him how he knew. "I could never forget the voice of my sister-in-law," he said fondly. I told him I'd found the kids, and I asked him about what really happened to Earnie. He said that Earnie and his third wife, Cathy, had been living in a boarding house. He then proceeded to tell me an incredible story about how Cathy and her *boyfriend* had killed Earnie, by giving him a hot shot (overdose of heroin). There was a witness, another boarder, who lived directly across the hall from Earnie and Cathy. It was New Year's Eve. Earnie had been drinking a few beers with another resident down the hall, and watching a football game. Just after midnight, Earnie reportedly went back to his own room to go to sleep. The boarder said he had his door open and saw Earnie's wife enter their room with the boyfriend, not long after Earnie went in to lie down. A few minutes later, the couple left, leaving Earnie alone. The boarder then went in to check on Earnie and found him dead. Mike said he and his mom had gone to the boarding house the day after Earnie died; they wanted to talk to Earnie's wife. The wife and the boyfriend were both there. Mike said that he and his mom overheard Cathy telling her boyfriend, "Don't worry, you'll get your money." Earnie's death was ruled a suicide. The family said that Earnie wouldn't have chosen suicide, and I agreed. Of course the cops did little in the way of an investigation; to them, he was just another junkie.

    The poor guy had chosen a hard life, just as I had, but he'd never sought recovery. Michael said that Earnie used to tell him that he blew it, by leaving me. Mike said that his brother was messed up from the war; he'd have bad flashbacks and would talk about the smell of death that he couldn't get out of his nostrils. I felt bad that my kids would never get to meet their father.

    As the plane made its decent into Detroit, I had butterflies in my stomach. When I stepped into the lobby, I saw a crowd of people standing there. I knew my kids were among them, but I was so nervous, I couldn't recognize anyone. When no one came toward me, I said to the crowd, "Would someone please come over here before I fall down fainting?" Right away, this handsome looking young man came to me and handed me a bouquet of white roses. Travis and I hugged and then my daughter hugged me too. There were several other people there with them. I was introduced to my daughter-in-law, my son in-law, my grandkids and Lisa's in-laws. It was overwhelmingly wonderful. We all walked over to baggage and got my suitcase, before heading to the parking lot. As we were walking, I was just staring at my children, looking at their features, looking for similarities. My son looked like his father. Both of them had black hair and brown eyes. My daughter's eyes had a beautiful almond shape to them. She had my eyes except that mine are green.

We went to dinner, and then Travis took me to his house, where I would stay for a week, before going to Lisa's. The first thing I noticed when I walked in his house was a fifth of Jack Daniels on the kitchen counter. Travis drank beer every night that I was there, but not the whiskey. I could tell, by watching the change in him after he'd had a few, that my son was an alcoholic.

It's hard to describe the difference it made in me, finally seeing my children. I can only say that I felt full and complete.

One morning, Travis came into the spare room where I was just waking up and said, "Ma, time to get up." That was to be the one and only time he called me "Ma."

My son, the cowboy, wore a black cowboy hat and loved horses. Apparently, my kids had been raised on a farm with horses. I enjoyed my visit with my son, his wife Julie, and my four-year-old grandson, Justin, who was instructed to call me "Grandma."

The week was up and my daughter came and took me to *her* house. She had a lot more questions for me about the past. I was open to a point about my drinking and drug use. I also wanted her to know that I'd worked very hard over the years, to better myself personally and professionally. I didn't feel it necessary to tell her about my suicide attempt and relapse, the year before. I think she was just happy that I was there, and to know that she had always been loved by me.

I fell in love with my three-year-old grandson, Brandon, and my two-year-old granddaughter, Kirsten. It was a very comfortable visit, and we were all on a natural high.

Lisa drove me to the airport when it was time for me to leave. When I was ready to board, she let me hug her, as she cried like a little girl. I would have liked to have hugged my daughter more during our visit, but she wasn't the touchy-feely person that I am. Yet I'd gone through that stage myself, so I understood that Lisa didn't feel safe enough emotionally. We were a lot alike, as were my son and I.

When I got home, my kids and I talked on the phone several times a week. They were as thrilled as I was about our reunion. When my son called to talk, it soon became apparent that he was inebriated, but I didn't dare question him about it. I didn't want to cause a rift between us.

Christmas was coming up. The plan was that I'd go visit my kids right after New Year's, because Lisa was having a Caesarean section for the birth of her third child, on January the 9th. There was no way I was going to miss that. Joe and I had a great Christmas together, and I was having a grand time buying presents for my kids and grandkids.

There was one thing I still needed to do for my son before I left for Michigan. I went to a veteran's surplus store with the copy of my husband's DD-214, his discharge document, which I'd received from the VA. It had a list of all the medals my husband had been issued. I told the man who worked there, a Vietnam vet, the story of how my kids never got to know their father, and how I wanted to give my son a special gift to remember his father by. The guy was great. He picked out an Army dress green jacket, and on it he pinned all the medals in the right places. Then I asked him to make two pairs of dog tags that would be identical to the real ones. Joe was with me at the surplus store. He knew what a powerful thing that would be, to hand my son that jacket, because he was a vet himself. I felt sad, because I remembered seeing those pins and ribbons worn by Earnie, such a long time ago.

Joe took me to the airport with my luggage and a duffle bag full of presents. When I landed in Detroit, I was much calmer, as I knew exactly who I was looking for. Travis was there to pick me up. The first thing I did after hugging him was to present him with his father's jacket. I could tell it meant a great deal to him. It was still early, so I suggested we stop by his place, pick up his wife and son, and go straight to my daughter's house to unwrap the presents I'd brought. It felt so good to finally be able to give my kids something. When I presented them with their father's dog tags, they were very touched.

My son-in-law, Bobby, took Lisa to the hospital to have her C-section. We were in the hallway of the hospital when my daughter was wheeled out of surgery. She'd had another girl. Since they hadn't picked out a name for her yet, Bobby went to the gift shop and bought a book of baby's names. He began reading them off. When he came to the name "Lacey," Bobby and I said, "That's it!" When they brought in little Lacey, it took me back to when Lisa was born. She looked just like her with her little heart shaped lips.

I asked Lisa if she was going to call her adopted mother, Beth, to tell her about the baby. They were still in touch with each other, although the DeWitt couple had moved to Texas, years before. Lisa said, "No, I don't want to talk to her, but you can call her if you want to." She gave me the number, and I went down the hall to the lobby.

I just stood there for a moment, looking at the pay phone, remembering the things my daughter had told me during our first phone conversation. According to Lisa, when she and her brother were very young, Beth had told them that their father was in prison, and that I had left them at some agency, with signs around their necks, saying that they weren't wanted. I remembered how angry Beth had been when I'd called her over twenty years before, wanting to know how my kids were. I despised this woman for what she had told my kids about their birth parents. Didn't she realize how that would have affected their self-image? *Beth DeWitt, it's my turn now*, I thought. I dialed the number. "Hello," a woman said. "Is this Beth?" "Yes. Who's this?" "This is Sheila...Lisa and Travis's mother. Remember me?" I said with a calmness that I didn't quite feel. There were a few moments of silence at the other end of the line. "Just thought I'd let you know," I continued, "Lisa had a baby girl." I honestly don't remember what I said after that, or what Beth said, except that she didn't say much of anything. I hung up, knowing that my intention had been to get back at her. It was dishonest, but it sure did feel good at the time.

My mom had sent my daughter a Lakota cradleboard that had been made by a friend of hers in South Dakota. When mother and baby were ready to leave the hospital, we put Lacey in the cradleboard and laced her up. My mom wanted my daughter to realize her Native blood. Lisa and Travis were told as children that their mother was Cherokee, but when you're not raised in the Indian way, as I had been, you really don't understand what it means to be Indian. My son had a tattoo on his upper arm, of a band with two feathers on it. That was his way of identifying with being Native.

The day after Lacey was brought home from the hospital, the phone rang. Lisa answered it and told me that Travis wanted to talk to me. Evidently, Beth had called him about the phone call. I was in no way prepared for his anger. That had been a fear of mine for years, when I would think about the day that I met my kids; how I feared that they would be angry with me, and that I wouldn't be able to live with myself. Travis told me that I had no business calling Beth, that she had called him in tears. What a manipulative bitch! How dare she hook my son into feeling sorry for her?

It was the last day of my visit. Travis had planned on taking me to the airport. He arrived early. When he walked into Lisa's house, he said to me very abruptly, "Are you ready?" as if he were talking to a child. I was stunned by the disrespectful way he addressed me. I quickly hugged my daughter, who had tears in her eyes, and left with my son. I felt horrible about leaving her like that.

Travis and I didn't say a word for the whole two-hour drive back to his house. When we got there, I went inside, sat down, and began to cry. I was in a lot of pain. Then Travis said, "Let's go for a ride." As he was driving he told me, "Those people raised us, they were our parents, and you have no right to upset them." Wow, that hit me right where I live. I stopped crying and went into a state of numbness. I shut down; it was way too much to take in. He'd taken her side and it was killing me. When we got to the airport, I was no longer numb. I was angry at Beth *and* my son. When my flight was called, he said to me with sincerity, "I'm sorry." I hugged him and without a word, I quickly turned around to get in line for my flight. I didn't look back. I had turned my back on my son.

By the time we landed in Phoenix, I could barely contain my anger. When I saw Joe standing there in the lobby, smiling away, happy to see me, I was really inconsiderate as I said loudly, "Fuck Michigan!" He was embarrassed and I didn't care. I didn't care about anything except getting drunk. My mother guilt had been triggered.

When we got home, Joe got ready for work and left. I knew he was concerned about my state of mind. But as soon as he was gone, I got in the truck and headed for the liquor store. The worst thing anyone can do is to drink on top of anger. I was in so much pain that I did what every self-centered alcoholic does, and that was to feel sorry for myself and blame everyone else.

I stayed drunk for days, calling my kids while I was in blackouts. One day, when I was sober, Lisa told me that she'd listened to a recorded message I'd left for my son that said, "I don't love you and I never wanted you." Good God…could I have said anything more hideous to my own flesh and blood? It was unforgivable.

Lisa had contacted my mom and told her what was going on. My mother called me and gave me a blast of reality. She said, "You may as well forget about ever having a relationship with your son, that's over, and you may lose the one you have with your daughter, if you don't stop drinking."

One day, I was driving around in a black-out and totaled my truck. I was booked on a DWI. After that, I was really a mess. I wasn't eating, and I was becoming bloated from the alcohol. After about two months, my body couldn't take anymore abuse, so I went to LARC, the detox center. The doctor examined me and told me that I had a fatty liver, which was causing the bloating. I weighed 165 pounds. My normal weight then was 140. When I'd gone on a drunken binge like that in the past, I always *lost* weight. But my liver was no longer able to process the booze I was consuming. The good news was that if I quit drinking, my liver would go back to normal. Within a couple of weeks of being in detox, my weight went back to normal, and I was feeling a lot better physically. So what did I do? I left detox and returned home to resume my drinking because emotionally, I was still hurting.

Joe had been busy working all that time, but when I got home from detox and relapsed again, so did he. Then he quit his job. We were soon in a crazy routine of drinking and fighting with each. All my social security money was going to buy booze, and soon there was nothing left to pay bills. When we were evicted, I contacted a friend of mine to help me put my belongings in storage, and I left Joe.

During the mid to late 90s, I was in and out of psychiatric units, detox, short-term substance abuse programs, and jails, but was never able to put more than three months of sobriety together at a time. My drinking kept me in the alleys and other hiding places that were known only to us winos. Joe and I found each other again and we lived in skid row together. We were so attached to each other emotionally, that the thought of splitting up was unbearable.

A favorite drinking spot for us drunks was next to a Buddhist temple. It was right on the corner of 7th Street and Indian School Road. We would hang out there all day, sometimes until the cops came and made us pour out our booze and take a hike. We were constantly being told by store managers, "You Indians get the hell out of here, or I'll call the cops." But not the Buddhists. They never seemed to be offended by the way we chose to live.

I was too proud to push a shopping cart and collect cans for wine, like a lot of the Indian guys did, but not too proud to dumpster dive for food and take sponge baths at the McDonald's Restaurant. And I always had a stash of clean clothes to change into.

My social security checks were going to Joe's parents' house. After I cashed my check on the 3rd of each month, the money only lasted a few days. I'd end up buying booze for Joe and all the other drunks we hung out with. When the money ran out, I started turning tricks again. I'd never imagined that I would ever go back to doing that. When you're desperate and sick for a drink, you'd be surprised at what you're willing to do. At first, Joe was hurt when he found out I was prostituting, then he was really pissed off. He seemed to think I enjoyed turning tricks. It made me sick to have to sell myself. I came to hate every man I had to hustle. And I was *really* pissed off at Joe. The way I saw it, he had no right to complain. He should've been doing a better job of taking care of me in the first place. Instead, he just hung out with the rest of the lazy, wino bums, waiting for me to come around with my whoring money to buy them all alcohol. They all loved me then, but as soon as the booze was gone, they'd all talk shit about me behind my back.

When I was about 45 years old, I remained sober long enough to get my own apartment. Comcare, the mental health clinic, had a contract with one of the apartment complexes, whereby, I only had to pay a small portion of my social security benefit for rent. Joe couldn't live with me. It was against the rules of the housing program. So he quit drinking and went to live at Tribal Lodge, a halfway house for Native males, and found a job working at another gym. I missed living with Joe and hated being apart from him. When he got paid, we'd go out to eat and see a movie. He was wonderful when he was sober and earning a paycheck. If I needed money, he'd give me all he had and keep just $5.00 for himself.

I spent my time going to AA meetings and visiting people I'd met in the various hospitals and psych units I'd been to. At home, I watched a lot of TV and would call my mom and my daughter, who had begun to trust me again. I tried hard to keep that trust.

One day, after several months of sobriety, I started thinking too much. That can be a dangerous thing for an alcoholic in early recovery. I wasn't able to get in touch with Joe. When I called Tribal Lodge, I was told that he hadn't made it home the night before. That could only mean one thing. I was still struggling with depression and panic attacks, it was worse when I knew that Joe was out drinking. I began toying with the thought of drinking, myself. I went back and forth with whether or not I should drink. Once an alcoholic begins that thought process, the drinking usually wins out. And it did. I walked the mile or so to Indian School Road and 7th Street. I bought a bottle of vodka and got drunk with the Natives living on the streets, some I knew, others I didn't. Then I bought more booze and invited a bunch of them back to my apartment. I didn't have to ask twice.

We were all sitting around in my living room, getting drunk on my beer, when I noticed this Chicano dude sitting there drinking too. He'd followed us to my apartment. Not really caring about it, I let him stay and drink. Then he left and came back, but went straight to the kitchen. When I went to see what he was up to, I saw him holding this small glass tube and smoking from it. I said, "What the hell are you doing?" He blew some smoke in my face. That night I began my love-hate relationship with crack cocaine, although it would be a while before I began using it daily.

Joe returned to my apartment one night, drunk, and since I was on a drunken binge myself, I disregarded the rules and let him move in. We started arguing a lot and he began hitting me. I had a thing about knives when I was drunk. I got all my kitchen knives and strategically hid them in all the rooms. If he tried to hit me again, I'd just stick him, I told myself. He found the knives and got rid of them all.

I often had trauma flashbacks when I was drunk, and it seemed that they only happened when I was in a blackout, like the time I was with Jacob and picked up the axe.

One morning, I woke up and looked over at Joe. He had a black eye. "What happened to you?" I asked. "You punched me in the eye with the tortilla roller when I was asleep," he said.

Another night, I was out drinking on the streets, when I saw a friend of mine that I knew from Salinas. He was drunk and invited me to his house to drink some whiskey. While there, he sold me a buck knife. I called Joe from my friend's house, telling him I was on my way home.

The last thing I remembered was walking in the front door, looking forward to seeing Joe. The next morning, I found myself on the floor. Not knowing how I got there, I asked Joe what had happened. He said that I'd walked into the bedroom when I got home, with the large knife in my hand—I raised it, and just as I was bringing it down on his head, he quickly rolled away, as I plunged the knife into the mattress instead. He said he threw me to the floor, knocking me out. I said I didn't believe him. Then he showed me the deep gash in the mattress. I could've killed him!

After that incident, it was time to quit drinking again. I decided to detox at the apartment. Joe decided to quit too. He'd just gotten a job at yet another sports club and had left for work that morning. He never got as sick from drinking as I did, and was still able to function. I will never forget that detox, because it was the hardest one I'd been through since the time I kicked wine and heroin. There was a whole other dimension to this one. When I later tried to explain this other worldly experience to others, they didn't understand and probably thought I was imagining things, except for the Natives I told. They knew all too well what I was talking about.

That first day, as I lay in bed, I went through the usual shaking, paranoia, and sweating. Later in the afternoon, as I began to drift off and enter that half-wakeful state, I heard my front door open, and the little bells that were tied around the doorknob, jingled. I felt and heard someone coming into the bedroom. An Indian man got on top of me as I lay on my back, and I couldn't move. Then I tried with all my power to push him off, and it worked. He was gone.

This was repeated with two more men, coming in and getting on top of me, and me pushing them off. At that point, I'd had enough. As I heard the footsteps of the fourth Native man entering my apartment, I knew I had to do something different. I had to use my voice to set a firm boundary. As he came toward me, I said, "Go away! You don't belong here. You have no power over me!" He vanished. By saying those words, I was also able to bring myself back to the earth plane and open my eyes.

Those men were bad spirits, trying to possess me, because I was vulnerable in my weakened state. They wanted me to keep drinking, but it didn't work. My power was stronger than theirs.

When Joe came home from work I told him what had happened, and of course he believed me. He told me to pray and boy, did I pray. By the third day, I was strong enough to leave the bed and began cleaning the filthy apartment. I had to do a little at a time and then rest. That was probably the last time that Joe and I lived together and functioned as human beings.

Three months later, Joe didn't come home from work. He'd gotten paid that day so I knew what he was up to. I, of course, joined him not long after.

While Joe and I were on our binge, he'd stay gone for days at a time, so I'd invite our Indian buddies over to drink with me. I hated being alone when I was drinking.

Eventually, I was evicted from the apartment because of complaints about the noise and because of all the physical damage. There was a hole in the front door where Joe had punched it because I wouldn't let him in when he was drunk and threatening me. The front window was smashed from me putting the broom handle through it. I don't know why, but I had a thing about breaking glass when I was drunk.

My last day there, I packed a suitcase with clothes and pictures of my family, and off I went to the streets. I was 46 years old, with nowhere to go *but* the streets.

I was staggering drunk with my suitcase, in the vicinity of my old stomping grounds late one night, when a Navajo guy stopped his car, asking me if I needed a ride somewhere. I said I didn't have anywhere to go, because I had no home.

Calvin took me to his place for the night. He'd been sober for a few years and didn't mind that I was drinking. He lived in a little rented room with a bathroom that was part of a larger house. He fed me hamburger and potatoes with a tortilla. That was a good Indian meal.

The next day he bought me some beer, and once I was drunk, I left my suitcase at Calvin's place and went to look for Joe. I found out that he'd left with some Vietnam vet alcoholic in his motorhome. They had gone to Oregon. He was the second soldier to leave me for Oregon.

I didn't know what to do. I went back to Calvin's and that's where I stayed, off and on, for several months. The guy was nice enough, but he was no substitute for Joe.

I started running into crack addicts and found a couple connections. I'd used crack for a short time when I was living in the apartment, but now it was serious business. I'd usually go to the crack house, get my hit, and got the hell out of there.

I couldn't stand watching them after they'd been up for days, constantly peeking out the window. I'd start feeling their paranoia. Hell, I had enough of my own. Sometimes, after I was high, I'd be walking down a dark street and feel the "shadow people" following me, and I'd start running.

After a year of smoking crack, I was well on my way to insanity. What sane person continues to buy a drug that does nothing but make them feel as if they were schizophrenic?

If I went too long without a hit, I went into such a deep depression, I felt like I was in hell's basement. Crack became the glue that held me together.

Hard core crackheads seemed evil to me, almost as if they were witches, or possessed. I'd probably been possessed myself when I tried to stab Joe.

I firmly believe that when a person is addicted, they are spiritually vulnerable. We all have a spiritual energy field around us. Even if we are going through something; depression, grief, or are very ill, it creates cracks in our energy field. A person who is drunk or high is not in their body, and is a sitting duck for bad spirits to enter and take over.

In between relapses, my case manager placed me in another hospital program for substance abuse. I really liked the program and began to think that maybe I could do this recovery thing, even though Joe was gone.

After treatment, I went to a women's halfway house called Crossroads for Women. I was going to meetings and working on my recovery plan, but missing Joe like crazy.

One day, I decided to take a chance and call his folks' house, in the hopes that he had returned from Oregon. I picked up the hand piece, put it to my ear, and hadn't even dialed the number when I heard a man say, "Sheila, is that you?" It was Joe! That was too weird. For some reason, he said, he had decided to pick up the phone at that moment. We had a strange bond that way. I was so happy to hear his voice. He was sober too. We started seeing each other again.

There was a woman's residential treatment program in Phoenix that I'd heard good things about. I knew I had issues that couldn't be addressed just by attending AA meetings, so I contacted the director and was given a day to come in.

The first thing the director did when I arrived was to give me a list of the rules regarding phone calls and visits. They were strict. I would have to wait a week before receiving phone calls and even longer for visits. It wouldn't have been bad if I could've trusted Joe to stay sober.

The program was in a beautiful Victorian-style house. I was in an upstairs bedroom with three other women. For the first week, I applied myself in all the groups and classes. I was the only woman there who had a history of long-term recovery and who'd been a counselor. As I was much further along on the path than they were, I soon became very disappointed in the type of treatment being offered. I'd been hoping for more qualified staff to conduct therapy focused groups and individual sessions.

One evening, I was upstairs sitting on my bed, when I began to feel strange. It wasn't a bad feeling, but I'd never felt that way before. I decided to go downstairs. As I went down the steps, I felt light, as if I were floating. Something was definitely happening to me. I was in a heightened state of awareness. I glided into the living room and observed the women with what I can only describe as, a "second sight." I was able to experience them with an unusual clarity.

One woman had been full of smiles that day. She'd just completed the program and was ready for discharge. As I looked at her then, I saw the cheerful face that she was showing us all, but then another face appeared: one of such fear that it was startling. I was sure that no one could see that but me, and I was probably right.

I continued to observe other women as I walked about the house, and saw that many of them were being phony with each other. I saw hidden secrets and the masks that they wore so well. We all wear masks to some degree. We are only human. Sometimes we smile, but our eyes tell a different story. That's not what I'm talking about.

What I saw that night were women whose faces were changing into expressions of fear, deep loneliness, and guilt. I even knew what they were thinking, and I knew what they thought about me. Wow! They didn't get who I was at all.

I went back upstairs to my room and sat on my bed, wondering what the heck was happening to me. I was alone, except for a Hopi Indian woman who was also sitting on her bed. I knew that if anyone could help me with what I was going through, it would be her. I was right. She told me that she'd gone through a similar experience herself.

It was a full moon that night. It felt like wind was rushing through me. I had a strong urge to be in water so I filled up the bathtub and got in. I thought about Joe and the world beyond that house, and it all seemed so far away. I sensed that I was regaining some part of my spirit that had been taken from me when I was a child.

There was a technique that was popular around that time called "soul retrieval." Soul retrieval work has its roots in Shamanism. Traumatic events can cause pieces of our essence, our soul, to become isolated, out of time and space, while we go on about our lives less whole.

Soul retrieval is an exercise that one would go through with a shaman or other qualified person. But what was happening to me was completely spontaneous. I hadn't put myself into a trance or done any breathwork.

I felt like I was one with my own spirit, and she was beautiful. The realization that she was my true essence was beyond words. All the other stuff, the trauma and drama and being an addict, were not who I was. I was shown that I didn't have to identify with that part of me. I never felt more connected to myself than I did then. I had a tremendous knowingness that, no matter what happened to me, I would be all right. I didn't feel panic or fear.

The next morning when I woke up, the Hopi woman came over to my bed and asked me how I was. I told her, "I'm still there." And "there" was a great place to be. The brunt of the experience lasted for about 24 hours, but it felt like it had been a month. I'd been out of time and space.

I realized that I didn't need to be in that program and informed the director of my decision to leave. I went upstairs, packed my bags, and then went to another staff person to get my medications. She said, "Honey, I guess you're just not ready." *Lady,* I thought, *you don't have a clue*! I ended up going to stay with a woman friend of mine.

I felt more "present" than I had in years. I was completely in my body, and vibrating with the energy of the Source of it all. I found myself giggling a lot, and realized that as a child, I'd never giggled, which told me that I must have regained a part of my child's fragmented soul.

I was high like that for about two weeks. Then I came back to this earth dimension. But I learned a lot from that spiritual experience. And then…I forgot. Five months later, Joe relapsed, and I followed. That's right, even after that life-changing experience, I felt the need to self-medicate.

About two years later I talked to a very wise woman about the intense spiritual experience I'd had. She explained to me that sometimes when we go through something like that, it can scare us on some level, especially if we haven't forgiven ourselves for the past, which then prevents us from loving ourselves. If we don't love ourselves, and are still in pain, it doesn't matter how much wisdom we possess. We're just not ready.

She went on to say that a part of me didn't want to own my own power, because then I'd have to take responsibility for it. I admitted that I was afraid of that kind of responsibility; I didn't quite know what it meant, and yes, it did scare me, because I knew that something about me was very different from most people that I knew and talked to.

I didn't want to be different; being different meant being alone. So I played dumb a lot and I used alcohol and drugs as a means of sabotaging my spiritual development. And in doing so, became more of a target for bad spirits because of the power and new awareness I possessed. So at the time of that particular relapse, I made an unconscious decision. I chose death...quick or slow, it didn't matter.

I stopped crack for a while and found the heroin connection. I lost track of Joe, because I started hanging out in the "barrio." I didn't care about dirty needles or HIV. I just wanted oblivion.

One day, I ran into Julio, who had become a heroin buddy. After he scored for me, we went to an alley to fix our dope. Right after I took my shot, I heard Julio say, "Oh, no!" I went down and didn't want to get up. He picked me up and made me walk. I kept saying, "I just want to go to sleep." Julio saw a friend of his and told him to drive me to the emergency room.

When we got there, Julio helped me through the double glass doors. I could hardly stand up. I was losing my vision, stumbling about, and said in a raspy voice, "Overdose." I barely made it through yet another close call. I was like a cat with nine lives. I think I had intended to die and would have, if Julio hadn't helped me. Any other junkie would've left me for dead in the alley.

When I was out of intensive care, I was transported to a substance abuse hospital program that I'd been to before. I was bedridden with a catheter, until the nurses felt I was stable enough to get up. The day I was able to get out of bed, I could barely walk. I also had a hard time with my speech and felt very confused. That overdose had done a number on me. I asked one of the nurses, "Am I going to stay this way?" She assured me that I'd get better, and in a few days, I was back to normal.

While I was there, I had blood work done. One day, the doctor summoned me to his office. He informed me that I had Hepatitis C. I knew I'd contracted it from dirty needles and didn't really care. I left the hospital after only a few days of treatment. I went right back to Julio and scored more heroin. But then, don't forget, I had a death wish.

I was going to jail on a regular basis. It started with me stealing booze. Most of the time I got away, but other times, I was caught. I would go into a 7-11 or a Circle K store, nonchalantly pick up an 18 pack, and just walk out, or in most cases—run. Sometimes, as I was dashing out the door, I'd tell the cashier, "I'm sorry, but I need it."

The first time I was arrested for prostitution in Phoenix, I spent two weeks in jail. The second time, I was given thirty days, and on my third offense, I did three months. If I were to catch another prostitution case, I'd be incarcerated for six months.

One morning, I was whacked out on crack, walking down some residential street in a bad neighborhood. I had a paper bag that contained a pint of vodka and a 40 ounce bottle of Buddy-weiser. I also had my crack pipe and a rock of cocaine in my pocket. A car full of young Mexican guys pulled up to me, and before I knew what was happening, I was sitting in the front seat of their car and it was taking off.

I had a moment of sanity and knew that I was in the presence of evil. I ordered them to let me out, and they just laughed. I tried to open the passenger door, and the driver reached over and grabbed ahold of my hair. I knew that I had to get out of that car. I wasn't one to scream when I was in danger. I'd usually just freeze. But what came out of my mouth as they were speeding away with me to my doom, sounded like it came straight from the deepest, most powerful part of me as I screamed, "NO!"

All of a sudden, my door was jerked open, and I was pushed out of that car. I just lay there for a moment, with the smell of burnt rubber in my nostrils. The paper bag of booze lay on the pavement. I was worried that it was smashed. I looked down from where I lay and spotted my left shoe, a few yards away. I started to sit up and saw that my left foot had the imprint of a tire on it. The skin on my left arm was stretched out and flat, just like in the cartoons. I couldn't believe it. They ran over me! I had to crawl my way to the sidewalk. I was able to stand, but the pain in my foot was excruciating. I hobbled over to where the paper bag was and was relieved to find that the bottles of alcohol hadn't broken.

Shortly after that happened, I quit doing drugs. I stole booze or found other ways to get drunk. I was tired of turning tricks, and I was beyond tired of getting raped. I'd already been raped about 60 times by then, in every manner imaginable, and by every race, except Asians. I was imploding with so much rage that it had turned into severe depression and I was giving up. I was coming to the end of myself; free-falling in a parachute with a malfunctioned ripcord.

Around that time I began getting messages from the spirit world. I used to hang around outside the Indian bar, hoping someone would offer to buy me a drink. One night, an Indian guy approached me and said, "Grandfather (the Creator) wants you to know that you'll be all right." A couple of weeks later, another Native man told me the same thing. I'd never met either one of those guys before.

I found myself walking down an alley late one night. I had a quart of beer and was looking for a place to drink it. I sat down near a dumpster and was soon joined by a couple of drunks who plopped themselves down on either side of me. The man on my left said he was Navajo and the one on my right said he was Hopi. For the next five or so hours, I had a conversation with the Hopi man while the other guy slept. He told me that I was going to make it...that it would be hard but I would have to be strong. I don't remember what else was said but I do know that it felt as if I were speaking with the man in another dimension.

I finished my quart of beer as I sat there listening to the Hopi man. Normally, I would've had to rush out to get more alcohol, but I didn't. As the hours wore on I was not in the least bit sick or shaky. I felt completely at ease. What was even stranger was that the Hopi guy was in his thirties, yet his voice was that of an old man's. As the sun was coming up, I looked over and the man was gone.

It was February 4th, 1999, and I was 47 years old. A drinking buddy had gotten me a motel room the night before, and left me with a couple of six-packs. That morning, I sat alone on the bed, drinking my beer. I looked over at myself in the mirror. My face looked like 100 miles of bad road. My eyes were vacant and lifeless.

My social security checks were being mailed to Kathleen's house. She was a young woman I'd met months before, when I lived for a short time at a Catholic shelter, run by the priests. Kathleen was a social worker, who did a lot with the homeless population. She didn't judge me for my relapses, and always gave me my check when I went for it. I knew it would be there that day. My plan was to cash my check, get a motel room, and score enough heroin to make sure I didn't wake up. This time, I was going to do the job right.

I finished the last beer and was still badly hung-over, but I had to leave that room and start hitchhiking to Kathleen's house. I walked outside to the parking lot and saw a van approaching me. It was being driven by a white guy with long hair. The man beckoned for me to come closer, and like the fool that I was, I did. He asked me if I was interested in some sort of sexual encounter. What I wanted was some hard liquor to stop the shakes. I said to myself, *Just tell him okay, as long as he agrees to buy you some alcohol first, then you can ditch him.* Well, once again, the Creator had his hand on me. I wasn't supposed to die that day. As soon as I agreed to the man's proposal, he stepped out of his vehicle and said, "Turn around and put your hands behind your back. You're under arrest for solicitation of prostitution."

The cold steel of the handcuffs pressed into my back, as I sat crouched in the back seat of the squad car. It would've been a good day to die, but as my Irish luck would have it, I was on my way to the slammer instead. My suicide was not to be, and I was pissed! If that damn cop hadn't been in that parking lot, my plan would've been executed, and all the madness would've been over: no more rapes, no more PTSD, no more coming to consciousness at noon with my body sick and shaking, consumed with terror, and no more fear about being killed in some hideous fashion. I knew I'd really be kicking hard from booze, and I was panic-stricken at the thought of being locked up for six months.

After I'd been processed and escorted to my bunk, I lay on it feeling utter despair, and waited for the alcohol withdrawals to begin. If that wasn't bad enough, my head was itching like crazy from the head lice I'd contracted, several months before. I knew I couldn't very well hide it, so I informed one of the guards. Another female guard came in and took me to a room to cut my hair. She said she'd never seen a case as bad as mine and that she'd have to shave my head. I cried, begging her not to shave it, because then the other inmates would know I had lice and I'd be humiliated. She didn't shave it off, but it was shorter than I'd ever had it before.

I wasn't put on a work crew, thank God, because I had fallen and injured my finger before my arrest, and torn some ligaments. I was in a "pod" with at least 200 women, enough women to where I could disappear and not be noticed. It was always noisy, and most of the women acted as if they were in summer camp, happy to have met up with all their chums.

In the beginning, I'd become overwhelmed with panic, and feel like I was going to lose it, I felt trapped. I tried to get back on my medications, but was denied because I didn't come in with them. Who in the hell gets busted and comes into jail with their medications on them? No one! I don't know how I managed to hold it together those first couple of weeks, but I did.

As the days turned into weeks, I was able to resign myself to the fact that I wasn't getting out of jail for a long time, and that I'd have survive however I could. I stayed to myself and read a lot. I learned how to play solitaire. I tried not to think about my life, it was too painful. I missed Joe, but wasn't able to get in touch with him.

I figured out a way to get my social security checks to go directly to the jail. Then I was able to buy candy and whatever else was allowed. I'd trade candy for tobacco whenever I could, and was lucky not to get caught. I had no visits the whole time I was there except for my friend Kathleen, who also wrote to me, offering her support.

For the first couple of months I had no plan to go straight when I got out. I was prepared to carry out my suicide. But sometime around May, I began to feel differently. I'd been volunteering for all the classes that were available to inmates, cognitive behavior, and substance abuse classes. I started feeling more positive about my future.

In June, there was an evening group that a fellow inmate suggested I attend. It was facilitated by an older man and his wife. The couple had a Master's degree in family therapy. The group was for women who had been sexually abused. I was curious, so I went. When the group started, we were all instructed to sit in a circle. Then the male therapist would go around to each woman and tweak her big toe. I'm thinking, *What the fuck is this?!* So I let him tweak my toe, and then he went on to the next woman. These women were giggling like silly girls the whole time. His wife was a meek looking thing who never spoke. She was basically in his shadow. I wondered about *that* relationship.

The next time I went to group, the therapist began making his way around the circle, tweaking toes. When he got to me I told him, "Don't touch me." He looked surprised. I was probably the first woman who'd challenged him. He had a silly smile on his face. I just looked at him as if to say, *Buddy, I got your number, you pervert.*

After the group was over, some of the women told me, "You should just let him do it and get it over with." "Fuck that," I said, "I did that most of my life, allowing people to do whatever they wanted with my body." I didn't go back to that group. The rest of the women continued going though, allowing themselves to be used for that man's sexual fetish, rather than speaking up.

For months, I watched as women came and went. A lot of them were on their way to prison. I learned that if I were to get another prostitution case, I would go to prison for two years, and would have to register as a sex offender when I got out. *Me?*—*a* sex offender?

One thing that really hurt was that I'd lost everything I had in my storage unit in Phoenix. I'd been paying it monthly, but failed to do so a couple of months before I'd been arrested, all because crack took priority. Everything I owned was in that storage unit. All of my pictures, pictures of my kids, the shield that my coworkers from the youth house had given me, videos of me singing at my mini-concerts, keepsakes—everything—gone! Then I thought, *When I leave here, I'll have nothing.* Like the line in one of Bob Dylan's songs, "When you ain't got nothin'—you got nothin' to lose." I'd just have to start over and grieve the things I no longer had. My intuition told me that because I had lost so much, materially, emotionally, and spiritually, I was going to gain that much more in my next recovery. I sensed that it would be far better than the time when I had nine and a half years.

I knew it was time to surrender to the Great Mystery, or die. I'd always had trouble with surrendering. It meant giving up the control. Then I thought about what a shitty job I'd done with all *my* controlling. I thought about all the times the Creator had spared my life, in spite of me.

I remembered how I would pray when I was on the streets, for the Creator to take my life, or help me find a way to live sober. My prayer had been answered; being locked up for six months was the best thing that could have happened to me. I had never really wanted to end my life. I just wanted the insanity to stop. I didn't want to die in the gutter, either. I didn't want to go out like that. That's not the legacy I wanted to leave my children.

I had contact with my mom while I was in jail. I'd asked her to call my kids and to let them know where I was. She was glad I was in jail, because at least she knew I was safe. She told me that she'd been calling my case manager for information she may have about my whereabouts, but that she didn't know what had happened to me. My mom told me that she'd been calling the morgues on a regular basis because she was afraid I was dead. Man, I knew I had to stop hurting my family. The guilt, the shame, and the grief, caught up with me and there was no way I could run from my feelings. I had to feel it all, right there in jail.

Most of the guards, male and female, were on a power trip. They enjoyed shaming us and took every opportunity to do so. There were shake-downs every couple of weeks; whereby, we'd all be ordered into the hall to sit on the concrete floor in silence, for an hour or two, while they tore our bunks apart and went through our measly belongings. Sometimes they took us into the large shower area, had us pull our pants down, and "spread um."

There may or may not have been rumors of drugs, but they never found anything, not that I was aware of. They would come into our pod at random times and yell at us, "You're nothing but a bunch of "whores and thieves." I'd think, *That's right—we're the ones Jesus chose to be his disciples, you assholes!* I had a lot of anger about being violated and humiliated. It was enough that we women had absolutely no rights, whatsoever. We didn't need the over-kill.

About a month before my release, I contacted Crossroads for Women. Luckily for me, there was a new director. I'd been told by the previous director that I couldn't return. I'd worn out my welcome after having been there several times before and relapsing. The new director, Amy, told me I'd be put on a waiting list. I said I'd sleep on the couch if need be, that was how badly I wanted sobriety. She sensed my sincerity, and said that if there were no beds available when I was released, I was welcome to the couch. What a relief. Once that was out of the way, I contacted Kathleen and asked her if she would pick me up on August 5th. She said she'd be glad to. I was actually happy and at peace for the last month I was in jail.

On August 4th, 1999, I slept very little. I knew what time the guards came by to wake up whoever was being released that day. About 5:00am, I saw Officer Mann walking down the rows of inmates. *Oh God, is she really coming down my row?* She stopped in front of my bunk and said, "O'Quirke, roll up!" Those words were like music from heaven. I woke up my Indian buddies, gave them my cosmetics and candy, and said goodbye. I walked out of that jail with one grocery bag full of court papers and a small black comb, the only things I had to show for 48 years of life, and shouted for joy when I saw Kathleen.

She took me to the halfway house, after stopping at Catholic social services to get me some clothes. As it turned out, I would be sleeping on the couch. I didn't mind at all. But the next day a woman left, and I had a real mattress to sleep on.

Of course, one of the first things I did was to call Joe's parents' house. As it turned out, he was back at Tribal Lodge and had been sober for a while. I was so relieved to see him that first day he came to visit me. I'd been so afraid that something had happened to him, or that he'd be with someone else. We began seeing each other again on a regular basis. His feelings for me were still as strong as mine were for him.

I reconnected with the mental health clinic the week I got out; I needed to get back on my medication. My psychiatrist put me on a new anti-depressant and hooked me up with a day treatment program for mentally ill clients. That program, along with the new medication, saved my ass.

For four months, I spent at least 20 hours a week in classes and groups. The educational classes taught me how to be aware of my PTSD and depressive symptoms, and how to prevent a relapse, as did the substance abuse classes. Of course, I'd taught classes on relapse prevention, but had not always practiced what I taught. The groups allowed me to process my feelings on a continuous basis and to delve deeper into my codependency issues.

I was in day treatment with clients who had a wide range of diagnoses: schizophrenia, major depression, PTSD, bi-polar disorder, borderline personality disorder, schizo-affective disorder and so on. As I observed the other clients, I was able to see myself in them. I began to recognize that there just may be something biochemically wrong with my brain, that medication could correct. I chose to see it as having a chemical imbalance. I'd blamed myself for my mental condition for far too long, and it was time to give myself a break.

Another thing that helped me was that I had a conversation with my brother, Matthew, about my denial around my diagnosis of major depression. He reminded me about our dad's mother, who'd been in a mental institution for the last 20 years of her life, and that her diagnosis was depression. *All right*, I thought, *it really can be genetic and not necessarily something that I should have been able to control.*

The therapists knew I was in a dysfunctional relationship with Joe and helped me to connect the dots. Intellectually, I knew that if I continued to remain with Joe, I would keep relapsing and end up in prison or dead. I wasn't strong enough to face that pain yet, but I was getting closer. During my time in the day program, when Joe "fell off the wagon," I had the support of the therapists to work through it. This allowed me to stay focused and connected to myself.

We were required to get an AA sponsor while at the women's halfway house. I was very blessed to get a woman, who had the vision to see what it was I needed to do, to break the cycle of continual relapse.

I'd had several AA sponsors over the years. I'd completed page after page of written assignments, just as the Big Book of AA instructed, and still I relapsed. One day, my new sponsor asked me point blank, "Have you made peace with your dark side?" "No!" I said emphatically. "I hate that part of me." "Well then, how do you expect to stay sober?" she questioned. The light bulb that went on in my head was a thousand watts. At the same time, I felt a presence telling me, *You better pay attention to this!*

I decided to make a collage. I collected several magazines and starting cutting out pictures of alcohol, drugs, a massive fire depicting my rage, a picture symbolizing prostitution, a woman who was in agonizing depression, guns, evilness, self-hate, and suicide.

As I was going through the process of making my dark side collage, I could feel the process working on me. I felt sick to my stomach and disgusted, as I saw the visual of the Sheila that I hated, staring back at me.

When I was finished, I shared it with my sponsor. "Now," she said, "I want you to look at each one of those images and have a conversation with that part of you; why you were that way, why you did those things, and so on. I started with the one that was my biggest source of shame...Sheila, the prostitute. *I know you did that because you were surviving the best way you knew how. And when you lived like that, I felt you deserved to get raped and beat up, because I hated you for what you were doing. I'm sorry I put you through that. I know that's not who you are, and I forgive you.*

I continued on with the rest of the images, and by the time I finished, I had compassion for myself and much less shame. That was one of the most powerful, healing pieces of work I have ever done.

Because I had never made peace with my dark side, I always had the fear of being found out. I no longer had that fear, because I was okay with those parts of me. After that, if *anyone* called me a bitch, I saw it for what it was—a manipulative gesture, to try to get me to back down—give in—or be *nice*. Oh, how I dislike that word…nice. I felt empowered from that very simple exercise, and was grateful that the Creator had put that wise woman in my path. I was finally getting free.

I made another collage, reflecting my light side. I still have that one today, but I did ceremony with the first one. I sat by a stream, tore it up, and released the pieces to the water, watching as they floated downstream.

One day, I was in my room when Amy, the director of Crossroads, told me I had a visitor. When I peeked into the living room and saw the pervert therapist from the jail, and his mealy-mouthed wife, I went to Amy and told her I didn't want to see them. After she sent them away, I told her all about the toe-tweaker. Amy was appalled. She had me write down everything I could remember about the man, and then she contacted the jail. The jail did an investigation into his background and found that he had forged his degree. He was terminated. I felt good about playing a part in preventing future female inmates from ever having to be in contact with that sick man.

Part Seven
Taking Back the River

I had nine months of sobriety when I finally got into my own apartment, with the help of my new case manager from Comcare. I needed transportation, so I bought myself an older vehicle. Then I decided to look for a job. I needed to feel productive. I found out through the grapevine that Indian Rehab was looking for a house monitor for the women's treatment center, Guiding Star Lodge. I contacted Carol, my previous employer, and she set me up with an interview. She'd known about my years of relapsing, because I often called her when I was sick and wanting help. I passed the interview and was hired. I was still receiving social security, but was allowed to work and still collect it for nine months. My new position paid $8.00 an hour. Combined with my monthly social security checks, I was bringing in over $1,500.00 a month.

Even though I'd worked at the women's lodge before as a counselor, I was excited and grateful to be given another chance. I worked the graveyard shift, and my duties included hourly monitoring of the residents and the premises, morning wake-up, room inspections, and dispensing medication.

Jill and I met when we were attending the day treatment program. One day she called me and asked me to come over. Jill had bi-polar disorder and was struggling with her symptoms. She had a beautiful one-year-old dog that was Chow and Collie. Jill asked me to take her dog because she wasn't able to care for him. I agreed to take Chester for her. It was difficult keeping such a large dog in an apartment, but I'd take Charlie to the park and let him run wild in the grass. I soon became quite attached to Chester.

It was a new millennium and no big deal, as far as predictions went. Joe was still at the Tribal Lodge and working at a gym. I didn't realize there were that many gyms.

264

He'd probably worked at them all by then. Sometimes, he'd spend the night at the apartment, but we weren't being intimate.

One night, he came by the apartment, drunk, and I told him I'd give him a ride back to his half-way house. On the drive there, he became verbally abusive. He called me a whore and brought up my prostitution. He said he could never forgive me for that.

I began to feel intimidated by his level of anger and decided to take him to the VA hospital instead. I pulled in, and as soon as I spotted a guard close by, I stopped the car and ordered Joe to get out. I told him that I couldn't help him, and that maybe the VA could. He finally got out, and I drove home. His dad had recently died, and I knew he was having a hard time with that, but I wasn't about to take his abuse any longer.

For a whole month I didn't hear from Joe. Not knowing what was going on with him was killing me. I felt compelled to do something, anything, to stop the powerlessness and helplessness that had such a grip on me. In the past, when I felt that way, I'd eventually relapse. I wasn't about to do that again. So I allowed myself to feel angry. At least when I was in touch with my anger, I felt more in control. I started thinking about all the times I'd tried to help Joe get treatment, all the support I'd shown him, all the money I'd spent on him. I thought about how I was the only one who had grown and changed, in all the years we'd been together. I was tired of hoping that Joe would change so that I could finally depend on him. I knew that the only one I could rely on was Creator God. Joe was no longer my responsibility. Despite the anger, disappointment, and grief I felt, I also felt relief. It was an opportunity to get back on track with my own program. I still loved Joe and wanted a healthy relationship with him, but not at the expense of losing myself. But in spite of my firm resolve to take care of number one, I struggled with trying not to worry about the man.

In the meantime, I'd been in touch with my daughter, and we talked on the phone on a regular basis. My son was still not talking to me. I'd written him a long letter, apologizing for the things I'd told him five years earlier. I did my best to *not* make excuses for my behavior over the past few years. I could only hope that one day, I would be able to see him and talk to him again.

It was February of 2000. My brother, Donald, who lived in Virginia, told me he was flying out to Reno, Nevada, with his wife and kids in a couple of weeks. He wanted to visit our brother, Kevin, who was living in Nevada, and Matthew, who lived in the Bay area in California. Frankie was going to school out in Maine at the time. Donald invited me to join them, saying it would be like a family reunion. That gave me an idea. I asked my daughter, Lisa, if she'd like to meet some of my family. She said yes, so I sent her a plane ticket. She'd be arriving in Phoenix; from there, we'd drive north to Nevada. Lisa was not afraid of a little adventure, but she was very brave to embark on the emotional journey that was before her.

Since I was going on my trip, I needed someone to stay with Chester while I was gone, and who do you think came to mind? That's right...Joe. Joe loved dogs, and he and Chester had been great pals. It was also an excuse to see him again, because I really missed him. I was afraid though, that Joe would say something that would send my emotions into further turmoil. If that were to happen, my visit with my daughter and family would be affected. He still had that much of a hold on me.

Joe seemed glad to see me. When he agreed to stay at the apartment, all the anxiety I'd been feeling, magically disappeared. It wasn't until that happened that I was able to feel excitement about my upcoming trip. Joe was the most mind-altering man that I'd ever been with.

After picking Lisa up from the airport, we went directly to where Joe was staying. I was feeling anxious again that he may be on another binge, but he was packed and ready to go. Joe had always been supportive of my relationship with my kids, and he was very gracious toward Lisa. She seemed to like him, too. Joe said later that he was amazed at the resemblance. "You two even walk the same," he said. I was in a hurry to get on the road, as it was getting late, and we had an eight-hour road trip ahead of us. I gave Joe some money for groceries and dog food. I knew Joe would take good care of Chester.

We arrived in Reno at about 4:00am. Donald met us in the hotel lobby and took us up to the room he'd booked for us. After a few hours of sleep, we were off in separate cars to Sparks, Nevada, to meet up with my brother, Kevin, at a restaurant.

I hadn't seen Kevin for several years. He was tall and handsome in his police uniform, and looked like my dad. He told Lisa, "You're the first baby I ever held." Kevin must've been about eight years old at the time. The last time my brothers had seen Lisa was when my dad died.

After a short visit with Kevin, we continued on to Red Bluff. Donald wanted his wife and kids to see where he'd grown up, and I wanted to share that experience with my daughter as well.

After going back to the house where we'd lived as kids, we all drove to the cemetery where my dad is buried. It had been almost 30 years since he'd died, and it was still emotional for me. Our next stop was Matthew's house, in the Bay Area. I told Donald to go on ahead; Lisa and I had one more stop to make and we'd meet up with them later. I drove to us to the cemetery where Earnie is buried. We searched and searched for his grave, then I heard Lisa say, "Here it is." Seeing his name on that tombstone was strange. It couldn't have been easy for Lisa, knowing that her father's remains lay there, a father she had no conscious memory of.

When Lisa knew she'd be going to California, she contacted Earnie's mom, Laverne. Lisa knew how I felt about the woman, but wanted to see her, nonetheless. And she had every right to see her. It was her grandmother.

When we arrived at Matthew's house, there were more introductions for my daughter. I hadn't taken into account how overwhelming it would be for her. Not only had she been to her father's and her grandfather's gravesites, she had, for the first time in her life, met seven of her blood relatives: three uncles and four cousins.

The next morning, Lisa and I said our goodbyes to everyone and went back up north to Sacramento for a visit with Laverne. When we arrived, it was dark. We were both nervous as we approached her house. When Laverne opened the door, she had us come right in. We sat down and made small talk for a while. Then Laverne talked about the circumstances surrounding Earnie's death. She told Lisa that Earnie and his third wife, Cathy, had a daughter, but didn't seem to know how to get in touch with the girl.

I thought it would be a good idea if Lisa met one of Earnie's brothers. I called the eldest brother, Bobby, who was anxious to meet with us. The visit with her uncle Bobby was good for her, because she was able to get a better idea of what her father was like, and how he ended up as he did. Bobby was funny, and it was good to see Lisa laughing and enjoying the visit. The next morning, we headed out for Monterey.

After we got a motel room, we went to the Fisherman's Wharf. It looked the same. What memories it still held for me. The next day, I took Lisa to all the places we'd lived when she was a baby. When we got to the last house, the one we'd lived in when the police took her and her brother away, it seemed like a lifetime ago, and yet, I could still picture everything clearly. It was bittersweet, because I'd found my children.

Lisa had brought a camcorder with her and was recording the entire trip. I told her that I wanted to make sure her brother, Travis, received a copy, since he wasn't there with us. Our next stop was Fort Ord. I wanted Lisa to record the hospital where Travis had been born. Unfortunately, it had just been demolished. I was disappointed.

When we finished with our trip down memory lane, there was one more stop that I wanted to make: the Salinas Human Services Department, where my kids had been placed with their foster family. I wanted some information, and so did Lisa. They still had records on file of my kids. What we found out was quite interesting.

It turned out that my kids had never been adopted by the DeWitts, even though the DeWitts had given them their last name. I started to get the picture. As long as my kids were in the foster care system, the DeWitts could collect money for them. So why bother to adopt? Lisa was shocked because the foster parents had told her that they were adopted. She wondered, "What else did they lie about?" I asked to see the letter I'd written to my children eleven years earlier, when I was leaving the state of California for Arizona; the letter I had hoped they would be given should they decide to look for me. It wasn't there.

On the drive back, Lisa told me that the DeWitts had given her and her brother fake social security numbers. One day, she said, a swat team had surrounded Travis' house, dragged him outside, and threw him on the ground at gun point. Afterwards, they realized that Travis was not their man, and let him go. Travis then called his foster mother, saying, "What the hell is going on? Whose social security number did you give me?!"

When we were getting close to Phoenix, I stopped to call Joe. I wanted to make sure he was sober. As soon as I heard his voice, I could tell he'd been drinking. I told him to make sure the apartment was clean. I didn't want to bring my girl back to a messy apartment. When we walked in the door late that night, it smelled of stale booze, and the apartment was filthy. Chester sure was happy I was home.

The next day, Joe cleaned up the apartment. I didn't want Lisa to feel uncomfortable because I was angry with Joe, so I played it off. That afternoon, Joe and I dropped Lisa off at the airport. On the ride back to my place, I felt sad. The journey I had shared with my daughter had ended, but I was also thankful that we were able to make that trip together.

I knew that I was getting closer to letting go of Joe, because I could barely stand him at that point. Knowing that

I had a decision to make, had me in a high state of anxiety. I knew I had to get some help.

I contacted one of the therapists I'd known from the day treatment program I'd been in. Stan was an older man from Chicago, where my dad was from. He reminded me of my dad. Not only did he have a fatherly air about him, he also had that all-too-familiar Chicago way of talking.

The day I met with Stan, I wasn't consciously aware of why it was him I needed to see, but it was perfect. I told Stan that I'd been feeling depressed and anxious about ending it with Joe. He asked me if I had completely let go of my father, and I said I didn't think so. I told him that in all my relationships, I seemed to choose men who were in some way, like my father. Joe was emotionally unavailable; he rarely shared his feelings with me unless he was drunk.

I told Stan that the hold that Joe had on me was debilitating, and I couldn't take it anymore. I wanted to be free. I knew that it went back to my father abandoning me, but I didn't know how to get past it. I'd done pieces of work on that very issue in the past, but I still struggled with it.

As I was sharing all this with Stan, I had the most painful sensation on the back of my neck and shoulders. It began to feel like something really heavy was forcing me down. I told Stan, "There's something on the back of my neck, and it hurts so bad." Then, all of a sudden, I was in touch with an enormous physical and emotional pain. I was sobbing as the pressure on my shoulders continued.

I was reliving the scene where my father told me that my mother was dead and that I couldn't live with him anymore. Yes, I had done some healing around that very experience before, but now I was getting to the actual wound of it, when I first dissociated from my body. I thought it would destroy me, it hurt so bad.

I was hardly aware of Stan at that point; however, I remember him saying, "Sheila, come back." But I knew I had to keep going; I had to go through it. I cried the tears that my four-year-old had locked away in my upper body. The more I let out, the less pressure I felt on my back. After about an hour of going through that process, I was able to return to the present. I had gone so deeply into the core of my grief, I ended up feeling very light, an enormous weight had been lifted.

Stan seemed relieved that I came out of it. I don't think he had ever witnessed anything so profound with a client. It didn't matter, because subconsciously, I knew that he would be the one to trigger that process that I so badly needed to go through. That primal pain was what kept me in addictive relationships.

On the drive home, I was in complete and total awareness. I was reminded of how my unexpressed feelings from the past, kept me from feeling fully alive and in the present. I was tired of making choices in the present, based on unresolved grief. I also understood that in order for me to experience my pain at such profound levels, I *had* to have been strong enough. I never went through a healing that I wasn't ready for and couldn't handle.

Many people think that they can just forget about a painful memory from the past, that it will magically dissipate. That is never true. If you don't believe me, watch people and the way they hold themselves, the way they carry themselves. Do they move their body in a relaxed manner, or are they rigid. Better yet, check yourself out.

My higher self had always known that just being clean and sober was not enough. For some people it is, but not for me. I wanted to go all the way to autonomy. I wanted to feel high, naturally, without the baggage that I'd carried around my neck, without the heavy cloak of sadness I'd worn, just because it was all I knew. I prided myself on having a lot of heart, when it came to facing whatever I had to, in order to be free.

Following that intense session with Stan, I had a newfound compassion for a four-year-old child, who knew how to protect herself, by shoving those feelings deep down and detaching herself from them, in order to survive.

I was finally ready to end my six-year relationship with Joe. I was no longer addicted to him.

I called my daughter and told her I was moving to Michigan. I had nothing left in Phoenix to hold me there. Phoenix had bad karma for me. It felt oppressive, dangerous, and full of so many bad memories.

I let Jill know that I was moving. She was feeling better and suggested that I bring Chester back to her. I knew I wouldn't have room in my car for him anyway. I cried, as I drove Chester back to his original owner. I'd only had him for five months, but I loved that dog.

All I was taking with me to Michigan was whatever I could fit in my car. The rest would be sold in a yard sale.

A couple of days before I left, I went to get an acupuncture treatment. I knew I needed one. When I got on the table, I told the doctor that I was letting go of a relationship, and that I hadn't allowed myself to grieve it yet. Wow, once those needles began to work, I began to sob deeply. I remembered when it was good between Joe and me. I remembered the times when I could talk to him about anything. I remember how he used to make me laugh. I remembered that we were to be married. I remembered how he always gave me a red rose and a box of chocolates on Valentine's Day. I remembered how he would take me to dinner and a movie. And I remembered how badly I had hurt *him*. All the while...I cried.

I was ready to begin a new chapter in my life, I felt strong and excited. I had my truckin' cassettes all packed to go in the front seat with me: Credence Clearwater, Linda Ronstadt, Pink Floyd, Stevie Nicks, Cream, the Shondelles, the Temptations, and other classic rock and oldies groups.

As I drove out of Phoenix, I didn't look back. The farther from Phoenix I got, the better I felt. It was almost exhilarating. I felt as if there was nothing I couldn't do.

I stopped in Lawton, Oklahoma, which was where my mom and her husband were living at the time. My mom had married a very good and gentle man, several years before. Charlie was a social worker from a tribe in Oklahoma. My mom was teaching special education kids at the time. They had both met Joe a few times and were glad that I had finally left him.

One day, I was sitting with my mom while she was on her computer. She had internet. I knew absolutely nothing about the internet. I didn't know Google from a curser. It baffled the hell out of me, but my mom was a wizard at it. All of a sudden, she said to me, "Let's try and find your birth mother's sisters." I was surprised by her wanting to do that for me. When I was growing up, those people were never talked about, yet I had always wondered about them. She still remembered their names. She looked up Juanita Reeves, my aunt, and several listings came up for the same name. She printed the list and gave it to me, so that I could write letters to each one, hoping that one of them would be a hit.

I arrived at Lisa's house around 6:00am. It was April, and still cold out. Lisa was just leaving for work. She assembled parts at an auto factory. My youngest granddaughter, Lacey, was awake in the living room with her dad, Bobby. She was about four years old and didn't remember me, but came right up to me to cuddle. She was the sweetest little girl. I brought my things in and went to bed, in the spare bedroom Lisa had cleared out for me.

A few days later, I wrote my letter to Juanita Reeves, made several copies, and then mailed them.

I settled into a routine at Lisa's house. Joe was on my mind a lot, and I still missed him. When I felt sad about him, I'd cry and let it go. While Lisa and her husband were at work, I stayed home with the kids. Brandon, Lisa's eldest, was eight, and Kirsten was seven. Because there was still snow outside, the kids and I played indoor games that had me running around the house like a teenager. We played hide-and-seek and Little Red Riding Hood. Sometimes I'd play my guitar and teach them songs like *Molly Malone*. One of their favorites was *American Pie*. The girls liked putting makeup on me and giving me silly looking hairdos. I enjoyed the time I spent with my grandkids.

The phone rang. Lisa answered it and said it was for me. The woman on the other end said, excitedly, "I'm your Aunt Waneen! She said that her sister, Juanita, had received a letter from me, and that she'd given Waneen my phone number. We talked for a long time. I had a lot of questions for her about my birth mother and about my nationality. We're Cherokee, she said. I needed to be sure about that. About a week later, my Aunt Juanita called me.

For the next month, the three of us had several phone conversations. One day, I received a package in the mail from Waneen. It was filled with pictures of Joyce, my birth mother, as well as pictures of my aunts, my grandmother, Erma, and my great-grandmother, Lillie. There were also letters that my birth mother had written to my

Aunt Waneen before her death. In all of the letters, there is mention of me as a baby. In a letter she wrote just weeks before her death, my birth mother stated, "You wouldn't know Sheila. She isn't even a baby anymore. She walks, doesn't take a bottle any longer, talks (if you could call it that), and doesn't wear diapers. I can dress her cute, now that she's walking. Still doesn't have much hair though. I have to go now to take her off her potty chair; when I put her on there she won't do anything but sing." Wow! I was singing?! I started my singing career much earlier than I'd imagined. In another letter, dated June 25, 1952, just two weeks before she died, Joyce wrote, "We (she and a lady friend) took the bus to town this afternoon. What a job! I wanted to find something to sew, but trying to look around and run after Sheila was too much. I'm going to have to get a rope and tie it around her when I go shopping." I sounded like a happy, inquisitive baby, and knew I was loved. It was bittersweet, reading her words. I silently thanked my mom for helping me locate my aunts. It gave me back a piece of myself that had been missing all my life.

While living at my daughter's house, I attended AA meetings, not because I needed to talk about my alcoholism, but because I wanted support. It was a place to go where I could process my feelings about Joe and about how it felt to be living in a different part of the country.

I knew that I had to get a job. I interviewed for, and was offered the position of house monitor, with a residential substance abuse program called Turning Point. It was a good 40 minutes away. Even though the pay was only $7.50 an hour, it was a job that would allow me to work in the field I was familiar with.

The program was on the outskirts of a small township called, Otter Lake, and sat right next to the lake itself. There was a circular drive that encompassed four buildings, which were surrounded by large beautiful trees. There was the newer administration office, the re-entry house and kitchen, the women's dorm, and the men's dorm. The women's dorm, built around 1920, was a large two-story building. It had been used as a TB ward, and afterwards, as a children's hospital and orphanage during World War II. I'd always loved old buildings with a history. After I started working there, some of the women clients would tell me that when they were standing in front of the house, they saw children's faces in the upstairs windows. Once, a client told me, that the spirit of a young boy with blondish hair was around me a lot. At times, when I worked alone during the evening shift, I would feel spirits as I walked through the building after lights out. I would just talk to them. It never felt eerie to me. But a few months later, there would be something that not only felt eerie, but downright evil, and would be directed straight at me.

Once the staff realized my abilities as a teacher and group facilitator, I was allowed to conduct my own groups. The residents liked my down-to-earth working style, and were more apt to open up with me because they knew I'd been a hard core addict like themselves.

I got tired of the long drive to and from work, and found a small, one-bedroom mobile home, in Lapeer Township. I'd brought my TV and stereo with me from Phoenix, but had no furniture. Slowly but surely, I acquired a table here, a couch there, and I settled into my new home. I had a large front deck. I would sit out in the sun, relax on the weekends, and listen to nature sounds. It was a far cry from the noise and barrage of gunshots that was a constant when I lived in Phoenix.

I'd been employed at my job for four months and really enjoyed working with women who were primarily from the Detroit area; whose drug lifestyle most closely mirrored the one I'd experienced. I was blessed to be a catalyst for their healing. Then one day, a woman entered the program who really disturbed me. She was African-American and younger than I. There was an evilness about her. As she acclimated to the program, I noticed that wherever she went, there were two other black women with her. Sometimes, she would come to the office by herself, when I was there alone, as if to ask me for something, but never did. I had been blessed by the Creator with many gifts and had a strong spirit, yet I was vulnerable at that time. I didn't have my footing yet, and that woman knew it.

One day, I told the client's counselor how uncomfortable I was around that woman, and that I didn't like her. I knew that something of a dark nature was being directed at me by the three black women. I was having dreams about bats flying around me, biting me.

One evening, I was the only staff person on duty. I announced that group was starting. I sat in my usual chair, as the women assembled in the living room. The client who gave me the creeps, sat directly opposite me. When her two cohorts came in and sat on either side of me, I knew I was being set up for something, because the three women had formed a triangle and I was caught in the middle of it. I looked at the evil woman across from me, and she knew that *I* knew. She had the most unsettling grin on her face.

No sooner had I begun the group, when the evil woman interrupted by saying to me, "My counselor told me that you don't like me. Why is that?" I was totally unprepared for her statement, and was shocked that her counselor had broken confidentiality with me. I felt angry and betrayed. The woman continued confronting me in my own group. I asked her to leave and she wouldn't. I finally said, "Then I'm leaving," and announced that group was over. I went into the staff office and called my supervisor. I told her she needed to come right over because I was going home.

When my supervisor arrived, I went to the parking lot to meet her. I told her what had happened. I also told her that I'd previously notified the director about how those women had been disruptive and problematic all along, but that nothing had been done. I was in a full blown PTSD episode. I said that I refused to work in an environment where clients were able to intimidate staff, and where staff sided with clients because they were afraid of them.

I went back inside, packed my things in a box, and left. When I got home, I called my mom and told her the whole story. When I told her about the bat dreams, she said to make sure I hadn't left anything behind that they could use to witch me with. Damn, I couldn't seem to escape witches!

I knew that those women thought they had won. But they hadn't; I was badly shaken, but I still had my power.

There weren't any other treatment programs in Lapeer, so I found a Mexican restaurant that was owned and operated by real Mexicans. I was hired on as the full time dishwasher. It didn't pay much, but I had a free Mexican meal every day.

My Aunt Waneen and I were still talking on a regular basis, and I decided that I'd like to visit her. She lived in Nebraska, while my other aunt, Juanita, lived in New Mexico. I had a little money saved up, so I quit my job at the restaurant, and drove to Nebraska.

As soon as I arrived in the small town of Creighton, I stopped at a pay phone and called my aunt to meet me, so that I could follow her back to her house. I was feeling excited about meeting this woman who was my birth mother's sister, the woman who knew me when I was a baby. I was standing near my car on the main drag, when I saw this very small woman walking toward me, smiling from ear to ear. I towered over her as we hugged.

We had a nice visit. She filled me in on some of the family history. She said that her mother, Erma, who was Cherokee, had what was called "the knowing." That's when someone knows when an event is happening, or when it's going to happen. She told me about times when my grandmother would tell her not to leave the house because a bad thing was going to happen. Waneen said she'd leave anyway, and sure enough, an accident or other such mishap would occur. Waneen told me that my grandmother would bleach her hands, to lighten them up. She was ashamed of being Indian. She also said that I looked like her. She gave me more pictures and some letters that my birth mother, Joyce, had sent her from San Diego, CA. The letters contained more tidbits about me, and gave me a better idea of the kind of person my birth mother was. I stayed with Waneen and her husband, Joseph, for about ten days, then returned to Michigan.

After being unemployed for a month or so, I decided to call the director at Turning Point. I figured that the witch would be gone by then, and asked if I could have my job back. As it turned out, they hadn't been able to fill my position, and were only too glad to have me return.

The "evil lady" and one of her sidekicks were no longer at Turning Point, but one of them, Felicia, still was. Felicia approached me on my first day back and seemed genuinely pleased that I had returned. Sure enough, she admitted that the three of them were doing witchcraft on me. She'd evidently been pulled into it by the other woman, and apologized for the part she played.

It was toward the end of November when the blizzard came. I had never lived with snow, and after the initial glistening whiteness, it lost its splendor for me. For the rest of that winter, I struggled with depression, due to the lack of sunlight. Driving in the snow was scary, with the black ice and having to avoid hitting deer. I wasn't enjoying the winter wonderland and couldn't see myself putting up with it year after year.

Although my son had begun talking to me again, I'd only seen him twice since I'd moved there. For the ten months that I'd been living in Lapeer, Lisa and I only saw each other a handful of times, and she rarely called me, nor I her. Our relationship had gotten better, and I enjoyed seeing my grandkids, but I began to realize something. The whole reason I'd decided to move to Michigan was because I wanted to develop a closer relationship with my kids. But I could see that they had their own lives with their own families, and weren't ready for me to come and be mom to them, and probably never would. I was all right with that.

I had my own interests, separate from my kids, and I missed being around like-minded people. Also, I wanted a relationship one day, but I couldn't see it happening in the land of the good ole' boys, whose level of conversation didn't go beyond talking about huntin' and drinkin' beer. I loved the natural beauty of Michigan and all that water, but I didn't even like the summer, which was always my favorite season, because of the man-eating mosquitos. And there weren't any Indians where I was living. I missed being around Natives.

It was around May of 2001, when I decided to leave Michigan and move to New Mexico. I needed the sunlight and I was definitely not going back to Arizona. I contacted several recovery programs in Albuquerque, but there were no job openings. I was feeling adventurous again and thought I'd just move to Albuquerque and find a job once I was there. My mom knew I was unhappy with the way things were going for me in Michigan, and offered to help me with the money I'd need to start over. I contacted an apartment complex in Albuquerque and secured a furnished apartment.

I was turning 50 years old. I wanted to spend my birthday with my two kids. The day of my birthday, Lisa came and picked me up and we drove to Travis' house. Travis drove the three of us to a nice restaurant, where I told them about my decision to leave Michigan. I said that I couldn't handle the weather and that it was affecting my mental health. My son also has seasonal depression, so he understood. I was sure that my leaving would take some of the pressure off my kids for us to be closer. It seemed that they were a bit relieved about my leaving. I told them how proud I was of them. The day was memorable for me, at least, in that it had been the only time the three of us had been together like that.

A few days before I was to leave for Albuquerque, I took Lisa's three kids to the circus. My grandson, Brandon, had said his favorite animal was the white tiger and I was pleased that he saw one there. There were ponies for the kids to ride. I just naturally assumed that six-year-old Lacey would like to ride one. I picked her up and sat her on one of the ponies. She was absolutely terrified, so I took her off. I was glad I was able to create some good memories with my grandkids. I took lots of pictures and sent them to the kids after I got to Albuquerque.

It was July and it was a dry heat in Albuquerque. As I was settling into my new furnished apartment, my mom told me about a family reunion that was taking place at my Aunt Cynthia's house. Cynthia, my mom's sister, lived on one of the reservations near San Diego, CA. Again, I asked my daughter if she'd like to come out and meet more of the family. She said she would, and arranged for time off from work. I should've asked my son, Travis, if he wanted to come to the reunion, but I didn't think he'd want to.

Lisa flew into Albuquerque and then we drove to California. I really enjoyed our road trips together. We called ourselves *Thelma and Louise*, from the movie.

I was glad that my mother and my daughter were finally able to meet. My brothers, Donald, Frankie, and Kevin were there as well. Lisa met Frankie for the first time. Frankie had recently moved to Reno, Nev. He was working in the VA hospital as a surgical tech. All of my aunts and uncles were there as well as my cousins and their kids. My mom gave Lisa the task of handing out name tags to everyone. She wanted her to feel a part of the family. After some initial nervousness, Lisa was able to do her job with confidence and grace.

I felt sad when I dropped Lisa off at the airport. I was really going to miss her. It seemed that we were closer when we didn't live near each other.

I started my job search. At the same time, I got busy putting together the documentation I needed to get licensed as a substance abuse counselor. Then I took the state exam and was issued my license.

As you may remember, I strongly disliked working in methadone clinics, and that's where I ended up. But it was a paycheck, and I continued to look for something more suitable. I'd heard about a program in the town of Bernalillo, that served several of the pueblo tribes in that area. It was called Five Sandoval Indian Pueblos. I would call the program on a regular basis, inquiring about positions. I was determined to work there. One day, I called the program and was asked by the director, Jack, to come in for an interview, as one of their counselors was resigning. I passed the interview and was hired at $12.00 an hour.

On my first day of work, I took a ride to Zia Pueblo with Roger, the counselor that I was replacing. The pueblo itself was spread out, and the oldest part of the pueblo was up on a hill and barely visible from the highway.

Roger filled me in on what he did there, but mostly I would have to learn as I went along. Roger said that he currently had about four clients and that that was normal. "Wow," I said, "What will I be doing all day?"

Indian tribes call the head of the tribe by different names. It's not like in the old western movies where they all go by "Chief." In the pueblo tribes, they are called governor. Eventually, I met the governor, as well as members of his council. There were other staff to meet, and eventually I'd meet everyone. I would be the only substance abuse counselor for the whole tribe, and that felt like a huge responsibility.

I spent close to two hours a day going to and from work. It was tiresome and a lot of money in gas. I knew I'd need to find a place to live in the town of Bernalillo, because it was closer to work. I'd never owned my own place, and my credit score wasn't too bad, so I contacted a mobile home agent. I went to look at a four-year-old manufactured home that he was selling in Albuquerque. I really liked it. There were two large bedrooms and two full baths. I completed the application and returned it to the agent. Later that week, he said I'd been approved. I couldn't believe it! The total cost of the mobile home was $25,000.00. My monthly mortgage payments would be $254.00. Once everything was in place with the purchase, I had to scramble to find a lot to put it on. I didn't want to be in a trailer park because I wanted privacy. I found the perfect place. It was on a quarter of an acre, and owned by a man who also owned the farm right next to it. He said, "I hope you like farm animals," and I just smiled. I knew they would make excellent neighbors.

I'd been telling my boss, Jack, that I wanted a dog. The day after I moved into my new home, Jack said to me, "Have I got the perfect dog for you!" He said that this dog had just shown up on his doorstep one day, and had never left.

It was Saturday, and I was excited as I drove to meet Jack and get my dog. We met at a gas station, and when he opened his car door, this beautiful golden retriever looking dog jumped out. I said, "Oh, my God!" This was definitely the dog I'd been waiting for, and evidently she felt the same, as she happily leapt into the back seat of my car.

I named her Molly. She was also part German shepherd. Her body was definitely that of a golden retriever, but her head was a shepherd's, because she had ears that stood up.

It was Monday and I left for work, leaving Molly in the house. I didn't want to chance her getting loose from the yard. After work, I pulled into the driveway and knew there was trouble, because I saw that the blinds on one of the windows was hanging and torn.

When I opened the front door, I was already mad, and not in the mood for the happy welcome of this big dog jumping up on me. I looked around the house to assess for more damage, and saw that she'd also destroyed the blinds from another window. My belongings were still in boxes, and none of them had been messed with, except for one small box containing my toiletries. It was completely dumped over. That was interesting.

The technician had come that weekend to hook me up to DIRECTV. Molly was there when he came. So you can imagine my anger at discovering that she had managed to rip the cable connection from my TV, in such a way, that it broke the connection on the back of the TV itself, leaving it inoperable. Man, oh man, was I ever upset, and Molly knew it. She just kept her head down and went into the spare bedroom to hide from my wrath. Every so often, she'd peek out into the living room, and then go right back into the bedroom, after seeing the mean look on my face. That dog knew exactly what she was doing and how to get back at me for leaving her alone. I thought Karma was bad…

As it turned out, Molly had severe separation anxiety. The next morning, I left her in the back yard, tied to a tree with a very long cord, and I left the metal gate open. When I got home, she was sitting in the front yard, waiting for me. She had bitten through the nylon cord but hadn't run away. So I felt comfortable enough, leaving her in the yard when I went to work. I'd just have to close the big cattle gate after I pulled out of the drive. That worked for the first few times. Then one evening, I came home, and there was no dog. She had escaped! After checking my phone messages, I heard a woman's voice ask, "Do you have a dog named Molly? She just wandered into my yard." That was the first of many calls I'd get about my Houdini dog.

I felt truly blessed to be working at Zia Pueblo. Sometimes I'd be standing on the porch of the building I worked in, and I'd watch the woman who lived across the road, shoveling loaves of bread into her adobe oven. Other times, when I was driving on the pueblo, I'd have to wait for wild horses to cross the road. It didn't get much better than that.

I had always been obsessed on my weight and had a distorted self-image, in that I saw myself as fat even though others would tell me otherwise. I didn't have a scale, because I knew I'd be on and off that thing every two hours. I was never bulimic or anorexic, just too fixated on how I looked.

Physical exercise was something I always had to force myself to do. It was a discipline. And I'm a firm believer in having at least one discipline. I started working out again with videos. When I became bored with that, I bought a treadmill and put it in the bedroom, and it just sat there. I put it in the living room so I could get on it while watching TV. Not happening. Then I got rid of the treadmill and purchased a put-it-together yourself, all-in-one, home gym. It was a bitch to put together. After a couple of weeks, my enthusiasm waned once again. The only time I had ever consistently worked out with any success, was if I joined a gym. The logic behind that was that if I paid to work out, I had to go. Curves for Women opened a gym right there in Bernalillo and I joined. I had no excuse now, especially since I passed it every day on my way to and from work. At that time I weighed about 165lbs. As the weight started coming off, I felt better about my body. I also felt more in control. Then it was time to do something about the way I ate.

I'd always had an issue around food. I loved my sweets and fried foods. I especially loved chocolate. I was always on some kind of a diet, and none of them worked. I decided to buckle down and get serious about my diet, but I didn't want to cut out chocolate and fried foods altogether. I had to have something to look forward to, right? I told myself that if I ate healthy during the week, I could reward myself on Friday and Saturday night with hamburgers, pizza,

Mexican food, and for dessert: ice cream and candy. During the week, I'd eat salads or make a chicken dish or a pot of stew to last all week. I disliked cooking, and still do. The less I have to do of it, the better. For lunch, I'd make myself sandwiches with cheese and avocados, or tuna. I didn't like lunch meat, and I rarely did any cooking that included meat. But I sure loved my greasy shredded beef tacos on the weekend, and so did Molly. She loved our Saturday ritual of going for takeout. If I got a hamburger, so did she.

I spoiled that dog, and she gave me nothing but unconditional love in return. There is nothing like coming home to a dog that has been eagerly waiting for you. When Molly would see me pulling into the driveway, her tail would be wagging and her hips would swing back and forth with such force and such pleasure, it made coming home something I really looked forward to.

Whenever I left work stressed out about some situation or person that had me all riled up, I was able to let it go when I saw my buddy. She put a smile on my face. She was pure joy and love and kept me in the present moment. She reminded me of what was really important.

I was in control of the coming home ritual. Molly knew that she had to wait for me to change clothes and unwind a bit, before any playing and petting got started. She was a very patient dog.

One Saturday morning, I left for a class I was taking. When I returned, Molly wasn't there. I'd been leaving the cattle gate open because she would always stick around the house. If I shut the gate, she'd dig her way out under the chain link fence, and not have a way to come back into the yard. So I was concerned when she wasn't there that day and I went looking for her.

I was becoming increasingly anxious as the hours went by and there was no sign of Molly. I'd only had that dog for six months, but my attachment to her was so strong that my heart hurt, fearing that she may be in trouble. If she'd been in the neighborhood, she never would have been gone that long. If she wandered into someone's yard I would've gotten a phone call. Maybe someone just took her. My thoughts were driving me crazy. I finally had to accept that she was gone, and I just sobbed. *This is worse than losing a man,* I thought.

It was about 10:30 at night, and I decided to look outside one more time before I went to bed. I opened the front door and turned on the porch light. I looked down the driveway and saw two piercing red eyes staring back at me. There she was, just lying on the ground. "Molly," I cried. "Where have you been?" I was flooded with relief. Tears were streaming down my face as I went to her. She looked exhausted as I helped her into the house. She was filthy and full of burrs. There was a canal on the other side of my street, and my guess was that she was chasing a critter and ended up being taken downstream toward Albuquerque. She must have gone a long way before she was able to climb out. I was amazed at how she remembered her way back home. My Molly was back, and all was right with the world.

I was seeing a psychiatrist in Albuquerque for my psych meds. I felt emotionally stable for the most part. My triggers came less often, and when I had a PTSD episode, it didn't last as long, and they were much less intense. I was making progress. It also helped that I wasn't in a relationship. I had my dog, and I didn't feel lonely, or have the need to be involved with a guy. I'd been sober and celibate for about four years at that time, and didn't miss sex. I was basically married to my job anyway, and felt I couldn't do both.

Living in the country was good medicine for me. I loved that I lived next door to animals. There were cows, sheep, donkeys, horses, chickens, turkeys and stray cats that were often having litters. A couple of times the chickens got over the fence into our yard, and Molly promptly killed them. Once a turkey flew into the yard, and Molly killed it too. I'd end up having to pay my landlord for the fowl. The way I saw it, Molly was just doing her job and was very territorial. What I worried about the most though, were the kittens. Molly hated cats, or for that matter, any critter that was small and moved fast. Once I opened the front door, and there on the bottom of the steps was something small without a head. "Oh gee, Molly, thanks for the present." I had no idea what it was. I dug a hole out back and buried it. Later that day, I went outside to check on Molly and saw that she had the thing next to her, she'd dug it up. It was covered in maggots. I put it in the dumpster.

One day, at a staff meeting, Jack announced that he was resigning. I would always be grateful to him for Molly. Our new director, Anthony, was a pueblo Native. I liked him right away, and it seemed like he was going to make some positive changes. He asked me how I was doing at Zia Pueblo, and I told him that I felt isolated there. He understood that. I said it didn't make sense for me to be there 40 hours a week if I only had four or five clients. I asked that he allow me to split my time between Zia Pueblo and the main office in Bernalillo, to which he agreed. The main office was actually on Santa Ana Pueblo grounds, and only five miles from my home.

I enjoyed working at the main building and teasing and joking with the staff, most of whom were Pueblo. I also liked the contrast of being at Zia because it was so peaceful there.

Sometimes, strange things would happen at my office. One day, I went to unlock my office door and found it open. No one else had a key to that office. When I went inside, one of my AA Big Books was lying on the floor in the middle of the room. I didn't think a lot about it until the next day, when the same thing happened. I mentioned it to one of the ladies who had an office adjacent to mine and she said that those kinds of things happened a lot there. During my lunch break I would shut my office door and meditate. Sometimes, my meditations would be interrupted; the computer would turn on or the shredder would start up, seemingly on its own. Once, it must have been time for me to come out of my meditation, because someone grabbed my knees and shook them, startling me back to consciousness. I looked forward to being visited by the spirits. I had a feeling that they were glad I was there, and that they liked me. I've never seen a spirit, but felt and sensed them a lot while I was at Zia and in my home.

My folks often stayed at my place when they were traveling through, on their way to L.A., to visit my aunts. My mom's husband, Charlie, agreed to take me as his daughter, in the Indian way. From then on, I called him, "pop." Charlie danced in pow-wows as a Southern Straight and Gourd dancer. He won at a lot of competitions. In my pop's tribe, they called the head of the tribe president. My pop was elected president of his tribe on two occasions, and served between 2004 and 2010.

I was still writing songs and playing guitar at home. I was ready to produce a CD of my music. I contacted Eagle Rock Studio in Albuquerque, and made an appointment to see the owner, who was also the producer. I walked into a state-of-the-art setup. I let the owner, Shane, hear the cassette I'd produced 13 years before. He wasn't all that impressed with the instrumentation. Shane knew that I needed someone to play the guitar parts and that I only wanted to sing. The guy was a great guitarist. He played every style and also played the mandolin. I was impressed. I also met Bob, the piano/keyboard player. Bob was from Boston and had a Master's degree in music. I heard him play a little and was very impressed with him too. So began the process of making a CD.

I had a great time with the whole production part of it and sang my own harmonies. It helped that Shane and Bob liked my music. They felt my songs were meaningful and not just a bunch of noise and silly words. Shane did say though, "Your voice is for rock and roll." But my limited guitar playing still kept me stuck in the basic and minor chords.

The photo shoot was fun. I wore a multi-colored peasant-style dress that I picked up at a thrift store. The shoot took place outdoors, amidst lush foliage. The photographer told me to just move around and to let myself go. I was a bit self-conscious at first, but was finally able to get into the flow of it. I took off my shoes and danced in circles hearing that click, click, click of the camera.

Once the pictures were developed, I located a graphic artist, Brandon, who put my CD cover together.

Six months and $3,000 later, I gave birth to my first CD. The whole process was wonderful and it felt like a huge accomplishment. Then that feeling of complete and utter fulfillment began to fade, as I lost myself once again, in my work as a counselor.

During that year, I really started feeling the effects of the hepatitis. I was getting used to being tired, but when I started having serious bouts of the sickness, I started to worry. Yet I wasn't worried enough to take the treatments. When I got sick, it would last about 24 hours, and I would feel like I was going to die. I'd had the flu before, but this was far worse. My doctor had been monitoring my lab work to see how the virus was progressing. It was multiplying rapidly in my body, but I continued to turn him down when he suggested I start the treatments. I'd heard horror stories about the Interferon treatment for HepC and didn't think I'd be able to handle it. So I continued to work out and eat healthy.

I'd never planted a vegetable garden, and that was something I really wanted to do. So I bought a shovel and spent a week digging and turning soil in my back yard. I planted carrots, lettuce, chilies, tomatoes, squash, corn, flowers, and gourds. After work, I loved going out there to water and watch little leaves coming up from the ground. I put a lot of time into that garden. But it was a disaster. Nothing I'd planted grew more than a couple inches, except the gourds. I had these beautiful gourds that climbed up the high chicken wire fence. *All right*, I thought, *maybe I'm supposed to do something with these gourds*. When they were ready to be picked, I brought them in and cured them in the bathtub with bleach, scrubbing away any mold that had accumulated. Then I carefully cut the tops off with a small hacksaw. Next, I cleaned the insides out and removed the seeds. I got out all my art supplies: pieces of leather, beads and water colors. I decorated my gourds with beadwork and painted butterflies, birds, animals, and flowers. Initially, my plan was to fix them up and sell them. But what ended up happening was that I developed a relationship with each of them. They felt so alive to me. I gave some to my family as gifts, but still haven't been able to part with the rest. The following year, I took some of the seeds from the first batch and planted them. I didn't even attempt my luck at another vegetable garden. *I'll stick with gourds*, I decided.

Off and on, I made jewelry to sell. I liked making beaded earrings and often used porcupine quills. A bead store opened up in Bernalillo, and I found myself looking at necklaces that were being sold on consignment. I thought, *I bet I can do that.* Always, my intention was to make a buck and it always backfired on me. I soon found myself addicted to making necklaces, and for the next two or three months, I must have spent $600.00 in that store, buying semiprecious stones and supplies. I sold some of the necklaces and beaded lanyards to the staff at work, but I didn't make my millions selling jewelry.

Another money-making opportunity presented itself, which was right under my nose. We had our own DWI School at the administration office where I worked. When I found out that instructors were making over $450.00, to teach 12 hours of classes to first offenders, I began the certification process. Within a couple of months, I was teaching my first class.

My spiritual life had always leaned toward the Lakota traditional ways, and I missed the sweat lodge. Whenever I sincerely asked for help and was ready to receive it, it often came to me in the strangest ways. Here's an example. I started getting mail that belonged to a woman named Kathy, who lived down the street from me. At first, I'd just put it back in the mailbox with a note that said, "wrong address." One day, I received yet another piece of mail for Kathy and decided to take it to her myself. I walked the four blocks to the address on the envelope. I knocked on the front door, but no one appeared to be home. Being nosy, I peered into her backyard and saw a sweat lodge. I was really intrigued. I wrote my phone number on a piece of paper, requesting that the lady call me. When she did, I inquired about her sweat lodge. I wanted to know if the sweat was run by a Native, and she said it wasn't. I asked her if she knew of any Lakota-run sweats, and she gave me the name and phone number of a Lakota man who lived a couple of miles away. I immediately called him. When he answered, I said, "Hello Henry, I'm Sheila." He sounded friendly and asked me to come over, so we could meet. When I arrived at his duplex, he was standing outside by his red truck, smiling, and walked up to greet me.

After we shook hands, he invited me to come inside. Henry was a nice looking man, of about 5'7. He wore his sparse hair in a ponytail. When he told me he was 66 years old, I was surprised; he looked young for his age and was in good physical shape. As soon as we sat down, I felt an immediate connection, and a sense of relief that I couldn't explain. I looked around in his living room and saw that it was filled with some powerful images and items, as well as some comical ones. Henry had a sense of humor.

Over the course of a couple months, Henry told me the story about how he came to be a pipe carrier. The Chanupa (Pipe) is very sacred; to be a pipe carrier, is a serious matter and a big responsibility. Many people buy pipes in Native shops, for their personal use, or to hang on their living room wall for fashion's sake; but that doesn't make them pipe carriers. I won't go into how the Chanupa came to the Lakota people, or be any more specific than that. If you want to know more about the Chanupa Wakan (Sacred Pipe), you may want to read the books: *Black Elk Speaks* or *Wallace Black Elk: The Sacred Way of Lakota*.

Henry and I had long talks about the Lakota way of living. He spoke his language to me and would explain in English. I knew he was a medicine man without his telling me he was. A real medicine person never says, "I'm a medicine man or woman." It's just not done. There are many "self-proclaimed" medicine people out there, and that is wrong. The same applies to those who claim to be healers. Those who have special abilities are called, "hollow-boned ones." In other words, the true power comes from the Creator, Wakan Tanka, not the human. My understanding of a true healer is that she/he is one who has been gifted with the ability to transmit the power of the Creator.

Henry and I became good friends. He was quite a character. He played a mean guitar and liked to tell jokes. When I was at his place and the phone would ring, it was usually someone calling for his help and *I* would be put on hold. Being a medicine man is similar to being an old-time doctor; he's always on call.

Henry had been asked to conduct a "Wopila," about ten miles outside of Bernalillo. The Lakota word for a sweat is Inipi. A Inipi Wopila, is a sweat that is conducted for the purpose of giving thanks, for a prayer that's been answered. Henry invited me to go with him. He never charged for anything he did. If a person wants the help of a medicine man, they offer him tobacco. My mom taught me that it's also customary to give a sack of potatoes, a can of coffee, or other food items that the medicine man can use. It is a very bad thing for a Native *or* a white person to charge others to participate in a sweat or other Native ceremony. Non-Natives shouldn't be running sweat lodge, period, unless they have been taught and are given permission.

I'd been to many sweats before, but this was to be the most powerful one yet, as well as the hottest. I really struggled in there and didn't think I'd make all four rounds. After the last round was over, I crawled out of the lodge and stood up shakily. I was barely able to walk. I felt like a little fawn, trying out my new legs. I was glad it had been a hard sweat for me, because I had been touched by the spirits in a good way and felt reborn.

I'd always wanted a soul connection with a man; one that transcended the physical. I became attracted to Henry. For me, there is a thin line between sexuality and spirituality. Intimacy can really develop when you connect with another on such a deep spiritual level. It actually showed me how much I'd grown and changed, because I was no longer attracted to the bad boy type. But...wait a minute. Henry was a Vietnam vet. And I was still attracted to soldiers.

I shared many personal things about myself and my life with Henry. Therein lies the danger for me. Whenever I opened up too quickly with a man I was attracted to, I gave my power away. It didn't matter that the man didn't take my power. I felt vulnerable just the same. Once I started giving my power away, I became dependent on his every word, every facial expression and that old, *I wonder what he meant by that*, type of thinking, came into play.

I felt that Henry was attracted to me as well, because I could feel sexual tension in the air. As time went on, I found myself being less authentic and less spontaneous. I feared that Henry may tell me to get lost, but I was already lost and in a lot of pain. My anxiety level was off the hook! Henry asked me one night, "How are you going to feel if a woman calls me in the middle of the night and I have to go to her house to help her?" I told him exactly how I'd feel—jealous! That ended any illusion I may have had about a relationship with that medicine man. I didn't want to come in second. But worse than that, I had to figure out how to go into a relationship without connecting it to past losses, and sabotaging it from the get-go. What I learned from that experience was that I still had work to do, more unresolved grief to heal, before I was ready for a relationship. That's why

I preferred being solo. But I also knew that by avoiding relationships, as I'd done for years, I was only postponing the healing that I needed to do. I also knew that there weren't many men out there who were secure enough with themselves, to fit the bill.

I began to detach myself from Henry. That was good, because one day, he informed me that he was moving to Nebraska. I was sad about that, because he had helped me in so many ways. I would miss my friend and I'd miss hearing the Lakota language being spoken.

I thought I'd better take advantage of him while he was still in Bernalillo, so I asked him to do a pipe ceremony for me, to which, of course, he agreed. Henry told me what I needed to do to prepare for the ceremony, and he never did anything without asking the Grandfathers and his "helpers." He said he'd get back to me when he knew what day it would be, and what colors I would use for tobacco ties. Tobacco ties, or prayer ties, are a big part of the Lakota traditional way.

Henry called me a couple of days later and told me what day it would be. He was told that I was to make fifty red, and fifty yellow, tobacco ties. I'd also need other colored cloth for another part of the ceremony. I headed for Wal-Mart and got the cotton cloth, a can of Bugler tobacco, and string. I cut the cloth into one-inch squares, filled each one with tobacco, put a prayer into them, and tied them with string in the way I was taught. When I finished, I was in an altered state.

It was two days before the pipe ceremony, and something unusual happened. I usually kept the cattle gate open at night because I was too lazy to close it. As I was driving out of my driveway to go to work that morning, to my amazement, there was a spider web that filled the entire length of that ten-foot gate. I then saw Iktomi (a large black spider) in the web, as I was passing through it with my car. I felt bad about destroying all the spiders work, but didn't attach any real significance to it, until the next morning. As I was driving out of the gate...there it was again! I'd remembered that Henry had told me that Iktomi, the spider, was one of his "helpers." Then it hit me. I called Henry and told him about it. I could *feel* him smiling. Iktomi, Henry said, was protecting me, as I was preparing for the ceremony. Wow! That was powerful.

Henry said I could invite a friend to the ceremony. I asked Mary, a young Pueblo woman. Mary was a co-worker and a friend. She and I had become close, from the time she came to work with our agency. She was a loving and down-to-earth woman, and I loved her like a sister, and still do. I made burritos, and Mary brought homemade guacamole and chips. After Lakota ceremonies, there is always a meal. The ceremony lasted quite a while. I had a lot of prayers and much to be forgiven for. That pipe ceremony was the first, and would not be the last, that I would participate in, but it was the most powerful one.

Work went on as usual, and one day, we finally got a clinical supervisor on board. Dr. Linda Sanchez was a psychologist, and the best thing that could have happened for our staff. She was a very wise woman in many ways.

One day, Dr. Sanchez and I were in Mary's office, and I was talking about an upcoming trip to South Dakota, for a "Red Road" gathering. I mentioned that whenever I was in another state, I felt freer to be my true self, because no one knew me. Linda said, "Sheila, no one knows you here," meaning the staff in our agency. I knew exactly what she meant and was glad to be "seen" for a change.

Dr. Sanchez became my friend, my mentor, and supported me in every way; in my job and in my life. She was always there to validate me. She knew about my PTSD and understood what my triggers were. Dr. Sanchez backed me up, whenever she felt that the director was being insensitive to my needs. There was a time when I was going through something of a profound, emotional and spiritual nature. Dr. Sanchez supported me in taking time off from work to heal.

It was in October, and I'd been triggered by a man. It happened about two months after Henry left for Nebraska. I'd met a guy through an online discussion group I belonged to. He was Lakota, a Vietnam vet, and a recovering alcoholic. I became attracted to his spirit; he seemed very traditional in his Lakota ways. We talked on the phone and there was an attraction on both sides. Then he was no longer the person I thought he was. He became rude and hurtful. It felt like a spiritual attack in many ways. It sent me into a tailspin, and I went into some very dark and gut-wrenching place within.

I spent five days in my home, which became like a cave to me. Talk about a dark night of the soul. I knew that whatever it was, I had to go through it. My analytic mind wanted to know why I was feeling so much pain and where it was coming from, but I had to get out of my head and just allow it all to unfold as it was meant to. I had to trust the Creator, and I had to trust myself. I had my medicines: sage, cedar, tobacco, and sweet grass. I prayed, I smudged, I cleansed my house, I cried out in pain and in anger.

During this whole process, I knew there were dark spirits in my house. I would see their shadows, peeking around corners, watching me. I often attracted those dark spirits when I was vulnerable and going through something very emotional. I was getting a bit fed up with spiritual warfare. But even in my weakened state, I knew that I was protected.

A Lakota woman I'd met, who lived in South Dakota, was aware of the battle I was having with myself. She told me that a pipe ceremony was being conducted for me, on the night of a full moon. So I knew, that in spite of the dark forces that were hovering around, waiting for me give up, that I was receiving help from the most powerful forces that be.

On the fifth day, I was feeling much better. I was sitting at my computer in the bedroom, with my back to the rest of the house. Molly always had to be in whichever room I was in, even the bathroom. Without turning around, I felt her come in and knew she was behind me. I turned around to look at her, and there was no Molly. *That's funny,* I thought, *I knew I felt her come in.* I went back to my computer and felt a very strong presence behind me again. I turned to see if Molly had come in, but again, she hadn't. Then, I knew. I was not alone. Whatever or whoever was in my bedroom, had a most loving and comforting presence.

When I returned to work, I felt great. As I said, my supervisor understood the necessity for the work I did on myself; however, Anthony, the director, had this to say to me: "I need to be able to depend on you to be *here*. You have a responsibility to this job and to your clients." I felt I'd be an even greater asset to my clients by continuing to heal and become stronger, but didn't tell him that.

A couple of days later, I was checking my email. There was one from a man whom I'd never met. He said he was Lakota, from Porcupine, South Dakota, and that Tunkasila (the Grandfathers) had told him that I "Walked in a sacred manner," and that I needed help. He said if I chose to not respond, that it would be okay. Well, I knew that Spirit worked in strange ways and used several mediums to give someone a message. I was floored! I just started to cry, because I had specifically asked for a Lakota teacher in my pipe ceremony with Henry, and here he was. I wondered why this man had waited until I had walked through my pain, alone, to give me that message. I figured that it was because the Creator needed me to realize the extent of my own power and to trust *Him* to help me. I responded to the man, "Who are you?" He told me, "I'm just a teacher who teaches teachers, to teach." *All right*, I thought, *why not?*

My mom and my pop had cautioned me about trusting other Indians who came into my life, telling me that they would help me in a spiritual way. My mom was afraid I'd be taken in by a so-called medicine person, and that my spirit would be taken. I'd wished that she had more faith in me, that she knew I wouldn't be that gullible. But she knew how trusting I was with the wrong people, so I really couldn't blame her for her fears. Yet, I kept the subject of my teacher to myself, I didn't want her to worry.

For the next several months, I was to undergo the most profound experience of my entire life. But I wasn't the best student in the beginning. After my initial trust in my teacher, I found myself questioning his motives. "What do you really want from me?" I questioned, after about a month of working with him. I'd become suspicious all of a sudden. He responded by telling me that the proof was in the fruit, that was borne from the tree. So I had to ask myself, was I being harmed by our teacher-student relationship? No. In fact, I had never felt more alive, nor had I ever felt more of a passion for living. And that's saying a lot for someone who's always seen suicide as an option. It's just that it seemed too good to be true.

My teacher was, by far, the most humble person I've ever known. "Our relationship is reciprocal," he'd say. "You are also my teacher, and I am your student." All he asked of me was to teach others who sought my help, in the ways that he was teaching me. He said that I was also a teacher who would teach others, and that they in turn would teach others, the things I was learning. He explained to me what it meant to walk, Canku Luta (the Red Road). The Red Road represents one who is walking in balance, living right, and following the rules of the Creator, with reverence. "It means living in harmony with all of creation," he explained. Walking the Red Road was not easy, but I believed it was the only way for me.

We communicated daily through emails and phone calls. I felt myself changing. I asked my teacher about that painful and otherworldly experience I'd gone through. I needed to know what that was all about. "You're being prepared, physically and emotionally, for what's coming," he said. "What do you mean? What is it that's *coming*?" I asked. "You are becoming stronger and will have the wisdom and the knowledge to help those who will seek your help, during the rough times that are ahead."

I was somewhat aware of the prophecies, future predictions regarding the end of days, but I didn't really understand my place in all of that, or why I'd been chosen to be of help. My teacher said that many are called, but that few are willing to do the work. He said it was because of the hard life I had led, and the changes I had made, that I was being called. I knew that to truly walk the Red Road, would mean making a complete commitment to that way of life. I had to ask myself, "Was I willing to make such a huge commitment?"

"There will be a time when you will feel like you are a snake shedding skin," my teacher said. About a week after he told me that, I was driving home from Zia Pueblo. I had the strangest sensation of wanting to pull something from my shoulders and down my arms. Then I remembered what my teacher had said. I was shedding old skin.

At that point in my work with my teacher, I was experiencing things on a whole new level that was not of the physical. It can be difficult for someone who hasn't experienced the life-changing transformations that I speak of, to understand what I'm talking about. But they were a necessary part of my spiritual evolvement.

I'd felt like the "call" was within me for several years: the call to be of service to others, to be a beacon to light the way, to be a teacher and a guide. There was a reason that I chose to live a difficult and traumatic life. I had to walk through the dark forest and face my demons and myself. I didn't do it without support, but there were many times when I had to do it alone, with only the Creator guiding me.

Always, when I reached the end of myself, when I felt that the pain could get no worse, I found the beginning of the Sacred—relief—healing—peace. I told myself years before, that if I was going to be clean and sober, I wasn't going to live a mediocre life and merely exist. I wanted to go as far as I could, down that rabbit hole of discovery and truth.

When I was counseling, I always made it a point to ask my clients, "Why are you here? Are you here to drink your life away—to just survive?" Many of them had never been asked such a question. I preferred to go straight to the heart of the matter.

My teacher always gave me homework and riddles to figure out. I would spend hours and days, trying to come up with the answer. My first assignment was, "What is the most important part of the wheel?" He said to picture a wagon wheel. "The center of the wheel," I answered. "Nope." "The rim?" "Nope." "The spokes?" "Wrong again." He finally gave me a clue, and I realized that the most important part of the wheel is not seen. It's what the wheel does that is most important. He always had to remind me that the unseen is more important than the seen. "Cante Iste, listen with your heart," he would tell me. Just as I finished writing this last sentence, I happened to look up at the TV. While I've been writing this book, I have been listening to a meditative music channel on TV. It helps me stay focused and grounded. It displays the name of the song, as well as the artist. Something made me look up just now, and you won't believe this, but the piece being played is by a Lakota man. The name of the song is "Listen with your heart!" I'll take that as a message from my teacher. Okay, big brother, I got that loud and clear. Wopila (Thank you). I love it when that happens.

My teacher told me to be aware of times when I had only the mouse's view of things. It was important, he told me, to have the eagle's view, to see the big picture and not to get stuck in so much earth plane pettiness: to remember what is really important, to be present enough to hear my guidance, and to remember that I'm not in charge, that there is a higher purpose for the things that happen. He'd get upset with me when I would tell him how angry I'd gotten with someone. He called them *sandpaper people,* because they would rub me the wrong way. "Never allow outside circumstances to control you." That was, and is, one of my most difficult life lessons.

In March of 2006, my teacher, who had been sick off and on for a couple of months, became seriously ill. I was really scared. I had become much too dependent on him as my lifeline to Wakan Tanka, and I was only just beginning my lessons with him. But he had told me earlier on, that we didn't have much time. When I asked him if he was going to die, he said that our relationship wouldn't end if he died, but that he would still be helping me from the other side (Just as he did a few minutes ago). That wasn't much comfort. He had become the single most important person in my life.

It had been about a month since I'd been in contact with my teacher, but I had gone through some powerful experiences that enabled me to have a deeper sense of "knowing" about myself, who I really am and how to stand in my own power. When I contacted his wife to find out how he was, she said that he was going in and out of consciousness. I told her to tell him what I had come to realize about myself since we'd last communicated. This was his response: "These things are those I was shown before we began our walk on Canku Luta Wakan. You have been timid, afraid, and very protective, and with good reason. Now, you have experienced the personal presence of the Wakan (Sacred) in your Ni (soul), and you know the source of the circle of life. Yes, little sister, you can ride the wind, you can honor the thunder, you are free of fear and lack of confidence. Those things that were so important, so satisfying, the bandages you used in the past, are gone and forgotten in the council fires between us and with Wakan Tanka, your Tunkasila. You did not learn anything from me, remember, I was the student learning to be the teacher. You taught me well. You taught me patience. You taught me not to react when doubted, wopila tanka (big thanks). Those teachings you feel you received from me, were directly for you, from Wakan Tanka, and you have received them and entered them into your circle of life. I am so very proud of you. I accept you as part of the heritage I leave on my earth walk. What you do, I will have a piece of. What you say, I will have a piece of. It is the energy we share. It is our relationship in the circle of life, and the self-empowerment granted to us by Wakan Tanka, that reaches out and gathers our brothers and sisters to the traditions and the old ways. I know that you *know,* that you know, as I promised you so long ago. Little sister, never ever forget or move your eagle eyes from the true provider of wisdom, no matter the package it comes to you in." He ended with, "Go now, hokahe! Wakan Tanka nici un" (May the Great Spirit walk with you).

My teacher went to the spirit world not long after that last message. I cried and cried for missing him. The relationship with a teacher can be very intimate. He knew me better than my own family did because of what his "helpers" and the Grandfathers had shown him. I will forever be grateful to this humblest of men. And I know he is with me still, protecting me, guiding me, and showing me what I need to do, to continue walking in a sacred manner. But sometimes, it can be very difficult.

In April of 2006, I decided to start the HepC treatments. My joints were beginning to hurt and my viral count had shot up to almost two million. Because of the strain of HepC I had, my doctor told me I would only have to be on the treatments for six months, instead of a year. That wasn't much consolation. I was a big baby when it came to being sick for even one day.

We had just hired a new substance abuse counselor, a Native man from Canada, so I felt it was a good time to take care of the hepatitis. I made arrangements with my work to take six months of medical leave, but told them I'd continue facilitating my weekly educational groups, a series of classes I'd developed for the program a couple of months before.

Anthony was not happy about my having to take such a long period off from work, but he couldn't prevent me from doing so. I'd been with that agency for four years while staff members came and went. I'd been stretched pretty thin by the demands of having to fill in for the lack of staff during the years, so this was my turn and my time, to take care of a serious medical condition.

My doctor informed me of the side effects of the Interferon treatments. He said that it was much like chemotherapy, but unlike chemo, whereby a person had a few days of feeling well, I would not. I'd be sick every day. The doctor also said that studies had shown that if a patient already suffered from depression, there was a chance of them becoming suicidal while on the HepC medication. Wow, this thing was sounding better and better all the time. I was set to begin treatments the first week of May. I was 55 years old, and that was not in my favor.

It was about 7:00pm and a week before I was scheduled to begin the Interferon treatments. I was sitting in my bedroom, meditating, when there was a loud knocking on my door. I didn't feel like answering it. I didn't want to be disturbed. But it continued. I thought I may as well see who it was, since my peaceful state had been so rudely interrupted.

I opened the front door. The young man standing there asked, "Do you have a big dog with a lot of fur?" "What? Yes!" "It was hit by a car," he said. "Oh, no," I moaned, as I held on to the wall to steady myself, to which he quickly responded, "It's still alive." I ran outside and saw Molly lying to the side of the paved road, in the dirt. I asked the young man to help me put her in the car. He refused and left; he was afraid she'd bite him, he said. Maybe he was the guy who hit her.

There was a lot of blood on the pavement, so I knew that Molly had been run over in that spot. The poor thing had managed to drag herself off of the paved road. I cried out, "Molly!" and her head came up immediately.

I went inside, grabbed a blanket, scooped her up as she cried out in pain, and laid her on the passenger seat. Her leg was bloodied and dangling. I wouldn't allow myself to think about how bad it was, as I drove the 20 miles to the hospital in a daze. I had to keep calling her name every time she closed her eyes. I wasn't going to let her die on me.

When I arrived at the veterinary hospital, I ran inside and yelled for help. Two of the vet techs came out with a small stretcher and got her from the car to the stretcher, as she yelped in agony. They rushed her inside and through the double doors to the treatment rooms.

As I waited for some word of her condition, I cried openly and paced the lobby. Finally, one of the doctors came out and told me that Molly's left hip was out of its socket, the toes of her right hind leg had been crushed, and the skin of the same leg had been torn away completely. The doctor assured me she was in no pain, as they'd given her medication and were stabilizing her. She would have to undergo surgery in the morning on her left hip.

Next it was, "How are you going to pay for this?" I could barely think straight and I was being asked about money. The doctor directed me to the financial staff person. I told the woman that I only had $400.00 in savings. She told me that if I qualified for the hospital loan I could get up to $1,000.00. She ran a credit check. I qualified for the loan of $1,000.00, which would go toward my dog's treatment. Then I wrote a check for $400.00.

As I drove home, I cried and I prayed that Molly would be all right. I couldn't believe what had happened. She never left the yard when I was home; she always had to be near me. She'd been hit right in front of the house. She must have dashed out to chase a cat. I was so angry at the person who hit her and then left her out there like that. How could anyone do that to my girl? I felt horrible that I hadn't shut that damn cattle gate.

I went to work the next morning and told the staff what had happened to Molly. Most of them knew her because I often took her to work with me. They were sorry to hear about the accident and some thought I should have her put to sleep. That was absolutely out of the question, even after I talked to the doctor that morning and was told I'd have to come up with an additional $2,000.00 for costs that were adding up as we spoke. Molly's lungs had filled with fluid during the night and they had taken care of that as well. If there was a way to save my girl, I was going to find it. Later that day, I went to a bank to apply for a loan.

When I got to the animal hospital after work, I was taken behind the double doors. As I approached Molly's cage, I saw that she was hooked up to an IV, and her right hind leg was wrapped. I opened the door to the little cage and squeezed my body half-way in. She opened her eyes. When she realized it was me she began howling. She was letting me know how scared she was and that she was really hurting. She howled for a good twenty minutes as I held her and told her, "Oh honey, I know, I know." It was so hard to see her like that.

The bank approved my loan, thank God. As soon as that check was in my hand, I cashed it and rushed it over to the hospital.

After Molly had been in the hospital for about a week, I received a call from her doctor. Molly's leg was infected from the open wound where skin had once covered it. The doctor said that if the leg were amputated, the infection wouldn't spread. I told her to take the leg.

I went to get my first injection of Interferon that week. "You may feel nauseous when you get home," the doctor said, but I didn't feel sick that day or for the rest of the week. I was so glad because I knew that when Molly was home, I'd have to be able to help her.

I'd been on medical leave for two weeks the day I went to pick up Molly. Before she was brought out to me, the vet tech gave me her medications, and instructions for her care. She had stiches on both hips and would need to wear the plastic cone around her head, so that she didn't lick and cause infection. I was outside by the car when Molly was brought out to me. She was walking on her front legs, and the tech had a sling around her midsection to hold up the rest of her body. Her left hind leg was taped up so that she couldn't use it, because it would pull the stitches out from the hip operation. The tech put her in the back seat, and we were off. When we got home, I had a hard time getting Molly out of the car and ended up dropping her on the gravel. My next door neighbor, a young man, was standing in his yard. I yelled for him to help me. As we carried her inside the house, he could barely look at Molly because of the appearance of her amputated leg. I was afraid he was going to faint on me. What a wimp.

I had everything set up for Molly and her care. I had an air mattress in the living room for me to sleep on so I could be near her. I had piled up several blankets next to it for her to lie on. I had a baby bottle to feed her water and frozen peas for cold packs. It would be a lot of work; like caring for an infant.

Around the third week of my own treatments, I began feeling ill. For the first couple of weeks, I'd been pleasantly surprised when I didn't get sick. What I hadn't been told was that it took a while for the Interferon to start building up in the system. The only good thing that I noticed in the beginning was that my joint pain was completely gone. I would have preferred the joint pain any day, to what was to come.

I went to work to teach my classes for about the first month or so, but had to stop because I was so sick. I'd heard that most people had worked while on the treatments, but I was not one of them. I became extremely anemic and weak. My emotions were becoming extreme. I was either so angry that I was raging, or I felt depressed and hopeless. I began to lose patience with poor Molly being sick, and the effort it took to help her recover. And Molly hated that plastic cone she had to wear around her neck. She'd pull it off and lick her stiches. When the hip on her good leg started looking red and puss-filled, I had to take her in for another operation to clean it up. When it did heal, the tape that bound her left hind leg was removed, but the leg had begun to atrophy. I had to massage it and do full range of motion exercises with it. She didn't like it, but it had to be done. I wanted her to be able to walk again.

As Molly got better, I became sicker. I'd take her to the deck in the back, set her on a blanket, and lie out there with her. She loved her backyard, and I knew she missed walking the perimeter. When she started moving around again on her own, she would just drag herself along, barely able to lift her one hind leg. After about five months, she was on her own and had healed completely. The more she used her back leg, the better she got at walking. My heart broke, remembering how she used to jump and how she loved to run.

My doctor had told me that the Interferon would affect my ability to fight off an illness or an infection. I was on antibiotics for a sinus infection a couple of times. I constantly had the taste of metal in my mouth and blood. I was having severe nosebleeds that I had a hard time stopping. I developed sores in my mouth, and it hurt to eat.

The year before, I'd gone to a training to learn an acupuncture procedure called Acu-Detox. Acu-Detox was a procedure that was first developed in New York and was found to have profound effects on heroin addicts, but it also worked for alcoholics. It involves the placement of five needles in each ear.

My friend and co-worker, Mary, and I, went to learn this procedure so that we could use it on our clients. While there, I was sharing some things of a spiritual nature with another participant. The woman said she was a minister with the Universal Brotherhood Movement. She said that I would be a perfect fit for the ministry as well. The movement sponsored and ordained ministers who were gifted in some way; who were not recognized in mainstream ministries. I thought a little about it but soon forgot, until one day, when I was talking to a man on the phone named Yellow Horse, who was Cherokee and Creek Indian. He also suggested that I become a minister with the Brotherhood Movement, and gave me the name of a woman he knew in Phoenix, who was one of their ministers. Well, when I hear something like that twice, I take it as a sign.

It was late summer when I contacted the woman, Janet, who described the ministry to me. After hearing my story, she agreed to sponsor me. The organization had its base in Florida, so I contacted them and asked for an application. I had to write about my life and the changes and healings I'd gone through, that enabled me in my work as a counselor. I had to share how I'd been gifted by Creator as a result of my personal growth.

Janet contacted me once my application for the Brotherhood had been received and accepted. She knew that I was sick and agreed to fly out to Albuquerque to perform my ordination in October. I invited three friends to be witness to the event: Dr. Linda Sanchez, my supervisor from work, and Mary. I also invited Brandon, the man who had done the graphics for my CD. He and I had become friends. Linda wasn't able to come, but gave me a very special card and gift.

I prayed and smudged the house before anyone came. I was feeling very weak, but also excited about the ceremony. Janet was right on time. It was good to finally meet her. She brought a friend with her, a Navajo woman.

Soon after my friends arrived, the ceremony began. It was a beautiful event. It felt as if I were getting married. I had vows to take and agreements and responsibilities to agree to.

When Janet presented me to everyone as Reverend Sheila, it became all too real, and I cried. At the end, everyone stood and we formed a circle. Molly had been lying down, but decided to get up and seat herself in the center of the circle. She looked up at us all and took in the wonderful energy, as Janet said a prayer.

When I woke up the next morning, despite my being ill, I felt a high that was unlike any I'd ever experienced. Just what I was going to do with my ministry, I wasn't sure. I was hoping that it would become clearer to me as time went on. But for the time being, my ministry would be my substance-abusing clients.

The Interferon had built up in my system to such a high level that it was really starting to show. People told me that I looked grey. When I was in the shower washing my hair, I'd watch as about fifty strands lay in the tub. I had bald patches and was seriously considering getting a wig. I cut my hair instead and wore hats.

It was the end of October. I had one more injection to go. I'd had my labs done at the three month point, and it showed I had cut the viral load by more than half. I was done! But I had a cough that wouldn't go away and I was feeling weaker.

When I went for my last doctor's visit that Friday, I expressed this to my doctor. He had me breathe deeply, as he checked my lungs with his stethoscope. He said that everything sounded good and clear. I went home wondering, "Why then, do I feel so sick? Why am I having a fever every night?"

That night I went to bed and fell asleep. I suddenly found myself sitting on the edge of the bed, having a conversation out loud with someone...a spirit? I was talking to this entity about wanting to give up...I was that sick. It felt as if this spirit was telling me to hold on. Afterwards, I looked around me, wondering what the heck had just happened.

By Sunday, I knew that something was terribly wrong. I called a neighbor, an older Mexican woman who adored Molly, and asked if she would watch her for me, because I was going to the hospital. Then I called an ambulance; I was too sick to drive. When it arrived, the EMTs had to help me step up into the ambulance because I was extremely weak. My medical insurance was with Lovelace, so I was taken to Lovelace Women's Hospital in Albuquerque.

I was given an MRI and told that I had a hiatal hernia, which was minor, and that I had double pneumonia. Who knew how long I'd had pneumonia? What the hell was wrong with Dr. Quack, that he missed something as basic as that when he checked my lungs?!

I'd been on so many antibiotics over the past few months that the doctors were concerned that my system would be immune to further antibiotics. I was deathly ill. I was put on the most powerful antibiotic possible and was on oxygen and an IV. I told the first nurse I had, that I wanted the nicotine patch, because I didn't want to go into withdrawal.

The second day I was there, I contacted my mom, my children, my job, and Mary. I didn't know if I would get well, so I felt I had to let everyone know. I was still running a fever, and that was a concern. I was barely able to manage getting to the bathroom by myself. I'd have to cart my IV on wheels, and a couple of times I didn't make it in time and wet myself.

Mary came to visit me the third day I was there. She was appalled when I told her that not once had my nursing assistants been in to bathe me, change my gown, or my bed sheets. She marched right out to the nurses' station, and I could hear her letting them have it. I was so sick; I felt helpless to stand up for myself. As soon as Mary left, the assistant came and took care of me. During my early years as a nurse's aide, I'd never treated a patient so carelessly.

The antibiotics were starting to work, and I was taken off oxygen. But I wasn't to be released until I no longer had a fever, and was able to get out of bed and walk. So I started getting up and walking short distances. I couldn't believe how much the pneumonia had taken out of me, and how sick I still was, but at least I felt I was going to make it. On the fifth day, I no longer had a fever and was discharged.

I got a new doctor because I didn't trust the old one. At my first visit, I had my lab work in hand when the doctor entered the room to see me. The first thing he said was, "You are a very sick lady!" Then I told him I'd just completed the hepatitis treatments and he said, "No wonder." He told me that my white blood count was seriously low. At that time, I was also suffering from diarrhea. The Interferon had caused me to have colitis, a digestive disorder. The doctor gave me a prescription for more antibiotics and suggested I go on the BRAT diet: bananas, rice, applesauce, and toast. The BRAT diet helps with diarrhea.

So now I'm home, still weak, and can't leave the house because of diarrhea. I'm wearing a diaper and feeling like my body is not my own. I just wanted to be done with all the being sick shit, literally. Thank God Molly was doing well, because I was sicker now than when I was taking the Interferon.

It was a slow process, but by January, I began to feel a lot better and my hair started growing back. That month I was well enough to return to work, but my doctor wouldn't let work full time until March. My latest lab work showed no sign of the hepatitis virus.

During the long period away from work, I'd had a lot of time to think. I thought about my career as a substance abuse counselor and how it wasn't that fulfilling anymore. But I had to make a living and would have to put off having my dream job, whatever that was, for a while. There was one change I could make, though. I was tired of living in the desert. I wanted to live in a place of beauty, with water and big trees.

I went online and found a position open with a residential program in South Lake Tahoe, California, called Sierra Recovery. They were looking for a lead counselor, so I sent them my resume. They called and said they'd like to interview me, but that it had to be in person. I felt confident that I'd get the job, and so I bought a ticket and flew there.

It was May, and I was blown away by the beautiful lake and the smell of the pines. It was intoxicating. During the interview, I was asked the standard questions, and felt I answered them thoughtfully, and that my answers attested to my knowledge and experience. I was informed that if I got the position, I'd have to work toward getting my California certification. I told them that as a lead counselor, I'd have to get at least $17.00 an hour to make it worth my while. They told me that they'd be in touch as soon as they made their decision. A week later, I received the phone call. I got the position and the salary I asked for. I gave my job two weeks' notice and handed in my resignation.

I had lots to do before I left for California. I put my furniture on craigslist and sold it all. Then I found a young couple who were willing to take over the mortgage on my home. I went to U-Haul and had a hitch put on my car. They hooked me up to a 5x8 foot trailer, the first of many trailers that I would tow, and Molly and I said goodbye to Albuquerque.

It was summer in Lake Tahoe, and the town was full of tourists. Luckily, I was able to find a nice, rustic, dog-friendly cabin to rent. My first day of employment was about familiarizing myself with policies and procedures of the treatment program. I was to be in charge of staff scheduling, which would prove to be a real headache. I was given a client caseload and got busy getting to know my clients and their histories.

Well, I got the water and the big tress, but on the other hand, I was encountering problems I hadn't anticipated. My credit took a nosedive due to the lapse in getting a paycheck. I'd written to all my creditors, explaining the situation, but there was no compromising with them. In addition, my place of employment, Sierra Recovery, was fast becoming problematic for me. I began feeling as if I'd made a mistake. But I refused to return to Albuquerque and feel like a failure.

I was continuously being undermined in my position as the lead counselor by my supervisor, and I wasn't getting the cooperation of the staff when it came to scheduling them. There were also counselors who were jealous of me because my position threatened them. Then, my supervisor began making unethical decisions in regards to the clients.

When the program director got wind of my plan to attend the next board meeting, where I was planning on voicing my concerns, she called me into her office and gave me my last check, which included shut-up money. I could have kept my mouth shut and just done my job and not complained, but that wasn't me. If I saw something that wasn't right, I had to do something about it, even if it meant losing my job. I wasn't willing to give up my ethics to work in another dysfunctional program.

I'd received my California Certification, the CADAC II, so I had options now. Unfortunately, there were no other treatment programs in South Lake Tahoe, so it would mean another move. As much as I disliked large cities like Sacramento, I didn't have a choice. At least there would be more job opportunities there. So once again, I was on the road with my forever faithful buddy, Molly, pulling a 5x8 foot U-Haul trailer.

I found a place to live right away. It was a little house with three small bedrooms, just outside of Sacramento.

Molly loved our new place. The backyard was about half an acre that ended at a creek. You'd have thought she'd be happy having all that room to roam around in...but no.

Twice, when I returned home from an errand, I found a notice on the door from animal control. She'd been picked up after having crossed a major boulevard. It's a miracle she wasn't killed, dragging herself along on three legs. She'd done the same thing in Bernalillo. Whenever I left her, she just had to be where there were people.

One evening, I let her out in the front yard, which was fenced in. After about an hour, I went to get her, and she was gone. She had escaped! She couldn't jump anymore because of her missing leg. She either squeezed through the wooden slats or dug her way out. I got in my car and went up and down the street calling her, but no Molly. I searched for a long time, then went back home, hoping she'd show up on her own. I was beside myself. I slept very little that night, because I kept going to look outside to see if she was there.

The next morning, I made a flyer on my computer with her picture on it, printed several copies, and posted them around the neighborhood. I was unbelievably depressed. I cried and prayed that she would come back, or that someone would find her. Molly had been my companion for six years, and I was desolate without her. I loved that dog so much. Most people don't experience the intensity of grief over a dog the way I did, and I wasn't ashamed of it.

That night, I sat in my recliner and tried to watch TV, but I couldn't concentrate on any of the programs. I kept looking out the screen door for any sign of movement. Molly had already been missing for over 24 hours, and I wasn't feeling hopeful. Here I was, in a strange city, with no job, no support system, and no paycheck coming in. And I was handling it. But I couldn't do it without my buddy with me. I didn't know how I was going to go on without her.

About 6:00pm, I heard a man's voice asking, "Is this your dog?" I jumped up and opened the screen door. There she was! I hugged the young man, saying, "You just saved my life!" A bit dramatic, I know, but that's how I felt. He told me that he lived across the street and that when he came home from work the previous night, Molly was in his front yard. He didn't know where she lived so he took her inside his house. The next morning he left for work, leaving Molly inside. When he returned home that evening, he let her out, and Molly ran over to my house.

My job search was going nowhere. When I was just about ready to throw in the towel, I found a job opening for a substance abuse counselor. It was with the Behavioral Health Program in a town called, Mariposa. They wanted me to interview right away.

Mariposa was east of Merced and was very rustic, nestled in the outskirts of Yosemite National Park. The facility itself was across the street from a creek.

After the interview, I went back home, and anxiously awaited that phone call. When it came, I was happier than I'd been in a long time. My new job was a county position, so it came with excellent benefits, as well as a $300.00 a month stipend. My pay was $17.00 an hour. I would be on probation for a year, after which I'd get a 5% raise.

My friend, Olga, who lived in Merced at the time, offered to let Molly and me stay with her until I found my own place in Mariposa. Mariposa was about thirty miles northeast of Merced.

One day, when I was at work, another staff person had heard that I was looking for a place to live. She said that she had a rental, and asked if I wanted to go have a look at it that afternoon.

We drove down a dirt road that looped around through trees and over a creek, to a house that lay completely hidden from the highway. It had a big deck in back that looked down upon the creek, with ducks swimming in it. I was already sold, just from what I saw of the outside of the property. When I saw the inside, I fell in love with it. It was so big and roomy. There were two large bedrooms, a fireplace and lots of storage and cupboard space. There were lots of windows to let in the light, and the view was gorgeous. I completed an application and practically begged the woman to rent it to me. She did, and I could've kissed her. The rent was only $800.00.

    I found out where the river was. One Saturday, I put Molly in the car and we drove there. I parked the car on the side of the road, and we made our way down a steep embankment to a patch of sand. Molly had never liked getting in water, which was weird; most golden retrievers and shepherds love the water. In Tahoe, I would shove her into the water at the beach. She would swim, but head straight back to shore. You should've seen me trying to get her into the tub for a bath. As soon as she heard me turn the tub faucet on, she was outa there…and tricking her, never worked. I'd have to capture her and pull her by her collar, then lift her big, heavy body into the water. Once there, she'd freeze and allow me to bathe her, with a look of sheer terror on her mug.

    The Merced River was clean and clear. I wanted to get in and do some swimming. I pushed Molly in, and suddenly, the current was taking her downstream. I jumped in and grabbed her, bringing her back to shore. *Well, so much for that,* I thought. Molly glued herself to that small bit of sandy beach while I swam a bit. When I decided it was time to head back, I looked up toward the road and wondered how we were going to climb back up that rocky embankment.

This 58 year-old lady and her three-legged dog were quite the sight, as we struggled to crawl up that hill to the road above us. Molly kept sliding down, and I kept pushing her back up, until she finally took hold and gathered momentum. I was right behind her, with rocks sliding down from under my feet. I had to grab on to small branches that stuck out between the boulders, but I finally managed to pull myself up.

Molly loved chasing critters. The poor girl would see a deer and be ready for a full blown run, forgetting that she could no longer do that, and would end up hopping with her three legs, but she'd be bookin,' despite her handicap. Molly, who seldom barked, began barking after dark when she was on the deck. When she started with her low "woof, woof," followed by three deep barks, I knew that there were deer or coyote nearby. Like me, Molly was in her element.

The first week of our living in the house, I would leave Molly on the back deck, while I was at work. But she soon destroyed the small wooden gate and down the steps she went, to freedom. Then one day, my coworker gave me a dog runner. I attached it to a couple of metal poles on the deck, like a clothes line.

I left one morning, with Molly attached to the runner. When I returned home, I went to the back deck to unleash her. She had escaped! The metal pole was bent from her trying to bring it down, and the leash lay mockingly, on the wooden deck floor. That darn dog had managed to unclip the leash that was attached to her collar. I called for her around our property, and soon saw her hopping up the dirt road toward the house, with her happy face on. I was so relieved to see her that I couldn't be mad.

Then I decided to leave her inside the house when I left for work. One day, I came home from work, went inside the house, and wasn't immediately greeted by my dear sweet Molly. I walked into the living room to find the sliding glass door lying on the deck. That dog had shoved the door off its hinges! Thank goodness it didn't break. From then on, I just let her run free on the property.

I loved my place. I would sit on my deck and watch the hawks as they swooped down, looking for food, in and around the pond. Once, I saw one dive back up with a snake in its beak.

I told my friends back in Albuquerque that I had finally found my dream house. I felt very blessed that things had finally turned around for me. I was so tired of moving, and could see myself living in that house for many, many years. It had the combination of everything I wanted and needed, to feel safe and at peace. It had natural beauty and quiet. It was spacious. I've always needed a lot of room to move around in.

One hot summer day, I came home from work to find a letter on my countertop. It was a 30 day notice to vacate. I immediately went into a state of shock. I called the landlord and wanted to know why I was being evicted. She told me that the home was going to be demolished. I couldn't believe I'd heard her right. "But this is the best place I've ever lived and it's my dream home," I sobbed.

As the days went by, I began experiencing all of my PTSD symptoms: depression, rage, and paranoia. The rug had been pulled out from under me and as usual, when I got a shock like that, I was badly triggered. I hadn't seen this one coming at all. I presumed that she was afraid of Molly destroying the place. As it was, I had to replace a screen door that Molly had demolished during one of her great escapes.

I found another rental that was a further drive to work. It was right off of the main highway and was $50.00

more rent a month. The three-bedroom house was newer. There was a grass lawn in the front with rose bushes. The roses didn't last long because the deer would eat them. There was plenty of space outside for Molly to go exploring.

I missed working with and being around Natives. I found out there was a program there in Mariposa called Miwu Mati, which served the tribes in the surrounding areas. One day, I went there to check it out. I met the receptionist, Judy, and I immediately liked her. I went there often after that, just to hang out. It was refreshing and comfortable being around other Indians. It was a nice change from behavioral health, where it was difficult for a *wild woman*, such as myself, to fit in.

Mariposa Behavioral Health received a grant to assist the Native outpatient program. I was chosen to work there one day a week as their substance abuse counselor. I was really happy about that. I already had a couple of Native clients that I was seeing at my office at the behavioral health location. I chose Friday as my day to work at Miwu Mati. When I didn't have a client, Judy and I would talk about our lives, and we became very close. Sometimes I'd take Molly to work with me. Judy enjoyed having her there.

Meanwhile, back at Behavioral Health, I was beginning to feel bored and unfulfilled again. But I had financial security with my position, and I told myself that I could retire in four years. The closer it got to the end of my year on probation, the more excited I got about that 5% raise. I'd been told by several of the staff that once an employee made it through probation, it was close to impossible to get fired. I was also told, "If they don't think you fit in, they can let you go for no reason, so don't get your hopes up." Well, I knew that wouldn't happen to me.

I had a client who volunteered to see me on a weekly basis at my primary office. Joseph was an alcoholic from one of the local tribes. He was doing some good work with me and was trying hard to maintain his sobriety. During one session, he shared about certain responsibilities he held within his tribe. He realized that in order to fulfill his responsibilities, he must stay sober. It was one of those sessions I often had with my Native clients; whereby, the level of talking was elevated to a higher plane. There was a powerful energy with us in the room that day. When the session was over, I told Joseph, "Now you know what you have to do." He left the office smiling and feeling positive.

The following week, I left a message at Joseph's house, reminding him of his appointment for that day; he was a no-show. The following day, Judy called me and asked if I'd heard about what had happened to Joseph. I said I hadn't. Judy said that the night before, Joseph walked across the road, drunk, and was struck down by a propane truck. He was dead! I couldn't believe it. It was so sad and such a loss. I was beyond tired of seeing my Indian people dying such senseless deaths, all because of alcohol.

It was April 4th, and a Friday. I was at the Tribal Program. My supervisor, Janna, who normally conducted our weekly supervision sessions at Miwu Mati on Fridays, called me and said she wanted me to return to Behavioral Health for our 4:00pm session. When I got there, she was very pleasant, telling me that we were going to meet in the director's office. I followed her, feeling confused and anxious. As soon as we sat down, the director looked at me and said, "You didn't pass your probationary period." I was stunned! "Can I ask why?" "No, by law we don't have to tell you. Here's your last paycheck. You're being paid through the rest of the month. You need to go and pack up your things." That was it. I walked back to my office, my legs feeling like rubber. Janna found me some boxes and I packed my belongings in a daze.

I drove straight to Judy's house. When I told her what happened, she was really upset. We were both angry that I wouldn't be able to serve the Native community at the tribal program. "Don't they know how much we need you here? Don't they care about the clients? They're really going to be upset," she said. I didn't stay long, but I felt that Judy was the only one I could talk to about what just happened. The next day, I applied for unemployment insurance.

Whenever I experienced the shock of being terminated from my employment, I went into survival mode. I wouldn't allow myself the luxury of falling apart. I got online right away to look for another job. A few weeks later, I received a letter from unemployment stating that I'd be receiving close to $400.00 per week. That was a huge relief.

Molly was having a hard time holding her bowels, and at times, she had difficulty getting up and walking. She was 11 years old, and I didn't know how much longer I'd have her with me. I made every day count, in case it would be the last. Nevertheless, she was still the same beautiful spirit who got excited upon hearing my car coming; who became animated when I played inside games with her. If anyone would have come to my front door over the past few years, when Molly and I were playing, they would have thought I was part dog myself. I'd get down on all fours with her and bark, or I'd run through the house while she tried to catch me. When I was in one of my moods, she would stay away from me until I came out of it. Molly loved massages, and I gave her many. She also liked meditative music and pow-wow songs. Both would put her right to sleep.

We had a very special relationship, and she was as attached to me, as I was to her. Sometimes, when I'd lie down next to her, she'd put her arm around me. Whenever I flew out of state I'd have to leave her at a kennel. The whole time I was gone, I'd be thinking about how I couldn't wait to get back to her. I loved those reunions.

It was 2009, and the country was in a recession. California was losing funding for many of their substance abuse programs, and the existing programs weren't taking on new hires. After several months of seeking employment within the state, and getting nowhere, I decided to look out of state. Only one program responded favorably to my résumé. It was in Rapid City, South Dakota.

Brian, who was Oglala Lakota, was the director of a program called Native Healing. It was a residential facility that had two components to it: substance abuse and codependency. Brian said he wanted to hire me and asked me to come out right away. So I took a chance and did just that.

I was excited as I made my way toward South Dakota. Before I left, I'd made arrangements to rent a three-bedroom mobile home in the town of Box Elder, just outside of Rapid City. After I arrived in Box Elder and got settled in, I put Molly in the car and went to meet my new boss and to see where I'd be working.

The Oglala Lakota Healing Program was comprised of two large houses, situated at the Sioux Sans hospital grounds. Brian gave me a quick tour, then told me it would be another week before I started working, due to some hold up at the main office in Pine Ridge.

Since I had some time on my hands, I decided to take a trip to Lincoln, Nebraska, to visit my friend Henry. He didn't have accommodations for Molly, so I had to put her in a kennel.

As soon as I arrived at Henry's house, he had me sit down to eat. He served me deer stew, and it was wonderful. After I ate, I put my things in the spare bedroom. When I went back out into the living room, we got caught up on what had been happening in our lives, even though we'd been in touch with each other during the past three years. Then he brought out his guitar and started playing his oldies, and I joined in to harmonize.

The next night, Henry performed a pipe ceremony for me. I was feeling good after the ceremony, until he told me that he had a lady in his life. I hadn't expected to hear that, but what's more, I hadn't expected to react the way I did to his good news. I should have been happy for him, that he'd found a good woman to share his life with. Instead, I said I had to have a cigarette and went outside to sit on the porch and smoke. He followed me out, asking me if I was okay. I started to cry, and told him that I felt really sad about him having a woman. He was very gracious about it and just let me cry and talk about how I felt. I hadn't realized that I was still very much attracted to Henry.

I received my South Dakota counseling certification shortly after I started working at the healing program. As a result, I was the only staff person qualified to perform certain client related tasks. I knew that *that* had to ruffle some feathers. But it was good to be around Lakotas. I must have gained five pounds in the first month because a couple of the staff ladies made fry bread on a regular basis, and it was hard to resist.

The program was not 12-Step based, but rather, a combination of traditional Lakota teachings and psychodrama. I understood the benefits of psychodrama; however, I didn't buy into the powerful techniques that were being used on our substance abuse residents. It was a 30-day program, and we were walking these guys through some intense grief and rage work, that most of them weren't ready to deal with, at such an early stage in their recovery.

It was in the beginning of January, 2010, that I began noticing a change in the way the other counselors interacted with me. I had felt at home with everyone, like I belonged, and that was important to me. Then, all of a sudden, I was being ignored and felt bad vibes coming from some of the staff.

As it turned out, one of the female counselors had been jealous of me because I was getting a bigger paycheck than she was. She admitted this to me one day in a staff group when she said, "I have a Bachelor's degree, and you just have the certification. I should be making more than you!" "Well, that's not my fault," I told her. What is more, not only did the woman have a B.A. in an unrelated field, she was much younger than I, and had very little experience in the field of substance abuse treatment.

Then, another counselor (in training) told me, "I don't like you, but I don't know why." "So what am I supposed to do with that?" I questioned. Oh, it was one thing after another. I saw no solution to my dilemma, especially since the *sandpaper counselors* weren't willing to resolve their issues with me. My depression was being triggered. It got to the point where I hated going to work.

On February the 4th, I told my supervisor that I could no longer be effective as a counselor in such a hostile work environment. I packed my things and went home to Molly. The next day was my sobriety birthday. I'd been clean and sober for 11 years, but I wasn't in a celebrating mood.

The program director called, asking me to reconsider quitting. But there was no way I was going to return. I wasn't willing to risk my mental well-being for any job.

I got on the Internet and starting looking for positions in and around Rapid City, and found nothing. I hated the thought of leaving South Dakota. It was such a beautiful and powerful place, but the more I thought about it, the more I realized that I missed Albuquerque. That's where my support system was. I knew I never should have left there in the first place. It had really cost me financially and emotionally.

As the days went by, I began feeling better just being away from that negative work environment. I'd joined the Curves for Women gym in Box Elder, so I continued to work out. It was the least I could do for my depressive state.

I called Marsha, a friend of mine in Albuquerque, and asked her if I could stay with her until I got back on my feet. She said that I could. I applied for unemployment right away and was sure I'd get it on the grounds of harassment.

On February the 20th, Molly and I would be "on the road again." She was 12 years old. She had been slowly losing her sight and her hearing. I told her to hang on because we were going home. There were a lot of people in Albuquerque who loved Molly; who would be thrilled to see her again. And I needed to be around friends when her time came to leave this world.

It was three days before we were leaving. I called U-Haul and reserved what I'd hoped would be my last 5x8 foot trailer, for my last move. I still had to find someone to help me pack it up.

I'd already taken Molly outside to go potty a couple of times that day, but she didn't even pee. That evening, when we returned from getting boxes, instead of her coming in the house, she went to the far end of the yard to lie down in the snow. I thought that was odd and called for her to come inside. She didn't want to. I went to her and coaxed her up, helping her walk up the ice-crusted stairs of the deck, and into the house.

I put food in her bowl. She went over to it, looked at it, and lay down next to it. A little later, she came over to me, stared into my eyes, and started shaking. I was becoming concerned at that point and said, "Molly, what's the matter baby?" I got on the carpet and had her lie down next to me. Somehow I knew to place my hands on her stomach. I channeled heat to that area and then began to massage her. I thought that she might be nervous about the move. Molly had always been sensitive to what I was feeling; she was probably just reacting to my being overwhelmed about starting over in Albuquerque. I let her lie there and I returned to my chair. Then she got up and tried to walk, but fell over. Now I was getting scared. *I'll bet it's an ear infection,* I thought, but then she started dry heaving and gagging. Something was very wrong, but I had no money to take her to the vet. It was getting late, so I decided to wait until the morning, and hoped that she would be fine by then. I didn't know what else to do. But neither of us slept that night. I could hear her bumping into things and hoped and prayed that it was only an ear infection.

The next morning, Molly wasn't any better. About 11:00am, she got up and was making her way to the front door when her body went rigid and she hit the floor with a thud. I rushed over to her. She was frothing at the mouth. I had to think. I couldn't lose it, not now.

I went into survival mode. Where was that damn animal hospital I'd seen? I grabbed the phone book and found the number. I called them, saying, "I'm bringing my dog in, she just had a seizure." "Okay Sheila," I said out loud, "get the car keys and your purse." I lifted Molly up, and rushed her out the door. Her head was flopping in my arms.

I shoved her limp body into the back seat of the car and tore off to the hospital.

I kept turning my head to check her. She was alive, but her tongue was hanging to the side of her mouth, and she wasn't moving. I prayed out loud as I drove those endless few miles to the hospital. I ran inside and yelled, "I need help!" An attendant followed me to the car, picked up my sweet Molly girl, and rushed her into a back room.

And I waited...and I prayed. Then the female attendant came out and asked me to follow her. I was numb as I walked with her to an empty room. The doctor would be in to see me soon, she said. I hated waiting...not knowing. The doctor came in and shut the door. *Oh, God,* I thought, when I saw the look on her face. I sat down. "She's been stabilized," she said. "We put her on oxygen and gave her an IV. She also has a catheter. At first we thought she may have eaten poison," the doctor continued, "but then we took an x-ray and found a large tumor in her stomach, it's cancer...and her kidneys are shutting down." I heard the words, but it was so surreal. "An operation would be very expensive," she went on, "and she's old...the humane thing to do...put her down." A gasping sound caught in my throat. *Cancer?...put her down?* It took a moment for that to register in my brain. *No, this can't be happening. Not now. Not when we're going back home to Albuquerque in two days. This doctor has stood here, saying the very same thing to dog owners hundreds of times,* I'm thinking. *But this is the only time for me...to decide my Molly's fate. I know what the right thing to do is...but...I'm not ready...* Then the word, "okay" came out of my mouth. "I'll bring her in so you can have some time alone with her," the doctor said, and left the room.

I fumbled in my huge purse for my cell phone. With shaking hands I dialed her number. "Mom," I sobbed.

"Sheila, what's wrong?" "I have to put Molly to sleep. Oh, Mom, it hurts so bad," I cried. "Oh sweetheart, I'm so sorry," she said. She knew how close I was to my dog. Just then, the attendant came in with Molly in her arms. "I have to go, they just brought her in."

The attendant placed Molly on the floor on a blanket, then left. I lay down next to her. Her eyes were open; they were glazed over and cloudy looking, but I was sure she knew I was there. She looked so helpless. I'd never seen such a distressed expression on her face before. I don't care what anybody says, dogs feel; therefore, they show it in their eyes.

Molly scared easily; I couldn't imagine how frightening this whole ordeal must be for her. "I'm so sorry Molly," I sobbed. "I didn't know you were sick all this time. I love you so much, honey. Thank you for coming into my life. Oh Molly, what am I gonna do without you?" I stroked her still-warm body. I looked at the body I knew so well: her big shepherd ears, her snout, her soft golden fur, her paws, her long bushy tail that was a catch-all for twigs when she was outdoors playing in the brush.

Just two days before, I'd taken Molly to the groomer, and she'd done a lousy job; her coat was all uneven. I remembered watching Molly as she stood, so patiently for the woman, on her three legs; how grueling it must have been for her, being so sick. I remembered seeing Molly looking at me, with pleading eyes that said, "Please get me out of here."

For years, I had tried to prepare myself for the day that Molly would die, but nothing could have prepared me for those last few moments with my faithful companion.

About five minutes later, the doctor and her assistant returned. Oh God, I needed more time. There was still so much more I wanted to tell her, and I wanted to hold her longer, and Jesus Christ, I just found out that she's dying!

The doctor was holding two syringes. She knelt down on the floor and gave Molly the first shot in her forearm as I held my hand on her shoulder. Then, the second one was administered. "She's gone," she said.

I don't remember getting up from the floor. The attendant took Molly's body away, but I don't remember seeing her do it. I *do* remember having a hard time answering the doctor's next question. "Do you want us to dispose of the remains, or do you want it cremated?" "Can I think about it and call you later?" I said. "I can't even think right now." "Sure," the doctor replied.

I drove straight to Curves and worked out. I didn't know what else to do. When I was through, I sat down in a chair next to the door and felt so lost. Laurie, the woman who worked there, came over and asked me if I was all right. I told her that I just came from putting my dog to sleep. "You mean that beautiful dog that was always waiting for you in the car when you were here?" I began to cry, and she held me. She was a dog lover herself. She then gave me the number of a friend of hers, Peggy, who'd recently lost her dog.

I told Laurie I was moving, and that I didn't know how I was going to pack up the U-Haul trailer. She said she had two grown sons that could help me. The Creator put an angel in my path that day, directly following Molly's passing.

I went home, and it felt so empty there. I couldn't remember the last time I felt so alone. Molly and I had been together for over eight years; it felt like we had always been together, and yet the time went by way too fast. I had never felt that kind of pain after ending a relationship with a man, partly because there were no bad memories.

So many people don't understand the bond between a human and a dog. Dogs are put into our lives for a reason.

They're gifts. They're great teachers and companions. They are always in the moment. Yesterday is forgotten and forgiveness comes quickly. All Molly wanted to do was to please me and to be wherever I was. She couldn't get enough stroking and massages. When I was sad, she was there for me. When my mood was too serious, Molly made me laugh out loud from my gut, by doing some of the funniest things.

I called my friend, Mary, in Albuquerque, and told her about Molly. Mary had been to my house several times and knew Molly well. She was the one I'd call, crying, whenever Molly went missing. Then I called my friend, Judy, in Mariposa. She cried with me because she knew how attached I was to Molly, and she loved Molly too.

I contacted the animal hospital and asked how much it would cost for a cremation, because I decided I wanted Molly's ashes. The entire bill was well over $200.00. I only had enough money for the U-Haul and for gas money for the long trip. I called my youngest brother, Kevin, and asked if he could pay for it. He contacted the hospital and took care of the bill. I was so grateful to him for doing that for me. I called the hospital back; they told me that Molly's body was scheduled for cremation that evening, and that I could pick up her ashes the next day.

When Peggy answered the phone, I let her know that Laurie had given me her number. After I told her about my dog, she came right over. She was the other perfect stranger, an angel, that was put in my path that day. Peggy took me to lunch and we talked about our mutual loss. It helped, knowing that another person was experiencing the same feelings about losing a dog. I wasn't very hungry and was still in shock, so I wasn't very good company. Peggy understood that. After lunch, we went back to my place, sat in the living room, and talked about Molly.

All of a sudden, a wonderful energy came into the room. Peggy felt it too and said, "Oh my God, she's here!" It was unbelievable, the love I felt and the pure joy. "She's okay, she's happy" I exclaimed. Molly had such a powerful and loving spirit. It filled the whole house! I felt lifted up, and was so happy she'd come to let me know she was okay and that she was still with me. It was immensely comforting.

Peggy knew I had more packing to do and said she'd be back the next day to help me. After she left, I called my psychic, Frank, in Albuquerque. I had to know about Molly. I had to know where she was. Frank was familiar with Molly because whenever I'd get a reading from him, I'd always ask about Molly. "She's showing me a scene where you're leaning over her and holding her shoulder. She has foam coming from her mouth." He even saw us at the hospital. He said that Molly left her body quickly, and that she nuzzled her nose in my ear, thanking me for letting her go. He saw her in a beautiful place, a meadow, with lots of flowers and tall grass. "She's got all four legs and is wagging her tail so hard that her whole hips are swinging back and forth. She's very happy."

The next day, I went to the animal hospital, pulling the empty U-Haul. I went inside and told the attendant that I was picking up my dog's ashes. She came back with a container that was covered with a soft, maroon cloth bag with a tie at the top. I took it from her. It was heavy. Molly was a big girl. I took it to the car and drove home in tears. I just couldn't stop crying.

Peggy and Laurie's sons arrived right on time. As they took boxes to the trailer, Peggy helped me pack the rest of my things, which I really appreciated. She knew that I couldn't think straight. I was really out of it. I knew I wouldn't have room for everything, so I gave some furniture and other items to all of them for helping me.

As I pulled onto the freeway heading east, I was no longer in shock, and the pain came, but it was bearable. I had the radio on and just let myself cry as much as I needed to, to all the sad songs that I heard. There was a song that would come on the radio when I was driving with Molly. It was called *Brown Eyed Girl*, by Van Morrison. Whenever that song came on, I'd sing it to Molly, because she was my brown eyed girl. *Brown Eyed Girl* came on within an hour of driving, and I really cried then. It could have been a coincidence, but when it played every couple of hours, I knew it wasn't. When my sobbing became howls, I could feel Molly there with me.

When I arrived in Albuquerque I went straight to my friend Marsha's house. She lived with her husband, her daughter, and her daughter's son. Marsha's grandson gave up his room for me. The next morning, Marsha's husband, Dick, helped me unload my belongings at the storage unit and drop off the U-Haul.

I was anxious to see Mary. When I walked into her yard, I was met by her husband, Daniel, and this black Labrador looking dog, who jumped up on me with pleasure. I went inside and talked with Mary for a bit, and then she asked, "Did you see our new dog?" "Yes, she greeted me when I came in. What's her name?" "Honey Bear," she said. As it turned out, Mary and her husband, Daniel, needed someone to exercise their dog during the week and I was hired for the job.

Thus began a most joyous occupation. I'd pick up Honey Bear and take her to the local dog park, a couple of blocks from Mary's house. The dog park experience was new to me. I was able to see the need for dogs to socialize and play with each other. I regretted that I hadn't exposed Molly to the dog park.

For the first couple of weeks, I would sit at the park and cry, for missing Molly. As time went on, I met some great people there and began to share with them the story of Molly and me. It couldn't have been more therapeutic. Honey Bear was a year old and had the sweetest disposition. She reminded me of Molly, and it was healing for me to be with her. Honey Bear took to me right off the bat. It was perfect for both of us.

I received notification from unemployment that I didn't qualify because I'd quit. I'd been so sure I was going to get it. Well, that changed everything. I applied for general assistance with the Human Services Department, but didn't expect to hear from them anytime soon.

It became apparent to me that Marsha had an agenda in letting me stay with her. Her daughter, April, was an alcoholic. Marsha had hoped that I'd be able to *save* her. The young woman would come home at all hours, drunk, sleep all day, and be hung-over and irritable when she came out of her bedroom. With all that I was going through emotionally, it wasn't a healthy environment for me to be in.

I told Mary about the situation at Marsha's house and she asked her mother, Clarisa, if I could stay with her. I hadn't met Mary's mother before, so I was a little apprehensive. As it turned out, Clarisa agreed to let me live with her and gave me the spare bedroom. I got along well with Clarisa and felt much more comfortable at her house; although, I hated that I had to live with anyone, and didn't like imposing.

I had a truck load of issues going on at once: lack of an income, unemployment, homelessness, the loss of my vehicle (I was unable to make monthly payments), and the death of my best friend, Molly. The only good thing in my life, was that I was clean and sober. That should've been a big deal, but it didn't feel that way to me. I was at an all-time low in my recovery. Yet, many people were struggling during that time; they'd lost their jobs and their homes, due to the recession. I tried to tell myself, "Hey, you're not the only one—sometimes shit just happens—life happens. So pick yourself up and get moving." But I felt like I was in the ocean, struggling to make it back to shore, and all the while, being pulled back out to the sea by the undertow.

All of a sudden, one day, I began feeling really bad, as if I were under spiritual attack. It worsened by the hour. I couldn't feel my limbs and I was thinking of suicide. I'd never experienced anything like it before, and I knew it wasn't PTSD. I was in big trouble. Something told me that I should go see a Native woman I knew, Alice, who would probably know what was happening to me and how to help.

By the time I got to Alice's house, I was hardly able to speak. "You've been witched," she said matter-of-factly. I sure was popular with witches. I knew what Alice said was true; I felt like I had no power at all, as if I was nothing but an empty shell. "Who could have done this to me?" I asked Alice. "I haven't been anywhere except to Wal-Mart." "That's probably where it happened. A lot of Indians go there. You were in a weakened state and a target. All that that witch had to do was make eye contact with you," she said.

Alice brought out her "medicine" and her eagle fan. She worked on me for about an hour. She said I would feel better by morning, and that I should spend the night there, where I'd be safe. I still felt strange when I went to bed, but by morning, my power was back. Alice gave me some corn pollen and told me how to use it. She said that the witches in the Southwest couldn't hurt me if I used the corn pollen.

Whatever works, I thought. I should've been smudging with sage all along, and maybe I wouldn't have been witched in the first place. *The next time I go to Wal-Mart*, I thought, *I'll wear mirrored sunglasses.*

Because I no longer had a vehicle, I had to utilize the bus system, and it was a nightmare. I was spending half my day either riding the bus or waiting for one, just to take Honey Bear to the dog park. So to help me out, Mary gave me an extra car that she had, a little 1992 Dodge. It was covered in rust, but it ran good.

I started feeling uncomfortable living at Clarisa's house rent free. So I contacted a women's shelter that I'd heard good things about. The morning that I called the Barrett House for Women, I was told to come in that morning for an interview. I presumed there was a waiting list, and was pleasantly surprised when the interview ended with the woman telling me to return that day with my belongings.

I was shown to my room and was pleased that I'd only be sharing it with one other woman. The Barrett House was a large facility, fairly new, and very homey. There was a big screen TV in the generous living room area, as well as a computer room.

My stay there would last five weeks. Getting hooked up with the Barrett House would prove to be the best thing that could've happened to me at that time in my life.

The week before I left the shelter, one of the case managers, Julie, told me that I qualified for one of their housing programs, due to my mental health disability. That sounded wonderful; except that one of the requirements for the housing program was that I had to be receiving a cash benefit from the state, at the very least, in order to move into an apartment. I'd be expected to pay rent. I'd applied for general assistance a couple of months before and was informed that it could take up to six months to receive the $245.00 allowance from the state of New Mexico. So on my last day at the Barrett House, I loaded up my car and was prepared to live in it until I could figure something else out.

That first night, I found a neighborhood that seemed fairly safe and slept in the car without incident. The next day, I picked up Honey Bear and took her to the dog park. I had to stick to my schedule. When we were ready to leave the park, we walked back to the car.

I quickly spotted the glass lying under the passenger's side of the car. In disbelief, I walked up to see what the hell had happened, and I looked inside. My purse was gone! I had everything in that large purse: my wallet with $90.00 in cash, my prescription glasses, my medication, my driver's license, my hair brush, and my address/phone book. I was beside myself. Not only had I lost some very basic and important items, but my car, which was now my home, had been compromised.

I took Honey Bear back into the dog park and began pacing and crying openly about my predicament, praying to the Creator to help me. That was as far down as I was willing to go—no further!

It was a good thing that I had my cell phone in my pocket. I called Nancy, a social worker that I'd spoken with the day before, who'd said she may be able to assist me with short-term housing. Nancy worked at a homeless program called St. Martin's, in downtown Albuquerque. I was sobbing as I told her what had happened. She suggested I drive to the program immediately. Not only was she able to get me temporary housing, she was also able to speed up the process of me getting cash assistance. It just so happened, she had connections in the human services department. Once that was in place, I contacted Julie from Barrett House and was able to start apartment hunting.

It was November 1, 2010. It felt so good to finally get my belongings out of storage, to have all my things in one place, and to be able to hang my pictures, and set up my altar. Molly's ashes became a part of my altar as well. I still cried for her and still felt a pressure in my heart whenever I thought of her. I don't know if you ever get over the death of a dog.

When I moved into my own place, my case manager, Julie, gave me a welcome home basket with all sorts of household items. A couple of weeks later, I came home to a beautiful bedroom set. I was finally home! Of course, I wasn't a fan of apartment living, but it was my own space.

I was having more good days than not. But I was still battling with depression. So I put together a treatment plan for myself. I knew I had to get back to basics if I was going to heal and move through this rough period of my life. I included the physical, emotional, spiritual, and mental aspects of myself, just the way I'd written treatment plans a thousand times before, for my clients. My diet needed to change. I returned to eating salads and fewer sweets. I began meditating again. I joined a gym and was back to working out three days a week. Getting acupuncture treatments became a weekly part of my schedule for several weeks, which helped me with an overall feeling of wellbeing. Journaling became a regular practice for me because it helped me feel connected to myself in the here and now. I paid particular attention to my dreams, because they gave me a clearer picture of what was going on with me on a subconscious level. I attended AA meetings until they were no longer useful. I got back into therapy and utilized the sweat lodge on occasion.

Then, I had to attend to the grief work. I had to accept the fact that I would never be a counselor again, and that was huge for me. Counseling had been my profession for over 20 years. I had to grieve that loss. Even though, toward the end of my career, I'd begun to feel burned out and longed to have a position where I felt more fulfilled, I never really saw myself doing anything else *but* substance abuse counseling.

I missed the person I was when I was working; that confident, savvy, inspirational woman. I was the kind of "grass roots" counselor that I always wanted for myself, but have never been able to find. I missed the rush I'd get when a light bulb would go on in a client's mind, when they finally understood something. I missed the successes I saw with my clients, and I missed seeing the Creator's hand in all that I did. But now, I felt like I was merely existing. I was in limbo and I didn't like it.

It took several months, but I came to realize I was exactly where I was supposed to be, in a place of healing and change. I wasn't supposed to feel useful to anyone but myself this time. The Creator was providing for me in every way and giving me the space I needed to just get better. It's said, that when one door closes, another one opens. I knew that the Creator wasn't through with me—there was still something else he wanted me to do, in the way of being of service to others. But I had to allow it to unfold, and not "Push the River," as my teacher would tell me. I had to go with the flow, trust the Creator.

My dog business was thriving. I never would have imagined that I'd be doing dog care. Creator knew that that was what I needed for my own healing and I was perfect for the job. I went from transporting dogs to the park to boarding them.

At one point, I put an ad on Craigslist in the women-seeking-men category. I met with about three guys and decided that I was merely looking for a distraction from focusing on myself, once again. *Been there, done that,* I thought. Besides, I knew that if I were to become involved in another relationship, the man had to be on a similar spiritual path. I was no longer willing to lose myself in a man. I wanted a man who would support my "mission" in life and not expect me to be his mother, his housekeeper, or his cook, while he sat in a chair all day watching sports on TV. And if I was meant to be single for the rest of my days, I knew I could do that and be quite happy.

Toward April, my depression began to lift. I was feeling more alive and at peace with myself. The internal and external work I'd been doing for the past year was paying off.

In October, my case manager, Julie, said that the Barrett Foundation was having their annual dinner and fundraiser, and that they always chose a client to speak about how their organization has helped them. She asked me if I'd like to be the speaker. I said it would be an honor.

The day of the gala, I put my hair up in a French twist and carefully applied my makeup. It had been so long since I'd dressed up for any occasion, and I felt elegant and beautiful, in my long, black, sequined gown.

As I walked into the hotel where the event was taking place, I felt more excited than nervous. Julie told me that I looked beautiful, that I was sparkling. It was quite the fancy affair. Everyone was dressed so nicely, and I felt like I fit right in.

I was reminded of such an occasion, 15 year earlier. I was at the University of Arizona in Tempe, at their theatre. I was standing backstage, waiting to sing three of my own songs. It was during the time when I'd been in and out of relapsing. I heard the announcer introduce me. I was dressed beautifully, as I began my walk toward the front of the stage. I thought to myself, *If those people in the audience only knew, that just three months ago, I was living on the streets, smoking crack and living like an animal.* Well, I sang my songs, but that thought led to another relapse, because I felt like a fraud.

This time was different, as Julie introduced me to members of the staff and the board. I was quite comfortable now, despite the fact that I hadn't worn high heels for 15 years. Nevertheless, I was able to walk with confidence and even felt sexy. At 60 years old I was still one hot mama!

A year before, I had been in such a different place. I was severely depressed and didn't know if I'd be able to have anything close to a normal life again. I couldn't imagine ever feeling as I did that night. In fact, it had been years since I'd felt such high self-esteem. I knew that it was only the beginning of better things to come for me.

As I walked up the stairs to the small stage to give my speech, I could sense how far I'd come. I realized that all of the hard work I'd done on myself over the years, had never left me. I stood before the group of over 300 strangers with dignity and humility. I briefly told them of my childhood, and of how I chose to live as a result of trauma I'd experienced. I told them about my struggle with PTSD and depression. I shared about my successes and about my recent losses. And finally, I let them know how much the Barrett House had helped me to get my life back. I spoke from my heart and I didn't feel like a fraud.

When I finished my speech, I was shocked by the standing ovation I received. Several people came up to me later and thanked me, saying, "You're a strong person," and "You're an inspiration to others, you make a difference." I was walking on air. At last, I knew I had a contribution to make to people of all walks of life.

Taking Back the River has been my final act of power. I own who I am today. I believe in myself. I am grateful for a life of hardship because I am able to share it with you. That makes it all worth it.

List of Characters

Several people move in and out of my life throughout the book. I've included their names and relationships to me, in order that you may have access to referring back as needed.

My brothers in the order of their birth:

Matthew: same birth parents
He lives in the Bay area and is an attorney.

Donald
He lives in Virginia and owns a construction company.

Frankie
He lives in Nevada and works as a surgical tech.

Kevin
He lives in Nevada and is a police officer and an instructor.

Earnie
He was my husband and the father of my two children.

Lisa
My daughter
She has three children and is a certified nursing assistant.

Travis
My son
He has two children and is a certified mechanic.

David
He was my first boyfriend after Earnie in 1972.
He lived in Monterey, CA, and was an abusive alcoholic.

Richard
We began a relationship around 1982.
He was an alcoholic/addict from Salinas, CA.

Brad
My friend
He was my sociology teacher
He lives in Salinas, CA.

Olga
My friend since 1977
We met while in treatment in Watsonville, CA.

Hector
Vietnam vet buddy who lives in Phoenix, AZ.

Joe
A significant relationship of six years
He lives in Phoenix and is an alcoholic.

Mary
My friend
We met while working as counselors in Albuquerque, NM.

Henry
My friend
We met in Bernalillo, NM.
He is an Oglala Lakota man and pipe carrier.

Epilogue

That's my journey so far. In case you're wondering...*Why the hell couldn't this woman get it right the first time...the second time...or the tenth? Why did she have to keep returning to drugs, to alcohol, to relationships with men that were terribly dysfunctional and dangerous, to succumb to far greater depths of despair and misery?* I don't have a simple answer to that. It just took me a long time to come to love and forgive myself. And it's by the grace of the Creator and my will to persevere, that I am here at all. I regret nothing, and I blame no one for any of the painful events of my life. Without those events, I wouldn't have had the opportunity to heal, to grow, to become strong, and to gain wisdom. By choosing to work through my past experiences, I've been gifted with a depth and compassion for myself and others that I otherwise, never would have had or known.

And I'm not done *yet*. As long as I'm breathing I will have hard lessons. It's all part of being in this school of life. I know now, that I have the power, the ability, and the spiritual help to get through anything.

As long as I put my own needs first, and continue doing the things that feed my soul, I will not self-destruct. As long as I speak my truth, I will not lose my voice—or myself. As long as I walk in a good way, with respect and humility, I will remain connected spiritually.

I have a wonderful life today. I'm seldom triggered by the events of my past. I feel safe and I know that I am spiritually protected. I feel contentment with my life. *I am finally at peace!*

My wish for you is that you too decide to make an act of power, as I did, and *Take Back the River*.

I will leave you with the lyrics of one of my songs.

I Want to Live before I Die © 2005 Lyrics by Sheila O'Quirke

The past is over… a half a lifetime gone,
    What's done is done, gonna sing a brand new song,
Up from the ashes…starting with today,
    No more excuses, letting go of yesterday.
And there's no one left to fight,
    I want to live before I die, I want to live;
Old haunts and traumas…never would have guessed
    I had it in me…to put it all to rest,
Old friends and loved ones…so sorry you died young,
    Can't blame myself no more…for me life's just begun.
And there's no one left to grieve,
    I want to live before I die, I want to live;
I want to be here…feel the earth beneath my feet,
    Walk in the sunlight…and be a part…of everything I see
Live in the moment…cause for now that's all I've got,
    Open my heart to you…not be someone…that I'm not.
And there's no one I need to please,
    I want to live before I die, I want to live;

No more wasted moments…of things I should have said,

    I want to be all that I dream…hold my vision straight ahead,

No time to worry…about things that don't mean nothing,

    It's the only life I got…gonna give it my best shot.

And there's nothing left to fear,

    I want to live before I die…I'm going to live before I die…I want to live.

www.ingramcontent.com/pod-product-compliance
Lightning Source LLC
Chambersburg PA
CBHW022049160426
43198CB00008B/169